"Vandana Shiva is one of the great minds and truth tellers of our time. This book is a chilling and meticulously documented exposé of the reckless and devastatingly dangerous use of philanthropy by the technophile capitalists who are clueless about the needs of living people and the living Earth. A must-read warning for anyone concerned about justice, Earth, and the human future."

— David Korten
Author of *When Corporations Rule the World* and *The Great Turning: From Empire to Earth Community*

Dispelling the myths that traditional agroecology is less productive than biotech factory farming and biotechnology is necessary for climate resilience, Vandana Shiva and authors confront the false narratives of corporate philanthropists and their biotech industry accomplices. Their lies are nothing less than environmental injustice for Indigenous people, small scale farmers, and women."

— Dina Gilio-Whitaker
Author of *As Long as Grass Grows: The Indigenous Fight for Environmental Justice, from Colonization to Standing Rock*

"Dr. Shiva has once again laid bare the emerging threats to our democracy and living planet. Shiva and authoritative contributors elucidate the dangers of genetic theft, protraction of the Green Revolution legacy, and terrifyingly bold genetic extinction technologies. The reader is left mortified and fully convinced that "Land Back" to Indigenous communities and a return to agroecology is the path to a livable future on planet earth."

— Leah Penniman
Co-Founder of Soul Fire Farm and author of *Farming While Black*

"*Philanthrocapitalism* is a remarkable effort, led by the great Vandana Shiva, to expose the growing dangers of capitalistic powers as they capture, control, and destroy many aspects of our lives. In a brilliant and vital work, authors seek to oppose the rising and dangerous powers of corporate dominion and fascism."

— Jerry Mander
Author of *Four Arguments for the Elimination of Television*

T0015423

"*Philanthrocapitalism and the Erosion of Democracy* takes an intersectional approach to examining the work of corporate philanthropy. It is a riveting read on why we should not trust billionaires to save vulnerable communities. Charitable giving shouldn't come with a catch."

— Leah Thomas
 Author of *The Intersectional Environmentalist: How to Dismantle Systems of Oppression to Protect People and Planet*

"A detailed exposé of how false climate solutions imperil our agricultural enterprise, undermine the sovereignty of the world's farmers, and affect the quality of our food supply. Shiva lays bare an account of elite corporate philanthropy's power to influence the direction of agricultural research with no public accountability."

— Peggy M. Shepard
 Executive Director and Co-Founder, WE ACT For Environmental Justice

"In an exceptionally important intervention, Vandana Shiva and colleagues expose the deceptions of the domination paradigm as it enters the late phase of its destruction of life, community, and the mental well-being of our children. This book provides an important signpost to reweave our human family and regenerate what has been depleted. We must collectively resist a system that concentrates wealth and power, leaving a few billionaires to speak as if they have our best interests at heart. Buy this book, it will support your ability to discern the falsehoods!"

— Gail Bradbrook
 Co-Founder of Extinction Rebellion

"A must-read for anyone fighting to reclaim food sovereignty, protect Indigenous knowledge, restore biodiversity, decolonize nature, and repair damage to the planet. The book not only identifies real threats to humanity and false solutions but also shows that we owe a debt of gratitude to the Indigenous communities preserving the most effective principles to heal, regenerate, and protect our ecosystems. This book teaches us to emancipate ourselves with dignity and freedom so we may live in harmony with nature."

— Fadhel Kaboub
 Associate Professor of Economics at Denison University, President of the Global Institute for Sustainable Prosperity

PHILANTHROCAPITALISM AND THE EROSION OF DEMOCRACY

*A Global Citizens' Report on
the Corporate Control of
Technology, Health, and Agriculture*

EDITED BY Vandana Shiva

FOREWORD BY David W. Orr

 SYNERGETICPRESS

Synergetic Press |1 Bluebird Court, Santa Fe, NM 87508 & 24 Old Gloucester St. London, WC1N 3AL England

Library of Congress Cataloging-in-Publication Data is available.

ISBN 9780907791911 (paperback)
ISBN 9780907791928 (ebook)

Cover Design by Amanda Müller
Book design by Howie Severson
Managing Editor: Amanda Müller
Project Editor: Sage Wylder
Printed in the USA

Table of Contents

❧

Foreword

❧

DAVID W. ORR

*"The idea is to pull off a digital version of the Enclosure
of the Commons and put huge powers into the hands of
an increasingly hardening police state."*
—Arundhati Roy[1]

"If brute force doesn't work, you're not using enough of it!" has been
proposed as the central operating principle of the modern world. It
is a plausible candidate because it captures the compulsive logic of
the marauder, empire builders, clear-cutters, strip-miners, corporate tycoons, militarists, and true believers of all kinds who shaped
the past two centuries. Brute force does not negotiate with history,
hubris, culture, biology, old knowledge, ethics, foresight, and the
unknown. It eschews humility, persuasion by reasoned debate, ethical limits, and abhors empathy, compassion, and the discipline of
place. In the fossil fuel era, the logic of brute force escaped from confinement and went on a planetary rampage and now pervades virtually all human activity. It masquerades as progress, but the disguise
conceals a darker reality. A prime example, at the far edge of insanity,
is the logically airtight, mathematically rigorous strategy of "Mutual
Assured Destruction," which informs our testosterone-saturated

---

1 Arundhati Roy, *Capitalism: A Ghost Story*. Chicago: Haymarket Books, 2014,
p. 31.

foreign policies and by which Armageddon hangs by an oh-so-slender thread. For what great cause, exactly, would one push the button to destroy the planet? What national interest, or reputational advantage, or great cause might be served? Who would be around to ponder such things and sift through the debris left by the most brutish of brute force weaponry?

Sometime after Adam Smith published *The Wealth of Nations* in 1776, the logic of brute force infected western economics, informing its underlying proposition that all men (mostly) have insatiable wants that justify tearing up the earth, polluting it, or frying it to death. By this logic, human survival is deemed uneconomical. But why would any even modestly sane person run the risks of destabilizing the earth's climate? It is impossible to comprehend the depth of nonsense in waters so turbid.

More pertinent to this book is the unfolding disaster of a global agribusiness system that operates by brute force as well. In return for a mess of pottage, industrial agriculture compromised the fecundity of natural systems, eroded soils, drained aquifers, polluted waters, destroyed once stable rural communities, created hundreds of dead zones in seas around the world, destroyed biodiversity everywhere, and erased the knowledge of better ways to farm, while creating a vast moral chasm between the overfed and the starving. The ironies of industrial agriculture stack up like cordwood; the unpaid full costs of cheap food for the rich are staggering; the moral costs are beyond counting.

Defenders of the system cannot rightfully claim they were not warned. There are warnings against overreach and hubris in the founding myths, literature, poetry, and scriptures of nearly every culture on earth. In western literature, for example, the monster in Mary Shelley's *Doctor Frankenstein* (1818), for one, is not the creature but its creator who refused to take responsibility for what he'd done. Melville's Captain Ahab in *Moby Dick* (1851) is a further warning about the penalties that accompany uncontrolled obsession in pursuit of ignoble ends. Dostoevsky's grand inquisitor gave a further warning about the perverse logic of necessity; in *Brothers Karamazov* (1879), the Grand Inquisitor says to a silent Christ:

> "In the end they [the people] will lay their freedom at our feet, and say to us, 'make us your slaves but feed us.' They will understand at last that freedom and bread enough for all are inconceivable together…they can never be free for they are weak, vicious, worthless, and rebellious."[2]

The strategy of the Grand Inquisitor is that of the petrochemical companies, agribusiness, and multinational corporations who will feed us in a manner of speaking but only in return for our acquiescence in the ruination.

In the nick of time, however, along comes Bill Gates and other "philanthrocapitalists" who, as luck would have it, promise to solve hunger, disease, poverty, and a rapidly destabilizing climate often by selling us more of the things that made them very rich. A Godsend, indeed, until one reads the fine print that, among other things, requires believing that the leopard has shed its spots and now wishes to feed those it once fed upon. A more enlightened and beneficent capitalism is possible, I think, but it requires capitalists to transcend self-interest and greed, which is not wholly supported by the record. It isn't just their hearts; however, it's their mindset conditioned by many years of accumulation to believe that money is necessary to solve problems. But for all of their puffery, philanthrocapitalists don't talk much about the root causes of the problems they purport to solve, or the politics of who gets what, when and how, or the fair distribution of wealth, or the destruction of vibrant rural cultures rooted in place. In Anand Giridharadas' words:

> "To question their supremacy is very simply to doubt the proposition that what is best for the world just so happens

---

2 Fyodor Dostoyevsky, *The Brothers Karamazov*. New York: The Modern Library, 1950, p. 300..

to be what the rich and powerful think it is . . . It is to say that a world marked more and more by private greed and the private provision of public goods is a world that doesn't trust the people, in their collective capacity to imagine another kind of society into being."[3]

What he calls "the Aspen Consensus" entails challenging the winners to do more good but never to do less harm.[4] The kind of absolution that theologian Dietrich Bonhoeffer once called "cheap grace."

There is a long, ironic, and mostly unhappy history of the very wealthy trying to do good, most often late in lives spent otherwise. To improve agricultural production and end world hunger, for example, the Rockefeller Foundation in the 1940s decided to launch what became known as the Green Revolution. It entailed the application of capital, machinery, chemicals, irrigation, consolidation of small farms, migration to overcrowded cities, and caused the destruction of "an agricultural system around which village life and livelihoods had revolved for thousands of years."[5] The Foundation leaders ignored repeated warnings, including those by University of California geographer Carl Sauer about overlooking the possibility "that native practices represent real solutions to local problems."[6] As it turned out, Sauer was right. The results of the Green Revolution have been a social, cultural, political, and ecological disaster.

One wonders, then, what great problems have been solved by philanthrocapitalism? After all the hype, the record—at best—is mixed. Most of what's grown by brute force agriculture goes to feed

---

3 Anand Giridharadas, *Winners Take All*. New. York: Knopf, 2018, p. 244.

4 Elizabeth Kolbert, "Shaking the Foundations," The New Yorker August 27, 2018. pp 30-34.

5 Mark Dowie, American Foundations: An Investigative History. Cambridge: MIT Press, 2002, p. 111.

6 Ibid., pp. 120-121; See also Linsey, McGoey, No Such Thing as a Free Gift. London: Verso, p. 217 on the Gates Foundation initiative the Alliance for a Green Revolution in Africa (AGRA).

the wealthy, often at the expense of people on the land, tropical forests, and biological diversity. And "What to make of the fact that growing philanthropy and growing inequality seem to go hand in hand," Linsey McGoey asks.[7] Increasingly philanthropy, she notes, deprives treasuries of tax revenues that could otherwise be better spent to help the poor. And, who holds the Bill Gates of the world accountable? Who weighs the difference between tax revenues not paid to the public treasury against the purported benefits of unsupervised philanthropy? The answer is no one. A more sensible approach to philanthropy is to recognize that "the state is better placed, for reasons of legal power and accountability, to do some things" that require a systems perspective, transparency, and ultimate accountability.[8]

The battle over land, common property resources, rural culture, and footloose wealth has entered a new and perhaps final phase, as the writers explain below. Bill Gates, through Ag One, is spending billions each year to monopolize seeds and control global agriculture in ways previously impossible. Agriculture was the last major sector of society rendered vulnerable to capitalism, but the advent of gene splicing and CRISPR technology, however, makes it possible and highly profitable to control the foundation of agriculture by controlling seeds and genetic material. The result is the brave new world of synthetic meat, genetically modified plants, and novel organisms of all kinds; a world of biopiracy, dependence, pesticides, and control beyond the wildest imaginings of any Grand Inquisitor. It also is a world losing vibrant rural communities, cultural diversity, biological diversity, and democracy—one shaped by "monocultures of the mind" warped by the ideology of brute force applied to genes, plants, animals, recalcitrant rural communities, and independent thinkers

---

7 Ibid., p. 18; See also Martin Kirk, Jason Hickel, "Gates Foundation's Rose-Colored World View Not supported by Evidence," Commondreams.org March 26,2017. Global poverty they argue has been rising dramatically due tax avoidance, mismeasurement, and the growing concentration of wealth.

8 Matthew Bishop & Michael Green, Philanthrocapitalism. London: Bloomsbury, 2009, p. 283.

like Vandana Shiva. Under the flag of feeding the world and armed with technology that can manipulate down to the fine grain of life, Gates and others are enclosing the final commons. That is a fight we must not lose.

In sum, we are kin to all that ever was, is, and ever will be. Vandana Shiva captures this ancient truth with an invocation: "We are the land. We are the soil. We are biodiversity. We are one Earth family deriving our common humanity and identity from the land and Earth as earthlings, sharing our common sustenance for life, breath, food and water through community and mutuality." Amen. The crux of the problem, she writes elsewhere, is "the Eurocentric concept of property [that] views only capital investment as investment, and hence treats returns on capital investment as the only right that needs protection...not labor, or care and nurturance."[9] The battle, then, is ultimately one about politics, which is to say about power and greed—justice and fairness within and between generations and species. It began long ago in the enclosure of common lands, forests, and waters and morphed into the enclosure of everything that could be fenced off to exclude common use, common decency, common justice, and a common future. It is ultimately a struggle to protect "a peoples' inalienable right to rule themselves."[10]

David W. Orr, Paul Sears Distinguished Professor Emeritus, Oberlin College currently Professor of Practice, Arizona State University. Author of eight books including *Earth in Mind* (Island), *Down to the Wire* (Oxford) and *Dangerous Years* (Yale) and co-editor of *Democracy Unchained* (New Press).

---

9 Vandana Shiva, *Reclaiming the Commons*. Santa Fe: Synergeticpress, 2020, p. 244; see also Peter Linebaugh, *Stop, Thief!* Oakland: PM Press, 2014; David Bollier, *Think Like a Commoner*. Gabriola Is: New Society Press, 2014.

10 Shoshana Zuboff, *The Age of Surveillance Capitalism*. New York: Public Affairs, 2019, p. 513.

Introduction

*Philanthrocapitalism and Colonization
in the Digital Age*

❧

VANDANA SHIVA

*We are the land. We are the soil. We are Earthlings. We are
biodiversity.*

We are one Earth family, deriving our common humanity and identity from the land as Earthlings, sharing our common sustenance
for life, breath, food, and water through community and mutuality.

When we care for the land and the soil, we reclaim our humanity.
Our future is inseparable from the future of the Earth. It is no accident that the word human has its roots in *humu*—soil in Latin. And
Adam, the first human in Abrahamanic traditions, is derived from
Adamus, soil in Hebrew. Land is what defines Indigeneity, identity,
community, country—our very being, our life, our freedom. The
ancient Bhumi Sukta, the prayer to the Earth in the ancient Atharva
Veda recognizes that the Earth is mother, and we are children of
the Earth.

> *"Impart to us those vitalizing forces that come, O Earth,
> from deep within your body, your central point, your navel,
> purify us wholly. The Earth is mother; I am child of Earth."*
> —Bhumi Sukta, Atharva veda XII. 1.12

For Indigenous people across the world, land is not just soil and rocks and minerals; it is living. It sustains the community and is sustained by people and culture. This reciprocal relationship between land and people—being cared for by Mother Earth and caring for Mother Earth—allowed Indigenous people to live on the same land over centuries without degrading the land. The Indigenous Australians farmed the land for over 60 centuries. Even today, despite two and a half centuries of colonialism, this relationship to land determines the identity and way of life of the Aborigines. This deep relationship between people and the land is often described as "connection to country."

As Dhanggal Gurruwiwi, a Galpu Elder from Nhulunbuy in the Northern Territory, explains, "The land and the people are one, because the land is also related....In our kinship system, as a custodian I'm the child of that land." In Indigenous cultures, the land gives us the law on how to live on this earth with other species for the well-being of all. The law gives us the knowledge and responsibility to care for the land, the purpose of being on the earth, and belonging to the earth community.

As Mary Graham writes about aboriginal world views, "There are two major axioms in Aboriginal (Indigenous) worldview. One is that the land is the law and the other is that you are not alone in the world." There is no anthropocentrism in Indigenous cultures: "And therefore, we concede to our fellow creatures, even our animal fellows, the same rights as ourselves to life on this earth."

Land is what defines Indigeneity: "Since time immemorial, First Nations have had an intricate, respectful, spiritually, and physically dependent, grateful, and protective tie to the land. The nature of this tie is not so much one of ownership but one of stewardship. They feel they have been bestowed with a responsibility for the land (and sea) and all of the creatures that inhabit the land with them."

Indigenous cultures have seen themselves being part as part of Mother Earth—not separate from her as masters and owners. We come from the land; the land is our Mother, who gives us care and for whom we must care. The land is our home, our place of belonging.

We belong to the land; land does not belong to individuals as private property. Colonization, fossil fuel industrialism, and globalization have led to a metabolic rift and rupture between humans from nature, Indigenous cultures, and the land to which they belong.

COLONIZATION, ENCLOSURES OF THE COMMONS, AND CREATION OF PRIVATE PROPERTY

Before colonialism, in India and in Indigenous cultures across the world, land was a commons, not private property. As Dharampal has reported, the Village community had supremacy over land and its use. The local community was the highest competent authority that made decisions on land use. The right to use land was permanent and hereditary as decided by custom and practice. The British violently destroyed our diverse, decentralized, democratic, self-governance community structures governing the customary practice of land rights and land use rights and imposed private property rights by institutionalizing "Zamindari," or landlordism. As Sir WW Hunter wrote in the Imperial Gazetteer: "The Indian Government is not a mere tax collecting agency, charged with the single duty of protecting person and property. Its system of administration is based upon the view that the British power is a paternal despotism, which owns, in a certain sense, the entire soil of the country."

In one stroke of a pen in 1793, Lord Cornwallis, through the permanent settlement, dispossessed the peasantry, tied 20 million small and marginal farmers and peasants into bondage to Zamindars created by the British to extract genocidal "lagaan" (taxes or rents). The British control over land and extraction of lagaan became the source of wealth for the empire and poverty and famine in India.

Over the course of 200 years, the British extracted an estimated $45 trillion from India through the colonial enclosures of our agrarian economies, pushing tens of millions of peasants into famine and starvation. The displacement of people from the land was one interconnected violent global process taking place at the same time across the world. The peasants in India and in England were both victims of the colonial process of enclosing the commons to create private property.

According to English Common law, the enclosure of a commons required the unanimous consent of the entire community. No authority had the right to alienate and enclose the commons. Even one member could block the enclosures. This right was fundamental and inalienable.

Between 1628 and 1631, head-on clashes took place between the peasantry and the lords of the manor on attempts to own the land. The Parliament started to pass laws to enclose the commons and undermine individual rights, passing 3,380 bills between 1770 and 1839 to reach this goal. It took two centuries of violence to enclose the commons in England.

ENCLOSURES OF THE COMMONS: THE "CIVILIZING MISSION" OF COLONIALISM AND THE "CREATION MYTH" OF CAPITALISM

Locke's (1632–1704) Treatise on Property was primarily a justification of the enclosures of the commons, creation of private property, based on the "civilizing myth" of colonialism that Indigenous people are primitive and need to be "improved" and the "creation myth" of capitalism, the manufacture of the illusion that "capital," a dead construct, is a creative force and creates wealth. Locke used the construction of "primitiveness" of Indigenous land use in Turtle Island to justify the creation of private property through the appropriation of their land and enclosures of the commons. As he writes in his second treatise: "For I ask whether in the wild woods and uncultivated waste of America left to nature without any improvement, tillage or husbandry, a thousand acres will yield the needy and wretched inhabitants as many conveniences of life as ten acres of equally fertile land in Devonshire where they are well cultivated."

Indigenous peoples of the Americas have been farming for centuries without leaving an ecological footprint. That they did no harm to nature is not "primitiveness" but ecological sophistication and sustainability. While developing the colonial myth of primitiveness of Indigenous peoples, Locke was also developing the "creation myth" of capital to justify the enclosures in England.

Locke wrote that property is created by removing resources from nature and mixing it with "labor." For Locke, "labor" was not the biological and physical work of the women and the peasants. The creation of property is based on the fictitious "spiritual" labor as manifested in the control of capital. "Intellectual property" and patents on seeds are a continuity of this false assumption of capital, a dead construct, as the creative force of production while defining the real creative forces—nature and people—as dead and inert inputs.

Mother Earth, as the very basis of life, disappeared as a creative force. The work of women, Indigenous people, and peasants disappeared as the creative source of production of the food we eat and the clothes we wear. Living economies based on the commons disappeared as land was grabbed, the wealth created by the earth and people were appropriated and extracted.

THE DIGITAL BARONS AS THE NEW LANDLORDS

A new enclosure of the commons and land grab is now taking place. The tech barons are the new landlords and feudal lords of the digital age. Leading the new tech feudalism and colonialism is Bill Gates, who has emerged as the biggest landlord of America, owning 242,000 acres of farmland across the US. Gates is not just buying land as a high-value "asset" to be added to the portfolio of investments through Cascade Investments. It is part of the diversification of the portfolio. Land, digital agriculture, and lab food (Impossible Foods) that makes "plant based" meat are the new investments. Above all, Gates is seeking control over the most important aspect of the real economy: land, food, and farming. This is a point made by Kissinger. Food can be used as a weapon; therefore, by controlling food, you control people. Land grab in the digital age is being presented as "helping family farmers by relieving them of the expensive burden of land ownership and freeing up the farmers capital for operating expenses."

Since the Green Revolution, corporations have been defining what is a "lucrative operation" for the farmer. But small farmers got into debt and lost their land. In extreme cases, when the debt trap drove them to losing their land, they lost their lives by committing suicide. I see the epidemic of farmer suicides in recent years both as a result of the hopelessness of being locked in a vicious cycle of indebtedness and a sign of loss and pain resulting from being forced to part from the land, from Mother Earth, from Mati Ma/Dharati Ma.

While tech barons like Gates distract us with new constructs like "dematerialization," like the early colonizers they seek to control the real economy: land, seeds, agriculture and food. Controlling the resources that sustain life is controlling life. It is very profitable business and investment for billionaires. But it is a new debt trap for farmers.

Gates now controls the 773,000 seed accessions collected from farmers during the Green Revolution and held in the CGIAR public gene banks. He seeks to create and control one CGIAR where the voices of farmers and countries do not count. Gates has created Gates Agricultural Innovations, also known as "Gates Ag One" to control the imagination of the future of food and farming.

People across the world have woken up to the destruction to the health of the planet and our health by large industrial farms and food systems and the need to have small farms which grow more food, conserve and regenerate biodiversity and the earth, and sustain more people. To push the food system further and faster down the violent unsustainable path of largeness, we need a new spin on "sustainability." As is claimed, "Gates Ag One aims to help poor farmers, especially in Africa and South Asia, get the tools, technologies, and resources they need to lift themselves out of poverty." If each acre can produce more food, that's good news for farmers. But it also means we can devote less of the planet's surface to farmland, which is good news for forests and ecosystems."

These were the claims made when the Green Revolution was imposed on Punjab in India and now on Africa through AGRA, the Alliance for the Green Revolution in Africa. However, as I have shown in my book, *The Violence of the Green Revolution*, farmers of Punjab got trapped in debt. As Tim Wise shows in his contribution, AGRA has created hunger in Africa.

Further, the claim that industrial agriculture produces more food is false. Industrial agriculture produces nutritionally empty commodities, not food. As Navdanya has shown, "yield" is a not an accurate measurement. Nutrition per acre is what matters. Biodiverse, regenerative organic farming is the proven path of increasing nutrition per acre by getting rid of poisons. It protects the land by regenerating the soil, biodiversity, and water. It intensifies biodiversity and nutrition, not chemicals and poisons.

Brushing aside centuries of sustainable agriculture knowledge and practice, Gates is promoting digital agriculture with partnerships with the Poison Cartel. The myths of the Green Revolution are being continued in Gates Ag One, that chemical industrial farming grows more food: "American agriculture today is being transformed as farmers employ new technologies and Big Data to help them manage their crops. That can mean better yields with decreased use of fertilizers and pesticides. Which in turn means less impact on the environment." In a world economy organized on the myth of limitless growth and limitless greed, there are no limits. There is a perpetual demand for more land to grow more commodities.

The Amazon is being invaded into not to grow food to grow GMO soya for biofuel and animal feed. Gates Ag One is a plan to grow a handful of crops on very large farms with drones and robots, intensive chemical use, GMOs, to produce "raw materials" of carbohydrates and proteins for lab food. Land grab translates into the end of farmers, an end to real food that comes from the land and nourishes us. Gates-linked Cottonwood Ag is one of the founding members of a new coalition of farmland owners, operators and environmental groups called Leading Harvest to impose one global monoculture of unsustainable industrial agriculture on the world through is working to come up with "verifiable standards for sustainable farming" and create "a kind of sustainability seal of approval certifying that a given farm meets environmental standards."

Our work in Navdanya has shown that food sovereign farmers practicing regenerative organic agriculture, fair trade and local circular economies can grow more food using zero chemicals, conserve more water by shifting to water prudent nutritionally dense foods like millets and organic farming and increase farmer incomes by stopping the hemorrhage to but costly chemicals and be locked into unfair corporate controlled trade.

Farmers need freedom, justice, and fairness. Navdanya farmers are earning 10 times more that chemical commodity producing farmers through defending their seed freedom, food freedom and economic self-reliance. Instead of supporting the Seed, Food and Land Sovereignty path that farmers and ecologists are calling for, Gates wants to further fragment farming, further centralize control, and further promote a fake science of sustainability.

An industrial, globalized food system is allowing farmers to receive only 1 to 5% of what the consumer pays. Instead of ensuring that farmers are paid fair prices for food they grow to nourish us, Gates wants to lock them into new systems and control and dependencies and push them to a zero-budget economy where they receive nothing for the nourishment, food, and health they provide society.

Instead, as the Leading Harvest group says, "farmers will be paid for sustainability...There will be incentives for things like using less water, fewer chemicals, and storing more carbon." In other words, farmers will not be paid for growing food and the incentives will not be for farming systems as a whole, but for fragments of the system which can be tied to the new "net zero" climate solution based on continued emissions with "offsets." This is a global food and agriculture dictatorship. Conditionalities under any condition violate democratic principles and human rights. Farmers are guided by Earth care. The culture of Earth care needs to be respected and rewarded.

Conditionalities to "climate sins" of continued emissions is morally and ethically bankrupt. It is the contemporary equivalent of the "indulgences" received by the catholic bishops and priests. Pollution is against ecological principles. Conditionalities based on fake science and fake solutions will accelerate the violence against the land, the earth, the farmers. It will, of course, create new markets, new rents, new profits for Gates.

Gates is seeking new forms of lagaan collection from farmers through more chemical intensive farming, more "Bija Lagaan" from GMOs and patented seeds, and new "data lagaan" by locking farmers into digital agriculture. He has called data the new gold. But the tech billionaires get the gold and the land. And farmers lose their land, livelihoods, and life. His dystopian vision is to drive diversity, health, and freedom to extinction by controlling complex systems of seeds, knowledge, agriculture, and food. He violently imposes the monoculture paradigm of industrial farms and agriculture which further perpetuate disease-creating globalized food systems.

RECLAIM THE LAND: LAND BACK AND MITTI SATYAGRAHA

Indigenous people around the world—from Australia to America and India to Africa—have resisted land grab. All our struggles for decolonization and movements for freedom have been movements to defend Mother Earth and our rights that flow from her. Small farmers of India have resisted land grab since the beginning of colonization. In regions of the Northwest of India, peasants resisted Zamindari and defended themselves as independent owner cultivators and small farmers. The peasantry led India's first freedom movement against the British in 1857 and ended the rule of East India Company. The crown took over 10 million people over 10 years beginning in 1857.

Peasant movements led by Sir Chotu Ram, the Agriculture Minister of the Northwest Provinces, defended their land rights through the 1900 Land Alienation Act in the North Western Provinces. In 1984, Punjab farmers led the resistance to the slavery of the Green Revolution and the threat to their land and freedom. Even the contemporary farmers struggle is in defense of the land of peasant cultivators. As they say, our struggle is for the soil and soul ("jameen our jameer") of India. Following Gandhi's footsteps when Gandhi started the Dandi March for the 1930 Salt Satyagraha (Civil disobedience against the British laws on Salt Monopoly making it illegal for Indians to make salt) farmers have started a Mitti Satyagraha (Soil and Land Satyagraha) against corporate controlled food and agriculture systems and laws to impose it, collecting it from every place where farmers' blood has been shed in defense of land and soil from colonial times to the present.

Indigenous people of the Americas have started the Land Back movement. The Land Back movement is restoring our relationship with Mother Earth, overcoming the colonial separation, reclaiming the sovereignty of the land and all her beings as living and members of one Earth Family, embodying land sovereignty by reclaiming our commons by reclaiming our potential to live as community.

Will the future be shaped by the new digital zamindars, or will we return to Mother Earth, *Dharti ma*, remembering that we belong to her as children? Will we take her instructions to protect her, and in the process, protect the future of humanity? Otherwise, our planet will be shaped by those who are finding new ways to run the money machine by using old colonial systems of land grab while small farmers are losing their land because of debt and mortgages due to capital-intensive industrial. The World Economic Forum and the billionaires of the world, have launched "The Great Reset," telling us, "You will own nothing, and you will be happy."

They are not joining the movement for returning to Mother Earth belonging to her, not owning her as property. They are not saying they will give land back to Indigenous communities from whom it was grabbed. Their version of the "Great Reset" is not suggesting that we live like Indigenous cultures as one Earth Family, free of inequality, injustice, and hierarchies.

They are not referring to reclaiming the commons when they say we will own nothing, which means, "We will own everything: your land, food, body, and mind." They are referring to a deeper colonization and privatization, including the commons of life, now aided with invasive digital technologies.

Leading Harvest is about the next step of extraction. Reclaim from the earth and from farmers. It is not about caring for the land to create an abundant harvest and sharing the gifts of the earth as commons. It is an agenda for the ultimate enclosure of all commons, privatization of the last resource, and all the life-giving processes of the planet. But we have a choice. We can use our living intelligence to return home. To return to the earth. To return to the land. To co-create with the land.

We need to return to the land, the soil, for reclaiming our true identity, as the ecological basis of our being. All we need to remember is the "law of return," of giving back to the land with love and gratitude. It is through the soil and the land we are connected to other beings. When we take care of the land, we cultivate the earth community, cultivating hope and justice. We meet all our needs while not depriving others of their share to the gifts of the land.

Systems of extraction demand more and more land to meet the needs of fewer and fewer people. That is why a billion people are hungry. Ever increasing numbers are homeless and refugees. We can reduce our ecological footprint while leaving no one hungry. My work in service to the earth through Navdanya over the last few decades has taught me that when we shift from an extractive economy to the economy of care and giving, we produce more for more beings. When we obey the law of gratitude, the law of return —which is the law of the land—the soil becomes more fertile, more biodiversity flourishes, we grow more food and healthier food, have more to share with others.

The land provides for all, and provides everything we need: our food, clothing, shelter, and even identity. We can meet our needs and the needs of all with circular economies based on solidarity, care, and generosity. Creation of local living economies rooted in the land is now an ecological, ethical, justice, and survival imperative. Returning to the land is the road to resisting getting caught in the web of power constructed by Gates and other philanthrocapitalists.

A GLOBAL EMPIRE

Disrupting a World of Traditional Knowledge, Sovereignty, and Biodiversity

❧

VANDANA SHIVA

A GRICULTURE IS THE culture of the land. Respecting and caring for the land has sustained societies over thousands of years. Diverse agricultural systems have been cultivated in different ecological climates and across a multitude of biomes, from mountains to coastal areas and deserts to rainforests. Such diversity and decentralization create the foundation for true freedom of living systems: nature, culture, seeds, agriculture, and the knowledge that encompasses it all. Nature knows no monocultures; cultures know no homogeneity and uniformity. This was the agriculture we inherited before industrialization took hold.

INDIGENOUS PRACTICES OF SUSTAINABILITY

Indigenous communities have evolved the most ingenious farming systems over time. Australian Aborigines created "the biggest estate or garden on Earth" by cultivating rice, barley, desert raisin, wild tomatoes, yams, greens, cooper's clover, grass seeds, Nardoo, bogong moths, and bunya nuts over 60,000 years ago.[i]

Indigenous peoples of the Amazon were gardeners and agroforesters who grew crops among trees. Jennifer Watling, an archaeologist at the University of São Paulo in Brazil, found evidence that millions of inhabitants in the Amazon carefully managed the soil and biodiversity, leaving both richer.[ii] Kate Evans says Amazonian forest management, "looks a lot like agroforestry—managing the land-scape, encouraging palms and probably other useful plants as well."[1]

In the Andes, Indigenous people grew peanut, cotton, and squash as early as 5,000 to 9,000 years ago.[iii] Andean peasants of Peru and Bolivia evolved more than 4,000 varieties of potatoes grown along-side maize, quinoa, squash, and beans.[iv] Around 1265 CE, Aztec farmers created floating gardens on the lakes of Chalco and Xochimilco that surrounded Tenochtitlan, their capital city.[v]

Native Americans began farming approximately 7,000 years ago. In Mesoamerica, they transformed wild teosinte into a diversity of maize (corn) varieties 6,000 years ago.[vi] By 1000 CE, Native American farmers had developed complex agriculture based on three major crops—maize, beans, and squash—that led to breeding a host of other plants which provided a diversity of supplemental crops.[vii]

In the Middle East, the land of the Fertile Crescent, the earliest records of farming date back 23,000 years.[viii] Cereals were grown in Syria as early as 9,000 years ago, and figs were cultivated even earlier. Prehistoric seedless fruits discovered in the Jordan Valley suggest fig trees were being planted around 11,300 years ago.[ix]

In Asia, agricultural systems evolved 40,000 years ago.[x] The origins of rice and millet farming date to around 6000 BCE. Over time, Indian Indigenous peasants transformed a wild grass, Oryza sativa, into 200,000 rice varieties[xi] and evolved a great diversity of crops with more than 30,000 plants and more than 10,000 species cultivated.[xii]

As Sir Albert Howard stated in his book, *Agricultural Testament*, "What is happening today in the small fields of India and China took place many centuries ago. The agricultural practices of the orient have passed the Supreme test—they are almost as permanent as those of the primeval forest, of the prairie or of the ocean."[2]

---

1 Evans, Kate. "Ancient Amazonian Societies Managed the Forest Intensively but Sustainably - Here's What We Can Learn from Them." *Ensia*, August 15, 2019. https://ensia.com/features/ancient-amazonian-societies-managed-the-forest-intensively-but-sustainably-heres-what-we-can-learn-from-them/

2 Howard, Albert. *An Agricultural Testament*. Albatross Publishers, 2018.

MONOPOLIES OVER SEED, FOOD, AND AGRICULTURE

A century of chemical-intensive industrial agriculture has destroyed the planet's climate systems, pushed millions of species to extinction, desertified the soil, and destroyed water systems.

One hundred years ago, the chemicals produced by IG Farben—who we know today as the "Poison Cartel"—were used in WWI, WWII, and in concentration camps during the Holocaust were sold then into agriculture as agrichemicals.[xiii]

These chemicals found fertile terrain in the 1960s when the Green Revolution was imposed on the Third World by the World Bank, US government, Ford Foundation, and Rockefeller Foundation. Vast areas of monocultures wiped out evolutionary diversity and innovation that was developed over thousands of years.[xiv]

Seeds, evolved and bred by farmers over millennia, were gathered up and stored in newly created institutions such as the International Rice Research Institute (IRRI) in the Philippines and the International Maize and Wheat Improvement Centre (CIMMYT) in Mexico. These institutions have matured into the Consultative Group on International Agricultural Research (CGIAR), which Bill Gates has now taken over as "One CGIAR." One CGIAR is to be subsumed into his newest venture, "Gates Ag One" or "One Agriculture," which aims to control the world's seeds. Any attempt to try and prevent this takeover of farmers' seeds from preserving their heritage has been bluntly thwarted, as in the case of India's most eminent scientist Dr. R.H. Richharia.[xv]

Thus, we have today vast monocultures of chemically responsive Green Revolution varieties of seed along with the conditionalities, credits, and subsidies that come with them. In the 1990s, the Poison Cartel, having introduced chemicals in agriculture, quickly adopted genetic engineering as a mechanism to patent seed. They freely modified and patented farmers' seeds housed in the CGIAR and other gene banks by simply adding the toxic Bt gene or the Roundup Ready gene.[xvi]

In "The Bill & Melinda Gates Foundation and the International Rice Research Institute Alliance," Chito Medina, a leader in the peasants' struggle for seed, food, and knowledge sovereignty in the Philippines, outlines how these movements demand the shutting down of the CGIAR institutions such as IRRI.

Monocultures of GMO corn, soy, cotton, and canola have spread over millions of acres. Monocultures have intensified along with the use of toxic chemicals. Agriculture became decoupled from food, and crops were reduced to commodities used primarily as biofuel and animal feed. As a result, seed freedom and food freedom movements that opposed globalized industrial agriculture have grown stronger.[xvii]

Civil society marches and the Tribunal and People's Assemblies[xviii] against Monsanto widely made the multinational company's innumerable toxic transgressions and violations known. Monsanto's long-term partner, MoBay, and the pharmaceutical giant, Bayer, bought the corporation, conveniently taking it out of the public eye.[xix]

Experience and research have shown that agroecology based on biodiversity, seed freedom, and food freedom is essential to the future of food and farming.[xx] The United Nation's International Assessment of Agricultural Knowledge, Science, and Technology for Development (IAASTD) seminal report showed that neither the Green Revolution nor GMOs could feed the world while at the same time protecting the planet.[xxi]

Nonetheless, blind to the thousands of years of farmer's innovation and dismissive of the voice of scientists and farmers, Gates continues with his vision of building an agricultural empire. Notwithstanding the scientific evidence of the Green Revolution's failure, he and the Rockefeller Foundation co-founded the Alliance for a Green Revolution in Africa (AGRA) in 2006.

Timothy Wise's contribution on AGRA, "The Gates Foundation's Green Revolution Fails Africa's Farmers" assesses the failure of the Green Revolution in Africa, which was previously unsuccessful and caused lasting negative consequences in Asia, Latin America, and the United States.

There is mounting evidence showing that industrially grown and processed foods contribute significantly to a chronic disease epidemic we are now witnessing everywhere.[3] But the impacts of the industrial agriculture system on health is not one that Gates is particularly concerned with.

The Cartagena Protocol on Biosafety was established 20 years ago to regulate GMOs in the interests of environmental safety and public health. Golden Rice was one of many GMO propaganda myths that the biotech Poison Cartel attempted to promote, as mentioned in Farida Akhter's contribution, "Bt Brinjal: Alliance for Crooked Science & Corporate Lies." GMOs have a history of failure, as with the first generation of genetically modified Bt cotton[4] and Roundup Ready crops.[5]

In 2011, India introduced a moratorium on the genetically modified Bt brinjal, which Gates then took to Bangladesh. Akhter gives us the real story. Despite these warnings, Gates leads the way towards disrupting our body's metabolic systems and gut microbiome with his funding of industrially processed laboratory fake food, starting with lab-made "breast milk" and the Impossible Burger. Lab processed food is really about creating patents on our food, not about feeding people like Gates and his biotech colleagues would like us to think.

Since 2015, Gates has been swiftly expanding his empire over seeds, agriculture, and food by engaging in and funding large-scale as covered in the articles on the biopiracy of banana and climate-resilient seeds in "Section III: Biopiracy." Through digital technologies, he is voraciously mapping, patenting, and pirating seeds worldwide, ignoring and eroding all international government

---

3 "Food for Health." *Navdanya International | Main Themes*. https://navdanya-international.org/key-issues/food-for-health/

4 "BT Cotton Failure Case Witnesses from India and Burkina Faso." People's Assembly, November 2, 2016. https://peoplesassembly.net/bt-cotton-failure-case-witnesses-from-india-and-burkina-faso/

5 Union of Concerned Scientists. (2013). The rise of superweeds—And what to do about it. https://www.ucsusa.org/resources/rise-superweeds

treaties on the protection of biodiversity. He continues to subvert and sabotage the seed sovereignty of farmers and entire countries.

In "A Treaty to Protect Our Agricultural Biodiversity," José Esquinas-Alcazar, the eminent "seed man" at the Food and Agriculture Organization of the United Nations (FAO) and architect of the FAO Seed Treaty, draws our attention to how digital genome sequencing is subverting the sovereignty built into United Nations agreements. Aidé Jiménez-Martínez and Adelita San Vicente also write about the undermining of the Nagoya Protocol under the Convention on Biological Diversity through digital genome mapping.

False claims of precision and safety were made for the first generation of GMOs. Today, similar claims are again being made about gene editing technology. Jonathan Latham explains how gene editing is by no means a precise "cut and paste" technology.[6] Instead, it scrambles the evolving tree of life by creating unexpected and yet unknown effects on organisms. In this anthology, he reports on the public relations firms that was hired to manipulate the United Nations over gene drives.

The European Court of Justice has ruled that gene-edited organisms are GMOs. However, Gates is hastily pushing for deregulation with no regard for caution of potentially dangerous consequences. The Gates Ag One initiative has declared that time—essential to assess and implement safety—is the enemy. Gates is rushing to impose untested seeds, foods, and medicines on humanity while undermining all scientific or safety assessments and destroying safe alternatives that have existed for thousands of years. Gates has no compunction in endangering people's lives and health in his pursuit of power and wealth.

Gates Ag One is an explicit declaration of his intent to create an empire over life, biodiversity, food, and farming. As one humanity, we must prevent this empire that builds on and reinforces the Poison

---

6 Latham, Jonathan. "God's Red Pencil? CRISPR and Myths of Precise Genome Editing." Independent Science News | Food, Health and Agriculture Bioscience News, April 25, 2016. https://www.independentsciencenews.org/science-media/gods-red-pencil-crispr-and-the-three-myths-of-precise-genome-editing/

Cartel's century of ecocide and genocide, pushing us faster down the road towards extinction. Choosing the path of diversity and life, as opposed to the violent path of monocultures and destruction, is our duty to the Earth and future generations. At stake is the biological and cultural diversity of the world from which we attain our health, democracy, and food freedom.

CONTROL OVER THE WORLD'S SEED BANKS

Since the onset of the Neolithic Revolution around 10,000 years ago, farmers and communities have worked to improve yield, taste, nutrition, and other qualities of seeds. They have expanded and passed on knowledge about the health impacts and healing properties of plants, as well as about peculiar growing habits and interactions with other flora, animals, soil, and water. The free exchange of seeds among farmers has been the basis for maintaining biodiversity and food security.

A great seed and biodiversity piracy is underway, not just by corporations—becoming fewer and larger through mergers—but also by super-rich billionaires whose wealth and power open doors to their every whim. Leading the way is Microsoft mogul Bill Gates.

When the Green Revolution was brought into India and Mexico, farmers' seeds were "rounded-up" from their fields and locked in international institutions to be engineered for chemical input responses.[xxii]

The IRRI in the Philippines and CIMMYT were the first to take the diversity from farmer's fields and replace it with chemical monocultures of rice, wheat, and corn. Other organizations quickly followed.

This hijacking of farmers' seeds is best highlighted by the shameful removal of India's preeminent rice research scientist, Dr. R.H. Richharia, as Director of India's Central Rice Research Institute (CRRI) in Cuttack, Orissa (which housed the most extensive collection of rice diversity in the world) for refusing to allow the IRRI to pirate the collection out of India. With his removal at the behest of the World Bank, Indian peasant intellectual property was hijacked by the IRRI in the Philippines, which later became part of the newly created Consultative Group of International Agriculture Research (CGIAR).[xxiii]

Farmers' seed heritage was held in the private seed banks of CGIAR, a consortium of 15 international agricultural research centers controlled by the World Bank, the Rockefeller, and Ford Foundations, and of course, the Bill and Melinda Gates Foundation (BMGF). Since 2003, BMGF has poured more than $720 million into CGIAR centers. CGIAR gene banks presently manage 768,576 accessions of farmer's seeds.[7] Taken together, CGIAR gene banks represent the largest and most widely used collections of crop diversity in the world.

The Bill & Melinda Gates Foundation operates a bit like the World Bank, using its financial power and prowess to control agriculture, influence government, and impact institutional agriculture policies. Being the largest funder of the CGIAR by far, Gates has successfully accelerated the transfer of research and seeds from scientific research institutions to commodity-based corporations. This has resulted in centralization which facilitates pirating through intellectual property laws and the creation of seed monopolies through regulations.

The urgency in this restructuring of CGIAR is reflected in the International Panel of Experts on Sustainable Food Systems (IPES-Food) open letter from July 21, 2020:

> "The process now underway to reform the CGIAR is therefore imperative and of major public interest. The 'One CGIAR' process seeks to merge the CGIAR's 15 legally independent but cooperating centers, headquartered in 15 countries, into one legal entity. The impetus has come from some of its biggest funders, notably the Bill and Melinda

---

7 "CGIAR Genebank Platform." CGIAR. https://www.cgiar.org/the-genebank -platform/

Gates Foundation, the World Bank, and the US and UK governments."[8]

The aim of One CGIAR—overseen by One CGIAR Common Board—is to become part of Gates Ag One, Gates' latest move in controlling the world's seed supply.[xxiv] Gates has indicated he will more than double the CGIAR present budget from $850 million to $2 billion per year.[xxv]

Despite the long-recognized failure of the Green Revolution in India and Mexico, Gates launched AGRA in 2006. The folly of imposing this technology in Africa is well-documented in the two following articles by Nicoletta Dentico and Tim Wise.

The Seed Freedom movement has called for the CGIAR gene banks to return stolen seed varieties to farmers. The lessons of the Green Revolution since the 1960s have shown us that the chemical path of monocultures has undermined Earth's capacity to support life and food production by destroying biodiversity,[xxvi] accelerating species rate extinction,[xxvii] and contributing to climate change.[xxviii] Furthermore, it has dispossessed small farmers through debt from purchasing external inputs and has undermined food and nutrition security.[xxix] The experience of the last half-century has made it clear that seed sovereignty, food sovereignty, and knowledge sovereignty are the only viable futures of food and farming.

Besides taking control of farmer's seeds in the CGIAR seed banks, the BMGF and Rockefeller Foundation are investing heavily in collecting seeds from across the world and storing them at the Svalbard Global Seed Vault in the Arctic Archipelago, the "Doomsday Vault," created to collect and hold a global collection of the world's seeds, in association with CGIAR and the Crop Trust.[xxx]

The Crop Trust, based in Germany, funds, and coordinates the Svalbard Seed Vault. In addition to the Bill and Melinda Gates Foundation, its funders include the Poison Cartel adherents CropLife

---

8 IPES food. "OPEN LETTER | 'One CGIAR' with Two Tiers of Influence?", July 21, 2020. http://www.ipes-food.org/pages/OneGGIAR

International, DuPont, Pioneer Hi-Bred International, Inc., KWS SAAT SE & Co. KGaA, and Syngenta AG.

The largest numbers of accessions stored in the Seed Vault are varieties of rice, wheat, and barley crops. There are more than 150,000 samples of wheat and rice and close to 80,000 samples of barley. Other well-represented crops are sorghum, Phaseolus bean species, maize, cowpea, soybean, kikuyu grass, and chickpea. Crops such as potatoes, peanuts, Cajanus beans, oats, rye, and alfalfa. The cereal hybrid, *Triticosecale*, and Brassicas represent between 10,000 to 20,000 seed samples.

CROP TRUST DONORS

DONORS	RECEIVED MONEY (US DOLLARS)
Australia	20,165,706
Bundesverband Deutscher Planzenzuechter	25,735
CropLife International	43,726
Czech Republic	40,000
Dupont/ Pioneer Hi-bred	2,000,000
Egypt	25,000
Ethiopia	25,000
Gates Foundation/UN Foundation	8,003,118
Germany	50,726,348
India	456,391
International Seed Federation	80,785
Ireland	4,144,250
KWS SAAT AG	35,589
Norway	31,491,161
Netherlands	489,000

DONORS	RECEIVED MONEY (US DOLLARS)
New Zealand	1,453,800
Republic of Korea	442,556
Slovak Republic	20,000
Spain	2,629,650
Sweden	11,886,620
Switzerland	10,992,704
Syngenta AG	1,000,000
United Kingdom	19,468,582
United States – before Farm Bill	42,825,073
United States – US Farm Bill	11,585,120
Subtotal	220,055,915
Concessional Loan	59,055,611
Subtotal	59,055,611
Grand Total	279,105,526

It should come as no surprise that Gates is also funding Diversity Seek (DivSeek), a global project launched in 2015 to map and patent the genetic data of the peasant's seeds—the seven million crop accessions held in gene banks—through genomic mapping.[xxxi] Biopiracy is carried out through the convergence of information technology and biotechnology, where patents are taken on seeds through "mapping" their genomes and genome sequences.

While living seed needs to evolve in situ (or "in place"), patents on seed genomes can be taken from seed ex situ (or "off-site"). DivSeek is designed to "mine" and extract data in seeds and "censor" out the commons. In effect, it robs peasants of their seeds and knowledge, it robs the seed of its integrity and diversity, it erases evolutionary history and the seed's link to the soil by reducing it to a simple "code." This genetic colonialism is an enclosure of the genetic commons.[xxxii]

The participating institutions in DivSeek are the CGIAR nodes and universities like Cornell and Iowa State University, which are being increasingly privatized by the biotechnology industry and the Gates Foundation. For example, BMGF funds Cornell's Alliance for Science, the corporate world's pseudo-science propaganda outlet, while Iowa State University promotes the unethical human feeding trials of GMO bananas. Other Gates-funded DivSeek partners include the African Agricultural Technology Foundation and Africa-Brazil Agricultural Innovation Marketplace developed by the Brazilian Agricultural Research Corporation (Embrapa).[xxxiii]

Through a new front corporation, Editas Medicine, BMGF is investing in an experimental genetic engineering tool for gene editing called CRISPR-Cas9.[xxxiv] Although the technology itself is immature and inaccurate, it has started a gold rush for new patents. As a result, the language of "gene editing" and "educated guesses" is creeping into scientific discourse.

Piracy of common genomic data of millions of plants bred by peasants is termed "big data." Big data, however, is not knowledge. It is not even information. It is privateered data—pirated and privatized. Seeds are not just germplasm; they are living, self-organizing entities, subjects of evolution, history, culture, and relationships.

In the 1980s, Monsanto led the push for GMOs and patents on seed and life. Today, the flag bearer is Bill Gates. In a nutshell, one billionaire gave free access to use his wealth to bypass all international treaties and multilateral governance structures to help global corporations hijack the biodiversity and wealth of peasants by financing unscientific and undemocratic processes such as DivSeek and unleashing untested technologies such as CRISPR on humanity.

Over the last two decades, thousands of concerned citizen organizations including the Convention on Biological Diversity (CBD), the Cartagena Biosafety Protocol to the CBD, and the International Treaty on Plant Genetic Resources Treaty for Food and Agriculture (ITPGRFA), have acted and written laws to protect the biodiversity of the planet, the rights of farmers to seed, and the rights of consumers to safety.

Contributors to this report outline how Bill Gates and his foundation routinely undermine international treaties created to protect biodiversity, farmers' rights, and the sovereignty of countries and communities of their seed and biodiversity wealth.

An Overview of Bill & Melinda Gates Agricultural Innovations

❦

NAVDANYA

Having become a billionaire through the deregulation of corporate globalization, Bill Gates is now leading the recolonization of Asian, Latin American, and African agriculture. Gates has taken the failed Green Revolution to Africa as the Alliance for the Green Revolution in Africa (AGRA) and has now launched the same initiative under the new name Ag One, this time pushing the new technologically updated Green Revolution to shape the future of agriculture.[i]

WHAT IS THE GOAL OF AG ONE?

In January 2020, a new initiative announced by the Gates Foundation called The Bill & Melinda Gates Agricultural Innovations LLC, or Gates Ag One, was launched. Gates Ag One was formulated to be a subsidiary of the Gates Foundation, led by Joe Cornelius, the previous director of the BMGF Global Growth & Opportunity Division. Interestingly, Cornelius came from being the Managing Director of Agriculture, Food, and Nutrition at Bayer Crop Science, following his previous position in the 1990s as Director for International Development at Monsanto.[ii]

Gates Ag One is hailed as a new non-profit to "bring scientific breakthroughs to smallholder farmers whose yields are threatened by the effects of climate change"[iii] and shrink the supposed "productivity gaps" present in Africa, Asia, and Latin America. It will work with the BMGF's Agricultural Development team and other partners across sectors to "accelerate the development of innovations" that are "needed to improve crop productivity and help smallholder farmers, the majority of whom are women, adapt to climate change."[iv]

The goal of Gates Ag One is claimed "to empower smallholder farmers with the affordable, high-quality tools, technologies, and resources they need to lift themselves out of poverty." According to the creation document, "yields on farms in these regions are already far below what farmers elsewhere in the world achieve, and climate change will make their crops even "less productive."[v]

Rodger Voorhies, president of the Gates Foundation's Global Growth & Opportunity Division, has said that Gates Ag One plans to work with partners from the public and private sector to commercialize "resilient, yield-enhancing seeds and traits." He adds, "We needed to accelerate the access to the kinds of products and services that low-income people and smallholder farmers need" due to the long time it takes for these new discoveries to move from invention to development, lab testing, and through regulation once commercially viable for the field.[vi] Voorhies explains:

> "We didn't think that research was flowing down to the crops that matter most to smallholder farmers in a timeframe that could reach them....But ultimately, the Gates Foundation did not see another way to ensure that early-stage discoveries, such as water use efficiency for crops that will face extremes of droughts and floods, are made accessible and affordable to smallholder farmers as quickly as possible."[vii]

In short, they are hoping to artificially accelerate the process of introducing "new technologies" to farmers through increased investment along with public and private partnerships while having total freedom in their business model as a separate entity from the Bill and Melinda Gates Foundation.

WHERE WILL IT WORK?

In a document released by the Gates Foundation itself, it is claimed that Ag One will work in "South Asia - with a population of about 1.8 billion - and Sub-Saharan Africa - home to around 1 billion people."[viii]

Their creation statement did not mention the implementation of the Ag One program in Latin America, called Ag Tech, through a partnership with the Inter-American Institute for Cooperation on Agriculture (IICA).[ix] The program's initiation point is planned to be in Argentina and then subsequently implemented throughout the rest of Latin America.

AG ONE, GATES GLOBAL COMMISSION ON ADAPTATION, AND TAKEOVER OF THE CGIAR SYSTEM

Overlapping behind several of the initiatives launched by Bill and Melinda Gates is a characteristic urgency that all new technologies and mitigation efforts must be pushed, adopted, and quickly implemented in the name of stopping climate change. This rhetoric stands to mask a wide section of initiatives, organizations, and funding schemes whose real purpose runs counter to any type of true climate change alleviation.

The same is true for Ag One, as the foundation is tied indirectly to another Gates initiative called the Gates Global Commission on Adaptation focused on pushing only technological solutions for adaptation and mitigation, through such things as filling the "data gap" of the Global South, creating smart green cities, and increasing development (along with return on investment) opportunities through these efforts.[x] Ag One was, therefore, launched as part of its 2019 year of climate action.[xi]

Along with Gates, the Global Commission on Adaptation hosts as its co-chairs two international organization heavyweights: Ban-Ki Moon, the previous 8th Secretary-General of the United Nations, who serves as the head of the organization's board and Kristalina Georgieva, the current Managing Director at the International Monetary Fund (IMF).

Forming part of Ag One's strategy will be the doubling of funding to CGIAR, an organization Bill Gates has had his eye on for quite some time. Hence, in September of 2019 at the UN Climate Summit, as part of the Gates Global Commission on Adaptation's "Year of Action," CGIAR announced the gift of more than $79 million through an investment coalition headed by Gates and made up of the World Bank, the UK, the Netherlands, the European Commission, Switzerland, Sweden, and Germany.[xii] According to the CGIAR announcement:

> "US $310 million [is to be given by] the Bill & Melinda Gates Foundation over the next three years to support CGIAR's shared agenda to tackle climate change and make food production in the developing world more productive, resilient, and sustainable. The foundation is the second largest donor to CGIAR after the US Agency for International Development (USAID), with investments contributing to work in crop breeding, seed systems, gender equity, livestock, nutrition, and policy."[xiii]

This aligns the vision of CGIAR with that of Ag One. The recently released Action Group on Erosion, Technology and Concentration (ETC) report states that a new System Reference Group (SRG), struck in 2018, has delivered its recommendations in July 2019, calling for the formal consolidation of the 15 CGIAR centers into one. The meeting of the 15 CGIAR chairs was convened at Bioversity International (BI) headquarters outside Rome in December 2019 to discuss the "mega-merger."

The consolidation would create one international board that would be responsible for all 15 centers.[xiv] The dangers seem imminent when one looks deeper and sees that Tony Cavalieri co-chairs the SRG, Senior Program Officer of the Bill & Melinda Gates Foundation, and Marco Ferroni, Chair of the System Management Board, retired as head of the Syngenta Foundation.

The unification is being pushed by the Gates and Syngenta Foundations, USAID, the UK, Canada, Australia, and Germany. Unification will mean a blurring of lines between private and public sectors. Private, profit-driven agendas will be clothed as the public agenda through the launching of Ag One.

This also provides unprecedented leverage in individual country policy and mass access to genetic seed resources. This hunger for influencing global food policy comes as no surprise as the Gates Foundation website states, "A key trigger of agricultural transformation is a conducive policy environment."[xv]

When reading the agenda of the newly launched Ag One, it is reminiscent of the rhetoric of the 2008 Alliance for the Green Revolution in Africa (AGRA), which essentially served to revamp the ghost of the already failed Green Revolution of the 1960s. Considering the multiple alliances with agrochemical companies, Ag One is meant to pick up AGRA's baton with a new tech twist and run with it to the rest of the Global South.

✳

THE GATES AGENDA
SUBVERTING OUR INTERNATIONAL TREATIES
AND UNDERMINING THE PROTECTION OF BIODIVERSITY

Convention on Biological Diversity (CBD) In 1992, the international community adopted this convention in Rio De Janeiro at the Earth Summit. The objectives of the convention were:

- ► Conserving biological diversity

- ▸ Sustainable use of resources
- ▸ Fair and equitable sharing of benefits that arise out of commercial use

Nagoya Protocol Under CBD, there are multiple protocols created. One of them is the 2010 Nagoya Protocol on access and benefit-sharing. The objective was to establish a legally binding framework for implementing the concept of access and benefit-sharing as birthed in the CBD. The protocol creates duties and obligations on the parties engaging with Indigenous communities for the use of genetic resources and knowledge.

International Treaty on Plant Genetic Resources Treaty for Food and Agriculture (ITPGRFA) Also known as the International Seed Treaty, the objective is conservation and sustainable use of all plant genetic resources for food and agriculture. It also involves the fair and equitable sharing of the benefits arising out of their use, in harmony with the Convention on Biological Diversity, for sustainable agriculture and food security.

Digital Mapping: Subverting Regulations on Access to Biodiversity
These international frameworks made to protect our biodiversity are being completely subverted through digital mapping of the genome. Biopiracy is being carried out through the convergence of information technology and biotechnology by taking patents through "mapping" genomes and genome sequences. While living seed needs to evolve in situ, patents on genomes can be taken through access to seed ex situ. This undermines farmers' rights as you don't need permission from them once the genome has been digitally mapped.

New GMOs: CRISPR and Gene Editing Gates has been pushing it for several years now, with a huge investment of $120 million. Gates used to fund others to get this done, but impatient with lack of progress, he now wants to do it himself.

Gene Editing is a Failed Technology Gene editing has been proven to be a failure because of how inexact and unpredictable it is. It was found that CRISPR introduced more than 1,500 single-nucleotide unintended mutations and more than 100 larger deletions or insertions into the genomes of mice.

Data Mining from Farmers Such experiments with data mapping are already underway. For example, in India, Digital Green, an initiative of the Gates Foundation, is described as "a global development organization that empowers smallholder farmers to lift themselves out of poverty by harnessing the collective power of technology and grassroots-level partnerships."[xvi] It is an NGO that focuses on "training farmers to make and show short videos where they record their problems and share solutions." It was first conceived as a project in Microsoft Research India's Technology for Emerging Markets. It has received $1.3 million from the Walmart Foundation. One project, the South Asia Food and Nutrition Security Initiative (SAFANSI), is funded by the World Bank. It also received the $400,600 Global Impact Award from Google in 2013. The Bill and Melinda Gates Foundation has put more than $10 million into this initiative.

This "data" from farms and farmers are being collected without their knowledge or prior consent. Problematically, this "data" is also closely connected to farmers' personal information like the farm location, yields, and other sensitive information. Farmers also have little say as to what even happens to the data being collected.

This brings in questions of data sovereignty as the data being collected is likely to be developed into products that are sold back to farmers as essential products for successful farming. The institutions that are pushing for this new data-ag and its regulation are directly or indirectly in the hands of the Gates Foundation. The most blatant example is the World Economic Forum's World Food Systems Summit (WFSS), which is to be headed by former Rwandan Minister of Agriculture and president of Gates-funded AGRA.

In the concept paper of the summit, there was no mention of agroecology, Indigenous peoples, or civil society. It specifically

mentions precision agriculture and genetic engineering as important for addressing future food security while also expressing vocal
support for the fourth industrial revolution around data.

For the countries where Ag One is looking to operate, there is very
little legislation, regulation, or concrete trade agreements around
digital data transfers, leaving countries in the Global South with
little capacity to handle this new influx of "data resources," leaving
them even more vulnerable to further predation by large corporations. Gates' digital agenda with Ag One will also serve to exacerbate
this already stark power inequality through the centralization of all
farming data out of the hands of farmers. This centralization also
then leaves the door open for further biopiracy, centrally managed
data that can only be accessed through paywalls, surveillance, and
further policing by big corporations of their product use and so on.

The pivotal example of these consequences is the biopiracy being
carried out through the convergence of information technology and
biotechnology by taking patents through "mapping" genomes and
genome sequences.[xvii] While living seed needs to evolve in situ, patents on genomes can be taken through access to seed ex situ. This
undermines farmers' rights as you don't need permission from the
farmers anymore once the genome has been digitally mapped.[xviii]

Making Time an Enemy: A Push for Deregulation   All of this is only
possible through an active agenda of deregulation. Using the rhetoric of climate change as the cause for extreme urgency, according to
Rodger Voorhies, president of Global Growth & Opportunity Division, "research and development take years to get from the lab to
the field, and while the Agricultural Development team funds the
development of new tools and technologies designed to meet the
needs of smallholder farmers, there were delays in translating these
discoveries to affordable products." He added, "we didn't think that
research was flowing down to the crops that matter most to smallholder farmers in a timeframe that could reach them."[xix]

But the only way this rush is possible for Ag One is through the
agenda of deregulation of biosafety. As the initiative announcement

states, its objective is to "get the products from the labs into the fields, faster and more massive than before." The objective of Ag One seems to be to fund these new innovative scientific discoveries with hopes of getting them through as quickly as possible to the point of commercialization with as little testing, assessment, and regulation as possible. One such example is CRISPR and gene editing, where they tried to bypass regulation altogether by claiming that gene editing is a non-GMO technology and is different from transgenic.

BUILDING ON EVOLUTION AND THE DIVERSE AGROECOLOGICAL KNOWLEDGE OF MANY CULTURES

There is an illusion that running faster on the chemical and Poison Cartel treadmill, now equipped with artificial intelligence and robots, will produce more food and feed the hungry. On the contrary, the tools and technologies of the Poison Cartel have brought the planet and the lives of farmers to the brink with climate havoc, species extinction, water crises, farmer incomes collapsing to zero, and food-related diseases killing larger numbers of people.

In the end, it appears that Gates' new Ag One initiative is the same wolf in different clothing. He is attempting to push faster and harder for the whole world to adopt his version of the already failed Green Revolution with a new tech twist. His is a completely disconnected worldview from the realities of small farmers and their need for food system sovereignty.

As shown, the future of agriculture is based on biodiversity, seed sovereignty, and agroecology, not on "Ag Tech" or "Ag One." We need to rise up, look past the corporate narrative and look towards time-tested Indigenous knowledge and agroecology to shape the future of agriculture based on biodiversity and cultural diversity. We need a rejuvenation of small farms with real people who care for the land, care for life, care for the future, and produce diverse, healthy, fresh, ecological food for all.

The Bill & Melinda Gates Foundation and the International Rice Research Institute Alliance

❧

CHITO P. MEDINA

B ILL GATES IS one of the wealthiest people on Earth, and he founded the world's largest philanthropic organization. The Bill and Melinda Gates Foundation (BMGF), organized in 2000, was reported to have total assets of $46.8 billion (as of 2018).[i] It has become the world's largest donor and the most influential player in international development, particularly in global health and agriculture policies, research, and programs. In fact, its control of agricultural development is far greater than the influence of most countries.

BMGF is the most significant private charitable donor to the CGIAR system and the third overall donor (after the US and UK), contributing 13% of the total budget.[ii] In recognition of its huge contribution, BMGF is the only private/non-governmental voting member in the CGIAR System Council.

Over 15 years, BMGF's direct grants to IRRI averaged $10.3 million per year, which amounts to 15% of IRRI's annual budget.[iii] Out of all IRRI's bilateral and restricted research funds for 2016, BMGF grants of $11.7 million constitute 18%.[iv]

The generous philanthropic contributions of BMGF towards alleviating poverty and hunger would be welcomed, except that such contributions carry a particular agenda. It attempts to bring simplistic solutions based on science and technology to address the complex problems of hunger and poverty. Such large-scale science and technology are, in fact, more aligned to corporate interests than the contexts and needs of poor farmers. Notably, BMGF lacks transparency and accountability. The philanthropic foundation is only accountable to its three trustees, Bill Gates, Melinda Gates, and Warren Buffet.

This paper analyzes the grants of BMGF to the Consultative Group on International Agricultural Research (CGIAR), focusing on one of its research centers, the International Rice Research Institute (IRRI).

THE INTERNATIONAL RICE RESEARCH INSTITUTE (IRRI)

The International Rice Research Institute (IRRI) was established in the Philippines on April 4, 1960, by the Rockefeller Foundation and Ford Foundation, "to feed the world" with a Malthusian approach to the issues. Its signature program was called the Green Revolution in rice. Implicit in the name of the program, the Green Revolution alluded to an alternative to communism in those years.

IRRI's Green Revolution in rice is composed of technology centered on "high yielding variety" seeds under conditions of high fossil energy-based inputs (fertilizers, pesticides, and machinery), irrigation, and production loans. It was successful in converting rural peasant farming into a capitalistic market economy. This helped pave the way for globalization and corporate control of agriculture and food systems.

In a broader picture, similar international research centers on agriculture, forestry, and fishery were established. In 1971, the Consultative Group on International Agricultural Research (CGIAR) was formed to serve as a coordinating body through which funds for international agricultural research could be administered to its 15 research centers. Being the biggest private donor to CGIAR, Bill

Gates now sits in the CGIAR Fund Council. The chair of CGIAR's System Council Board, Juergen Voegele, is Vice President for Sustainable Development of the World Bank.

IRRI, as an international research organization, appears to be public. It projects as an unquestioned public interest institution, but it is not. IRRI is a nonprofit organization. Research donors are governments, foundations, and business corporations. It has tremendous power to influence the direction of agricultural research, but it lacks public accountability. In fact, IRRI in the Philippines is protected by law (Presidential Decree 1620) and is not accountable for any adverse effects of its research and technology.

Who determines IRRI's Agenda? Gone are the days when science was unquestionably for the public good. IRRI is always on the path of the "modernization" of agriculture, which is unmistakably industrial farming. Its agenda is guided by corporate values, influenced by corporate representatives, and often determined by its funding sources. In fact, there is a funding mechanism (Window 3 funds)[1] wherein the donor designates funds to individual research centers for specific purposes.[2] It used to be called commissioned research, but perhaps realizing the very private image of the term, they now call it bilateral restricted funding. This means that the funds provided by the donor are for predetermined specific activities and outputs. Often, any commercial results are reserved for the funding donor.

BMGF FUNDING TO CGIAR AND IRRI

Over 13 years (2008–2020), BMGF has granted a total of $1.136 billion in funding to 12 CGIAR research centers and the CGIAR system organization (Table 1). In fact, it contributes 13% of CGIAR's entire budget. From 2008 to 2020, BMGF funded 15 IRRI projects with a

---

1 Window 3 (W3) are project investment funds allocated by funders that they and partners define and which are coordinated with larger investments.

2 https://www.cgiar.org/funders/trust-fund/#:~:text=Window%203%20(W3)%20%E2%80%93%20Project,aligned%20with%20system%2Dwide%20investments.

total of $1.54 million (Table 2). Over the years, the foundation has been contributing an average of 15% of IRRI's budget per year. On a yearly basis, BMGF contributed 18% of all research grants in 2016[v] and 64% of all the Bilateral Restricted research grants in the same year.

Table 1. Project grants funded by Bill and Melinda Gates Foundation to the CGIAR and its research centers (2008–2020)

Agricultural Research Center	No. of Projects	Total Grants (US $)
Int'l. Maize and Wheat Improvement Center (CIMMYT)	25	280,155,682
Int'l. Food Policy Research Institute (IFPRI)	27	174,869,347
Int'l. Institute of Tropical Agriculture (IITA)	26	158,602,630
International Rice Research Institute (IRRI)	**15**	**154,544,972**
Int'l. Crops Research Institute for the Semi-Arid Tropics (ICRISAT)	11	127,934,330
International Potato Center (CIP)	11	90,588,729
Int'l. Livestock Research Institute (ILRI)	16	65,907,489
Int'l. Center for Tropical Agriculture (CIAT)	13	29,229,888
World Agroforestry Center (ICRAF)	3	18,917,317
Int'l. Water Management Institute (IWMI)	1	9,012,826
Africa Rice Center	3	6,004,502
Bioversity International	3	5,097,884
Center for Int'l. Forestry Research (CIFOR)	0	0

Int'l. Center for Agric. Research in the Dry Areas (ICARDA)	0	0
WorldFish	0	0
Subtotal (Research)		**1,120,865,596**
CGIAR System Organization	4	15,494,677
Grand Total		**1,136,360,273**

There are at least five big research projects funded by BMGF in IRRI:

- ▸ *The Realizing Increased Photosynthetic Efficiency (RIPE) program* started in 2008 and lasted for seven years, where BMGF contributed $19.4 million. It was touted as an innovative scientific research program attempting to make rice, a C3 plant, into a C4 plant through genetic engineering in order to make it more efficient in photosynthesis for higher grain production. C4 super rice was projected to produce 50% more yield and significantly contribute to global food security. To date, except for some knowledge gained, there is no tangible C4 super rice produced.
- ▸ *Golden Rice* is an IRRI project funded by BMGF. The first phase lasted from 2010 to 2017 with a total grant of more than $10 million. The second phase lasts from 2017 to 2022 with a total grant of $18 million. It aims to be able to reach the approved commercial stage in Bangladesh and the Philippines by then. Despite strong opposition, overwhelming funding to push Golden Rice is too big to reckon with in the fight against this GMO.
- ▸ *The Stress Tolerant Rice for Africa and South Asia (STRASA)* project focusing on the development of seed systems tolerant to drought, submergence, salinity, iron toxicity, cold, and biotic stress. The first and second phases were implemented from 2007–2010 and 2011–2014 with $20 million for each phase. A third phase lasted from 2014–2019 with a

budget of $32.77 million. Perhaps the most publicized output is Swarna-Sub1 rice or scuba rice. The gene used here came from the naturally occurring local Indian rice variety Swarna, which was bred to modern varieties using marker-assisted selection.

▸ *Transforming Rice Breeding (TRB),* which was implemented from 2013 to 2018 with a budget of $12.5 million. It focused on rice germplasm development and networking of trial and testing of newly developed varieties.

▸ *The Accelerated Genetic Gain in Rice in South Asia and Africa (AGGRi) Alliance* organized from the merger of STRASA and TRB with a new funding round of $34.99 billion from BMGF. It aims to modernize and unify existing rice breeding efforts, strengthen its partnership with the National Agricultural Research and Extension System (NARES), increase rice yield, and improve the livelihood of rice farmers in South Asia and Africa.

Another significant BMGF supported program where IRRI is involved (IFPRI and CIAT are the project holders) is Harvest Plus, otherwise referred to as Challenge Program. This program started in the early 1990s, and BMGF started supporting it in 2003. It is a large alliance of nine CGIAR research centers, universities, private sectors, NGOs, along with other international and national agricultural research institutes. This program aims to develop crops to provide higher levels of micronutrients such as iron, zinc, and vitamin A through biofortification. Rice biofortification is done through conventional breeding, transgenic biofortification (Golden Rice), and gene editing.

In its networking mechanism, IRRI is the convenor and secretariat for the Global Rice Science Partnerships (GRiSP), which is also indirectly supported by BMGF through other programs. This network influences and unifies all research activities on rice science.

Lastly, IRRI is the secretariat of the Hybrid Rice Research and Development Consortium (HRRD), which was organized in 2007. HRRDC laid down the foundation for a direct relationship between IRRI and private seed companies, with the former providing parent lines to the latter. GRiSP, AGGRi Alliance, and HRRDC are big networks for the consolidation, diffusion, and with it, influence on rice research, development, and farming.

Table 2. BMG Foundation Funding Granted to IRRI from 2008 to 2019.

YEAR	AMOUNT (US DOLLAR)	PURPOSE OF PROJECT
RIPE Program (Realizing Increased Photosynthetic Efficiency)		
2008 (to 2012)	11,017,675	To increase yield by increase the photosynthetic efficiency of rice (44)
2012 (to 2016)	8,375,747	To increase yield by increasing the photosynthetic efficiency of rice (43)
Golden Rice Project		
2010 (to 2017)	10,287,784	To address the problem of Vitamin A deficiency among millions of people in the Philippines and Bangladesh (83)
2017 (to 2022)	18,000,000	To develop and deploy healthier rice varieties genetically engineered to improve the nutritional and health status of the poor in Asia, particularly in Bangladesh and the Philippines (63)
STRASA (Stress Tolerant Rice For Africa and South Asia Project)		

YEAR	AMOUNT (US DOLLAR)	PURPOSE OF PROJECT
2011 (to 2014)	20,000,000	To develop and disseminate stress-tolerant rice varieties for smallholder farmers in Africa and South Asia (37)
2014 (to 2019)	32,770,000	To reduce poverty and hunger and increase food and income security for farm families and rice consumers in South Asia and sub-Saharan Africa, through the development and dissemination of high-yielding rice varieties tolerant of abiotic stresses (61)
TRB Project (Transforming Rice Breeding)		
2013 (to 2018)	12,500,000	To significantly increase the efficiency and genetic gain in irrigated rice breeding programs by using modern breeding tools and approaches to increase food and income security of resource-poor farmers and to ensure rice food security in Asia and Africa (61)
AGGRi Alliance (Accelerated Genetic Gain in Rice in South Asia and Africa) merged TRB and STRASA		
2018 (to 2023)	34,990,000	To unify existing rice breeding efforts targeting South Asia and Sub-Saharan Africa into a system capable of sustainably delivering genetic gain in farmers' fields (60)
Other Project Grants		
2008	22,128.658	To decrease hunger and poverty in South Asia by increasing rice, wheat, and maize production (43)

YEAR	AMOUNT (US DOLLAR)	PURPOSE OF PROJECT
2009	96,869	To support the Conference in Beijing, China, in connection with the IAAE conference (30)
2010	600,000	To monitor the diffusion of improved crop varieties in rainfed areas of South Asia (40)
2013	690,327	To conduct a pilot survey to monitor varietal adoption and rice production in South Asia (12)
2014	3,359,914	To increase rice productivity in South Asia and improve agricultural policies (54)
2016	880,000	To help Indian and Bangladeshi rice breeding programs deliver higher rates of genetic gains in the farmers' fields by improving product design, shorten breeding cycles, increase selection pressure, and improve heritability (50)
2019	954,527	To evaluate the effectiveness of the organization and identify potential improvements in strategy, management, and partnerships that could enhance the rate of genetic gain delivered to smallholder farmers (16)

THE OUTCOME OF IRRI SCIENCE

The introduction of IRRI's modern rice varieties through the Green Revolution has caused genetic erosion wherein a majority of local rice varieties in rice-growing countries have disappeared. In Indonesia, around 1,500 traditional rice varieties and landraces disappeared between 1975 and 1990.

In India, some 30,000 rice varieties are down to just 10 varieties in 75% of its rice.[vi] 99% of rice fields in Pakistan were planted with only four High Yielding Varieties (HYV)[vii] and at least 85% of the rice fields in Burma, Indonesia, Philippines, and Thailand are occupied by HYVs.[viii]

The associated biodiversity in rice fields was also displaced due to monocultures. Edible fish, snails, crustaceans, and plants were killed by pesticides. Due to intensive planting and reliance on synthetic fertilizer and soil nutrient imbalance, depletion became prevalent. Pests and diseases had periodic outbreaks due to high nitrogen levels, overuse of pesticides, and crop management practices. Water, soil, biodiversity, and humans were poisoned by pesticide residues. The expensive inputs of fertilizers and pesticides became an economic burden to farmers, and many became bankrupt. The pervasive modern rice technology developed by IRRI, supported by aggressive government extension work, made farmers forget how to grow rice.

IRRI is a tool for privatizing farmers' seeds. They have collected 132,442 rice accessions from farmers and stored them in a gene bank, with duplicates in the Svalbard Seed Vault in Norway. They value farmer's rice varieties because of their genetic diversity but never acknowledge the associated farmer's knowledge. The seed diversity that farmers developed is neither officially recognized nor honored. Instead, IRRI in partnership with Diversity Seek, are doing genome sequence mapping of the seeds in the "public seed banks" and taking patents. By genetic characterization, IRRI and DivSeek are dematerializing the farmer's seeds and committing biopiracy of seed commons because they are dealing with non-material dimensions (gene sequences) of the farmer's seeds.

Rice science in IRRI is now biased towards technologies that are covered by Intellectual Property Rights (IPR), particularly in breeding, genetic engineering, gene editing, and towards synthetic biology. Examples include genetically engineered vitamin A rice, gene editing for zinc enhanced rice, phosphorus starvation tolerance gene (PSTOL1) to solve phosphorus deficiency, looking for rice gene to reduce methane emission, and many more.

These are cutting edge science projects but there are so many practical, ecological, and cost-effective alternatives. These approaches are in fact aligned with corporate interests of commodified seed products, and conversely, farmer's loss of seed control, undermining localized, practical, safe, sustainable, and affordable approaches.

IRRI's solution to climate change is the exploitation of genetic resources mainly through biotechnological approaches. This approach creates uniform genetic makeup rather than diversification in breeds, varieties, species, and management approaches. As such, this is not reliable in unpredictable circumstances caused by climate change.

Restricted research can be assumed to be beneficial to IRRI because it adds to their research fund portfolio. However, it might have the opposite effect. It is the research fund donors that benefit because they are, in effect, subsidized by IRRI through its existing resources such as salaries of researchers in plantilla position, laboratory equipment, and the use of other existing facilities. In some of the restricted or commissioned research, any commercial results are reserved for the funder.

THE CORPORATE HIJACKING OF RICE SCIENCE

With the huge funding granted for agricultural research to produce modern science and technology in order to address hunger and poverty, we might be tempted to praise Bill Gates for his humanitarian character. However, there are serious concerns beneath the veneer of his philanthropy. His big actions have a particular framing that is inconsistent with the root causes of hunger and poverty. His narrative is of a Malthusian framework where solutions can emanate purely from technical and scientific developments. Poverty and malnutrition are far more complex than that—it is the structures that perpetuate these problems which must be fixed. Often, poverty is brought about by precarious assets and livelihood, discriminating social relations, lack of security, disempowerment, and lack of democracy. Fixing such socio-political problems with expensive technological solutions will not work no matter how sincere the philanthropic donor might be. It only aggravates and perpetuates the problem it is intending to solve.

Supporting modern farming with the use of chemical fertilizers and pesticides will only create more environmental, socio-economic, and health problems as shown by the outcome of the first Green Revolution. Even if there will be successes in chemical farming or industrial agriculture, they would be ephemeral because they are not sustainable. Other than productivity, Mr. Gates is missing equity (intragenerational justice) and sustainability (intergenerational justice), which are equally important in rural development.

Mr. Gates' strong push for GMOs and its modern versions of gene editing and synthetic biology creates more serious and intense problems. Health problems associated with exposure to GMOs have been elucidated in scientific literature, yet proponents like Mr. Gates deny the problems. Contamination of biodiversity and the environment have been reported in scientific literature, but the proponents refuse to open their eyes. Unreliability of the genetic mutilation processes have been reported, yet proponents refuse to listen. And so, people wonder, "Why?" Because GMOs are patented, and it would be advantageous to the biotech seed and agrochemical companies. Corporate interest in GMOs is undeniable and with the full support of Mr. Gates for GMOs, he is inevitably promoting corporate interests.

With funding in agricultural research, BMGF and IRRI (and CGIAR) easily influence and co-opt the National Agricultural Research and Extension System (NARES) of governments across the IRRI network, through advice, staff training, seed distribution technology. For example, the Global Rice Science Partnership (GRiSP), another program collaboration of IRRI, lists 302 NARES partners. This means that national research and extension institutions harmonized and homogenized in framing, focus, and approaches, thereby setting aside other approaches that are more sustainable and equitable. For example, organic approaches to farming, agro-ecology, permaculture, etc. would be labeled as second-class science because they do not conform to the cutting-edge science of Mr. Gates. With such homogenization of approaches, any unforeseen or unintended results would be more catastrophic.

Bill Gates, through his foundation, has hijacked agricultural science in rice, turning it into a corporate science. First, it focuses on the very expensive cutting-edge science of genomics, gene editing and synthetic biology that can't be afforded by most NARES in many countries. Secondly, the resulting technology (seeds) are covered by intellectual property rights (IPR) that can be turned to a business entity for corporate benefits. Farmers buy the seeds at exorbitant prices, making the farmers poorer while the corporations accumulate huge wealth. If the cycle goes on, it creates corporate philanthropy.

Corporate power has extended so well in science that any finding against the interest of corporations can be suppressed by interested parties. Situations have been uncovered where corporations hire scientists to make biased research to counteract any independent science that would be damaging to their business. They can simply turn down publication of research results inimical to the interest of corporate business.

Currently, no assessments have been done into whether the intentions of BMGF are indeed successfully achieved. Generosity does not automatically make positive results and success on societal objectives. Because of the potential magnitude of impacts of BMGF philanthropic funding on research and policies, there is a need for transparency, accountability and mechanisms of assessment.

The "generous" philanthropy of BMGF is actually more generous to corporate interests than the poor and hungry. It pursues industrial and chemical farming which are expensive and unsustainable. One thing is sure, the science and technology emanating from the BMGF's support makes biotech, agrochemical corporations, and agribusinesses control agriculture and food. It is corporate philanthropy.

II

PATENTS, GENE EDITING, AND DIGITAL SEQUENCE INFORMATION

Seed Ownership Through New Gene Editing Technologies

✣

VANDANA SHIVA

TODAY, WE ARE witnessing an acceleration of technological revolutions in all fields, the concentration of economic power in the hands of a small number of super-wealthy individual's organizations and competing forces throwing all caution to the wind in their haste for unfettered profits and power. Such is the case with gene editing.

Bill Gates is a big player in both promoting the old, failed GMOs, including the GMO banana, Golden Rice, Bt eggplant, and new GMOs based on gene editing and gene drives.[i]

Life is organized creative complexity. Living organisms are complex, self-organizing, and evolving systems. When genes are added, edited, or removed through genetic engineering, the self-organizing capacity of living systems is disrupted. But the self-organizing organism will nonetheless continue to evolve. How it will evolve is unpredictable and unknown.

To impose a mechanical reductionist paradigm on evolving living systems creates new hazards and unpredictable consequences, as evidenced in the widespread failure of the first generation of GMOs.

Gates' mechanistic view of life likens it to a Microsoft program. Cutting and pasting living organisms is simply the next step in patenting and owning the next commodity.

As is typical in our times of post-truth information, Gates and the biotechnology industry are pushing new technological tools—gene editing and gene drives—as precise and time-efficient technologies. Although these methods are unpredictable and unreliable, they are used as a magic bullet for every problem in agriculture and health. In their haste, they sidestep any regulation and don't give a minute's thought to ethical, moral, and safety concerns.[ii] For them, each magic bullet will become a patent which will bring immeasurable profit.

CRISPR, the new diamond in genetic engineering, has been described as "a relatively easy way to alter any organism's DNA, just as a computer user can edit a word in a document."[iii]

Gates has been quick to invest and promote CRISPR technology by funding the two leading biochemists developing the technology: Jennifer Doudna of the University of California, Berkeley, and Feng Zhang, of the MIT McGovern Institute and the Broad Institute.[iv]

It is a simple yet powerful tool for editing genomes in seemingly any organism on Earth, including humans, which allows researchers to easily alter DNA sequences and modify gene function.[v] It should come as no surprise that the technology is eliciting major concerns and serious ethical and moral questions.[vi]

The paradigm of genetic engineering is based on genetic determinism and genetic reductionism. It is based on a non-acceptance of the self-organized evolutionary potential of living organisms and treats them rather as a Lego playset. But this is not child's play. Life is complex, self-organized, dynamic evolution—it is autopoietic.

As Jonathan Latham cautions, CRISPR "can induce mutations at sites that differ by as many as five nucleotides from the intended target."[vii] In other terms, CRISPR may act at unknown sites in the genome where it is not wanted. This shows how unreliable and misinformed the assumptions and projections are that genome editing techniques like CRISPR are precise, predictable, therefore safe, and in no need for biosafety regulation.

Bill Gates and 13 other investors have poured $120 million into a "revolutionary" gene-editing startup, Editas Medecine, a new company co-founded by Feng Zhang that is focused on CRISPR genome editing systems.[viii] The piracy of common genomic data of millions of plants bred by peasants is termed "big data," but big data is not the long-held intellectual knowledge of farmers. It is biopirated and privateered data.

A representative from Editas has stated, "Investing in intellectual property is one component of how we are building the company to be a leader in genomic medicine."[ix] Its lead investor is a newly created firm called BioNano Genomics (BNGO), which has a select group of family offices led by Boris Nikolic, who was previously a science advisor to Bill Gates. Both Editas and the Gates offices confirm that the Microsoft billionaire, who is the world's second-richest man, is a major investor in the genomic firm BNGO.[x] Thus biotechnology, information technology, and financial technology are being integrated into one mega-machine, transforming life into a money-making casino.

It is worth noting that Doudna and Editas (Zheng), both heavily funded by Gates, are engaged in a patent battle on CRISPR technologies. No matter who loses, Gates wins.[xi]

The attempt to deregulate new gene-edited GMOs and rush them commercially on the market falsely assert that they are "natural." However, new research has established that gene editing is not "natural," that it can, in fact, be tested and should be regulated for biosafety as a GMO.[xii]

The European Court of Justice in July 2018 ruled that CRISPR is a gene modification technology and needs to be regulated like all GMOs:

> "In today's judgment, the Court of Justice takes the view, first of all, that organisms obtained by mutagenesis are GMOs within the meaning of the GMO Directive, in so far as the techniques and methods of mutagenesis alter the genetic material of an organism in a way that does not occur naturally. It follows that those organisms come, in principle, within the scope of the GMO Directive and is subject to the obligations laid down by that directive."[xiii]

This ruling was put to the test in the UK when the House of Lords voted against a Trojan amendment 275 in the Agriculture Bill, which was pushing to introduce and define gene editing as "natural."[xiv]

It can be assumed the industry hopes that the introduction of the new gene-edited GMOs will cover up the failure of old GMOs—the failure of Bt cotton to control pests and the failure of Roundup Ready crops to control weeds. Nonetheless, industrial agriculture is still faced with managing the unmanageable problem of superpests and superweeds.

CRISPR technology also poses serious health risks. Two studies published in 2018 found that editing cells with CRISPR-Cas9 could increase the chance that the cells being altered could become cancerous or trigger the development of cancer in other cells.[xv]

Like the former director of the US National Institute of Health, some high-ranking scientists have called for a self-imposed ethical moratorium on CRISPR until more effects are known, particularly on these germline mutations that could potentially be passed on through generations.[xvi]

The risk of unintended permanent mutation in CRISPR technology calls for the precautionary principle and a moratorium until we fully understand the risks involved and the potential for harm and mutation to the human body and other species.

CRISPR could potentially permanently alter an entire population. Once out, there is no going back. A failure to properly anticipate all the effects and consequences could be apocalyptic.[xvii]

Gene Editing:
Unexpected Outcomes and Risks

❦

DR. MICHAEL ANTONIOU

MORE PAPERS HAVE been published on unintended outcomes and risks of gene editing in medical research on human and animal cells and laboratory animals compared with plants. The results have implications for the gene-editing of farm animals. The problems found with human and animal gene editing are increasingly being confirmed in plant gene editing.

The unintended mutational (DNA damaging) outcomes summarized below occur after the gene-editing tool has completed its task of creating a double-strand DNA break. The mutations occur as a consequence of the cell's DNA repair machinery, over which the genetic engineer has no control. So even if scientists eventually succeed in avoiding off-target mutations, most of the unintended mutations described can still occur at the intended gene-editing site.

This lack of full control of the gene-editing procedure, as well as gaps in our knowledge of outcomes, point to the need for strict regulation of gene editing in food crops and farm animals. Regulation must start from consideration of the genetic engineering process used to create the gene-edited organism, "process-based regulation," so that regulators know where things can go wrong and what to look for.

✳

NEED FOR REGULATION

New GMO plants do not have a history of safe use and should not be exempted from biosafety assessments.[i]

Changes Induced by Gene Editing Different Than What Happens in Nature Gene editing makes the whole genome accessible for changes, unlike naturally occurring genetic changes.[ii]

Unintended Mutations Below is a selection of studies showing different types of unintended mutations resulting from gene editing that can affect the functioning of multiple gene systems. The consequences are an alteration in the plant's protein and biochemical function, which could lead to poor crop performance and/or the production of novel toxins and allergens or higher levels of existing toxins and allergens.

Off-Target Mutations Gene-editing tools, especially CRISPR, are prone to causing mutations (damage) to the organism's DNA at locations other than the intended edit site ("off-target mutations"). This can alter the function of other genes, with unknown consequences to biochemical composition and function.[iii]

Large Deletions and Rearrangements of DNA at Off-Target & On-Target Gene-Editing Sites Large deletions and rearrangements of the plant's genome, which can involve thousands of base units of DNA, have been observed following CRISPR gene editing. These mutations can affect the functioning of many genes, leading to alterations in the plant's protein and biochemical composition.

Creation of New Gene Sequences Leads to New RNA & Protein Products Iteration of the genetic code of the targeted gene can produce mutant forms of the protein it encodes for and new RNA or new protein products. These outcomes can lead to changes in the plant's biochemistry.[iv]

Gene-Editing Process-Induced Mutations The gene editing process taken as a whole (including plant tissue culture and GMO transformation procedure) induces hundreds of unintended mutations throughout the plant's genome. This can affect multiple gene functions with unknown consequences to protein biochemistry and metabolic activity.[v]

Insertion of Foreign & Contaminating DNA into Genome at Editing Sites Following the creation of a double-strand DNA break by the CRISPR gene-editing tool, the repair can unexpectedly include the insertion and rejoining of the broken DNA ends of the recombination template DNA used in SDN-2 and SDN-3 or the insertion of contaminating DNA present in materials used in the plant tissue culture. This insertion of extraneous DNA in the genome of the plant, which can take place at off-target sites as well as the intended on-target editing site, has the effect of introducing new gene functions and disrupting the function of host genes. These effects can combine to alter the biochemical function of the plant in unexpected ways.

Reports describe the insertion of the whole plasmid DNA molecules that acted as the recombination template for the SDN-2 or -3 procedure.[vi] The insertion of these plasmid DNA templates will invariably result in at least one antibiotic resistance gene being incorporated in the genome, as these are a component of plasmids. This risks the transfer of antibiotic resistance genes to disease-causing bacteria in the environment and, more worryingly, in the gut of the consumer, which would compromise the medical use of antibiotics.

Megadiverse Countries as Providers of Genetic Resources & Digital Sequence Information

❦

AIDÉ JIMÉNEZ-MARTÍNEZ AND
ADELITA SAN VICENTE TELLO

THE CONVENTION ON Biological Diversity (CBD), which came into effect in 1993, has three main objectives, "The conservation of biological diversity; the sustainable use of its components; and the fair and equitable sharing of benefits arising from genetic resources."[i]

According to Article 1 of the CBD, these objectives may be achieved through "appropriate access to genetic resources and by appropriate transfer of relevant technologies, taking into account all rights over those resources and to technologies, and by appropriate funding."[ii]

As stated in Article 2 of the CBD, the definition of "technology" includes "biotechnology," which is defined as "any technological application that uses biological systems, living organisms, or derivatives thereof, to make or modify products or processes for specific use."[iii] It is evident that this technology depends on genetic diversity, which is found in megadiverse countries such as Mexico. In December of 2016, three important international meetings took place simultaneously in Cancun, Mexico:

1. The 13th meeting of the Conference of the Parties (COP) of

the Convention of Biological Diversity (CBD)
2. The 8th COP of the Cartagena Protocol on the Biosecurity of Biotechnology
3. The 2nd COP of the Nagoya Protocol (NP) on Access to Genetic Resources and Associated Traditional Knowledge

In all three of the meetings, emphasis was placed on "the very worrying shift towards a predominantly mercantile view of nature and the growing influence of the business sector at different levels of the organization, in conferences, projects, and activities of the Convention and its associated bodies. The participation of the business sector in the CBD through the Global Partnership for Business and Biodiversity is becoming increasingly important."[iv]

In fact, it was during one of the meetings of the COP that the hosting delegation first began to promote the use of "integration of biodiversity" as a concept. This term quickly became mainstream in the COP and its official language, English, while in Spanish, it began to be interpreted as the integration of biodiversity according to its exchange value, or in other words, its commercial potential.

Conversely, Mexico was the first of countries that ratified the Nagoya Protocol to show the world how it might be implemented; it was applied to the maize species called olotón, a hugely important variety owing to its ability to "fix nitrogen" in the atmosphere. The Mexican Secretariat of Environment and Natural Resources (SEMARNAT) "welcomed the fact that in Mexico the benefits established by the Nagoya Protocol (NP) were already being reflected, particularly with regards to the legal certainty needed for the use of genetic resources, by establishing measures to prevent their improper use."[v]

In these same meetings of the COP, it became evident that digital sequence information (DSI) was an increasingly important topic for attendees. Several debates were sparked on this particular approach to the storage of genetic information. It was so significant that the 196 countries present at the meeting "agreed to investigate how digital sequence information might be used in new forms of biopiracy."[vi]

DSI facilitates "digital biopiracy" because it allows for the downloading of genetic sequences of plants, microorganisms, and seeds from the internet, which can later be used to recreate physical DNA using methods taken from synthetic biology. This may be done without considering any potential benefit for the countries and communities from which the organisms originate and in which this genetic information is based. DSI may include the following: sequences of nucleotides that form part of deoxyribonucleic acid (DNA), sequences of ribonucleic acid (RNA), amino acids that form proteins, chemical compounds derived from genetic information (metabolites), and even environmental information or information related to ecological interactions between sequences (epigenetics), as well as any other resulting information.

Today, there are millions of DSI in public and private databases. These sequences can be used and modified for commercial purposes and patented without following any of the basic principles established by the NP. In other words, their use does not necessarily imply any financial or non-financial benefits to the parties that provided the resources. They may not even require Prior Informed Consent (PIC) or Mutually Agreed Terms (MAT), much less the fair and equal sharing of the benefits that result from the use of genetic resources.

DSI is intrinsic to "physical" genetic resources, and the two are therefore inseparable. Gaining access to DSI without following the main regulations of the NP encourages biopiracy and leads to unilateral economic benefits, which miss the most important aim of the CBD, "the conservation and sustainable use of biological diversity."[vii] It is precisely for this reason that it is important to recognize that DSI should be considered as valuable as any "physical" genetic resource.

Furthermore, the present low cost of genetic sequencing and the free availability of DSI in databases are both factors that are contributing to a reduction in the need for "physical" access to genetic resources.

In Cancun, a very important agreement was reached: to request opinions from governments, civil society, Indigenous and local communities so as to know their opinions on the theme of genetic resources as well as to establish ad hoc groups of technical experts to analyze these discussions.[viii]

This agreement was envisaged as a starting point from which to begin analyzing the implications of digital sequence information. It must be recognized that "the members of the CBD took an enormous step forward in addressing the controversial theme of digital biopiracy as a means of attending to the many legal gaps that exist in the Convention on Biological Diversity. Although it's true to say that some Northern countries with powerful biotechnological industries (such as Canada) tried to have the theme of digital biopiracy removed from the discussion agenda, ultimately, everyone agreed that the issue warranted deeper scrutiny and that this would be addressed as part of future meetings."[ix]

It is crucial to recognize that open access to DSI has been fundamental to scientific research, resulting in studies that expand our knowledge of the many different aspects of genetic resources both in evolutionary and taxonomic terms and in relation to diversity and conservation. Similarly, it has played a fundamental role in the development of medicines and the diagnosis and molecular identification of organisms of biomedical interest, particularly in the field of public health, amongst others.

However, open access to this information has also been considered res nullius, a legal term translated as "nobody's thing," which means that digital databases containing genetic information uploaded by researchers are freely available to companies and other parties who generate intellectual property rights over sequences with no regard for the existing ancestral work and knowledge that Indigenous communities hold.

The use of DSI implies great responsibility, and its possible repercussions require ethical principles. Therefore, in order to fulfill the third aim of the CBD, those researchers who upload sequences onto digital platforms must commit themselves to provide data that helps in the traceability of the DSI, as mentioned above. Finally, it must be said that open access does not mean unrestricted or unregulated access because, at least theoretically, one could benefit from and make use of DSI obtained through unethical or bad practices.

As a megadiverse country, Mexico is an important provider of genetic resources and many different DSI kinds. It is acknowledged that biodiversity continues to be the inheritance of Indigenous and local communities who, using the profound knowledge built up over centuries and practices such as seed exchange and the sustainable management of nature, have managed to create and recreate biodiversity in line with their cosmologies which imply a positive and harmonious relationship between communities and their environments. For this reason, it is clear that there is a need to promote biocultural heritage as a strategic position, particularly for megadiverse countries, who are more likely to be providers of genetic resources and, consequently, DSI.[x]

However, in past decades, successive neoliberal governments in Mexico (1982-2018) opened many of the nation's vital resources up to the transnational market, and among those were genetic resources. It is calculated that "since 1996, [the Mexican government] has authorized 4,238 permits for scientific collection,"[xi] and many of these authorizations have resulted in profiteering. Access was even provided to sensitive genetic resources such as those found in maize. Access to the genetic wealth of this particular cereal and the growing interest in its commercial potential was also demonstrated by a joint visit made by Bill Gates and Mexico's richest man, Carlos Slim, to the International Centre for the Improvement of Maize and Wheat (CIMMYT) in Texcoco, State of Mexico.[xii]

They announced, "the investment of 25 million dollars by the Bill & Melinda Gates Foundation and the Carlos Slim Foundation to CIMMYT, which, founded in 1943, had been an initiative of the Mexican government and the Rockefeller Foundation, in which the father of the Green Revolution, Norman Borlaug, had worked."[xiii]

The current government, which was democratically elected in 2018, is determined to work for the poorest in society, to protect the sovereignty of the resources that belong to the nation, and ensure that Indigenous communities are the true beneficiaries, thereby recognizing their central role in the conservation of biodiversity. In this way, the government is working to include Indigenous communities in local legislation—and the guidelines set out by the NP—thereby reinforcing biocultural heritages and visions. Regarding DSI, it is essential that criteria are specified to establish with clarity what the commitments and obligations of users of DSI databases should be so that they might be obliged to share the benefits and not avoid those measures indicated by the NP.

If regulation is often one step behind technology, then time is of the essence, and the issue of access to DSI must be discussed and analyzed in the 15th COP through the lens of biculturalism. The challenge for all participating sectors is to face the issue head-on. Although it will not be easy, not doing so risks rendering the NP meaningless.

III

BIOPIRACY

Biopiracy of Climate Resilient Seeds

🌱

NAVDANYA

BIODIVERSITY CREATES THE resiliency needed in seeds to recover from climate disasters. The biotechnology industry and the Gates Foundation are intent on using the climate crisis as an opportunity to push GMOs while biopirating and patenting climate-resilient seeds—strengthening their monopoly on the world's seed supply.[i]

Chemical agriculture and the globalized food system are responsible for 40–50% of all the greenhouse gas emissions that contribute to climate change.[ii] Both centralized systems and chemical-based monocultures are much more vulnerable to failure and collapse in unstable and extreme climates.

It stands to reason that GMOs and monopolies are not the answer to mitigating or adapting to climate change, nor for reversing biodiversity erosion, because they are embedded in chemical monocultures that create centralized and monopolistic control over the seed supply.

✳

HOW THE GATES FOUNDATION PRESENTS THE BIOPIRACY
OF FLOOD TOLERANT RICE AS "INNOVATION"

Problem In areas of Asia and Africa where rice-growing farmers depend on rain-fed agriculture, rice productivity is low and unstable due to stresses such as flooding, drought, and poor soils.[iii]

Flooding regularly afflicts over 6 million hectares in South Asia[iv] and as much as a third of the rain-fed lowland rice-growing areas in sub-Saharan Africa.[v] Neither newer rice varieties nor the traditional varieties of farmers can survive prolonged submergence underwater. There is a need for new rice varieties that can withstand a range of environmental stresses.

Innovation Harness the knowledge of leading global, regional, and national agricultural researchers and combine it with local know-how to develop and distribute submergence-tolerant rice to small farmers.

Through Stress Tolerant Rice for Africa and Asia (STRASA), the International Rice Research Institute (IRRI) partners with researchers at the Africa Rice Centre, an African research organization, and national scientists in low-income countries, creating submergence-tolerant rice varieties that can "hold its breath" underwater.

STRASA developed improved varieties through identifying and using traits that allow rice to make better use of oxygen even while submerged, therefore, coping with this stress that can devastate crops.[vi]

However, climate resilience is a complex trait and cannot be "engineered" using crude tools that transfer single gene traits from one organism to another. What corporations and the Gates Foundation are doing is taking seed varieties from farmers with known climate-resilient traits that are in public gene banks, mapping their genome, and creating patents based on guesswork and speculation on which part of the genome contributes to the known trait.

Like Columbus, who, by setting out for India, getting lost, and arriving in the Americas, "discovered America," Gates and Monsanto are "discovering" climate resilience.

Just as the narrative of Columbus' discovery erases the Indigenous people who lived across the American continent, the patenting of climate resilience erases breeding techniques and the biodiversity that farmers have given us. It erases the source of the seed, the culture of the seed, the commons of the seed. It is an enclosure through piracy—biopiracy. Patenting life through genetic engineering is rapidly giving way to patenting life through mapping the genome.

Navdanya's Community Seed Bank in Orissa has conserved more than 800 rice varieties, multiplying and distributing salt-tolerant and flood-tolerant varieties. The "innovation" to evolve these climate-resilient traits has occurred cumulatively and collectively over thousands of years. These traits and crops are a commons.

However, the biotech industry is now presenting traits, evolved by nature and farmers over centuries, as the "invention" of "scientists." For example, they renamed the flood-tolerant property of seeds such as Dhullaputia from Orissa as the submergence tolerant gene (or Sub1A). They proudly state that:

> "Using marker-assisted selection (not transgenics), the researchers were able to isolate the submergence tolerant gene, Sub1A, and then transfer it to a rice variety that is grown on more than five million hectares in India and Bangladesh, known as Swarna. Most rice can tolerate flooding for only a few days, but researchers say the new variety, Swarna-Sub1, can withstand submergence for two weeks without affecting yields."[vii]

This is a scientifically flawed description based on genetic reductionism because flood-tolerant traits, similar to other climate-resilient traits such as salt tolerance and drought tolerance, are multi-genetic traits. They cannot be identified with a "Sub1A gene" because it is not simply just a singular gene which they have referred to as "Submergence tolerance 1 (Sub1) Quantitative trait locus (QTL)."

Marker-assisted selection identifies the genetic sequence that is always linked to varieties that share a trait.[viii] Such varieties are then selected for crossing conventionally with varieties like Swarna. Farmers who have bred the traits did not need the marker-assisted selection to breed for climate resilience. The diversity and pluralism of knowledge systems and languages to describe and name processes or organisms must be recognized.

Gates steals centuries of breeding by farmers and describes it as new flood-tolerant rice that will offer relief for the world's poorest farmers.[ix] This is how the Gates Foundation redefines the biopiracy of flood-tolerant rice from India's farmers as "innovation," with the consequence that farmers as breeders disappear, meaning the source of flood-tolerant traits disappears. They become recipients of that which came from them in the first place. This is the regime of Bio Nullius (building on the concept of Terra Nullius) to imply that the minds of farmers are empty, their seeds are empty, and "innovation" only begins when Gates and Big Money take over.

Adapting to an unpredictable, changing climate requires diversity at every level. Biodiverse and decentralized systems have been shown to be more resilient in times of climate change and have more flexibility to respond.[1]

We also need biodiversity at the level of knowledge systems.[2] Biodiversity of knowledge implies that we recognize the ever-evolving

---

1 Shiva, V., & Leu, A. (2018). Biodiversity, Agroecology, Regenerative Organic Agriculture: Sustainable Solutions for Hunger, Poverty and Climate Change. Westville Publishing House. https://books.google.com/books/about/Biodiversity_Agroecology_Regenerative_Or.html?id=Shyh wgEACAAJ&redir_esc=y

2 The International Commission on the Future of Food and Agriculture, Manifesto on the Future of Knowledge Systems: Knowledge Sovereignty for a Healthy Planet, Regione Toscana, Arsia, 2008, https://navdanyainternational.org/wp-content/uploads/2016/04/conoscenze_ing.pdf

knowledge of women, farmers, and tribal citizens that comes from their life experience, and intimate connection with the Earth, and local ecosystems, as well as its biodiversity. We need to recognize the emerging sciences of agroecology and epigenetics.

At the ecosystems level, agroecology is also a systems paradigm. This is the real science of agriculture and food production, not biotechnology. We also need biodiversity in our economic activities. We need local food systems, regional food systems, national food systems, while some trade can take place at the international level.

Finally, we need biodiversity of political systems and decision-making. Centralized and bureaucratic systems are like dinosaurs. They are not flexible; they cannot adapt and evolve. We need flexibility, which comes from diversity. Biodiversity in politics is what we call Earth Democracy.

BIOPIRACY CASE STUDIES
GMO Bananas

❦

VANDANA SHIVA & NAVDANYA INTERNATIONAL

THERE PERSISTS A creation myth that is blind to nature's creativity and biodiversity, as well as the creativity, intelligence, and knowledge of women. According to this myth of capitalist patriarchy, rich and powerful men are the "creators" and can pirate our knowledge and biodiversity. They can own seeds, plants, and life through patents and intellectual property. They can tinker with nature's complex evolution over millennia and claim that their trivial, yet destructive, acts of gene manipulation to "create" life, "create" food, and "create" nutrition.

GMOs have been the means to own and control life through patents. When patents are taken on biodiversity and knowledge, evolved and conserved over millennia by Indigenous cultures, it is called biopiracy.

In the case of genetically modified bananas, it is one rich man, Bill Gates, financing one Australian scientist, Dr. James Dale at Queensland University of Technology, Australia, who knows one crop, the banana, to impose inefficient and hazardous GM bananas on millions of people in India and Uganda. People in these regions have grown hundreds of banana varieties (and other crops) over thousands of years. The contribution written by Mantasa is an excellent account of how "Dr. Dale's globe-trotting GMO bananas are a globe-trotting case of biopiracy and biocolonialism." Gates funded Dr. Dale to push iron-enriched GMO bananas on India that would reduce iron deficiency in anemic women in India and prevent death in childbirth.

Nature has given us a cornucopia of biodiversity that is rich in nutrients—malnutrition and nutrient deficiency result from destroying biodiversity and, along with it, abundant sources of nutrition. Pushing the Green Revolution in the name of increasing farm outputs for a burgeoning population of consumers has spread monocultures of chemical rice and wheat while driving out biodiversity from our farms and diets.

What survived the onslaught were uncultivated wild crops like the amaranth greens and chenopodium (called bathua in India), which are rich in iron while optimizing the growth of other crops despite being sprayed with poisons and herbicides. Instead of being seen as iron and vitamin-rich resources, they are treated as "weeds."

As monoculture of the mind took over, biodiversity disappeared from our farms and our food. The destruction of biodiverse-rich cultivation and diets has led to a malnutrition crisis, with a large percentage of women now suffering from iron deficiency.

India's Indigenous biodiversity offers rich sources of iron. Below is a list of sources in mg per 100 grams of food:

Amaranth	11.0
buckwheat	15.5
neem	25.3
bajra	8.0
rice bran	35.0
rice flakes	20.0
bengal gram roasted	9.5
bengal gram leaves	23.8
cowpea	8.6
horse gram	6.77
amaranth greens	up to 38.5
karonda	39.1
lotus stem	60.6

The solution to malnutrition lies in growing nutrition; growing nutrition means growing biodiversity. It means recognizing the knowledge of biodiversity and nutrition among millions of Indian women who have received it over generations as the "knowledge of their grandmothers."

> "The knowledge of growing this diversity and transform-
> ing it to food is an integral part of women's knowledge—the
> reason for Navdanya creating a network for food sovereignty
> and putting it in women's hands" – Mahila Anna Swaraj

There is a curious urge among the biotechnology brigade to declare war against biodiversity in its center of origin. An attempt was made to introduce Bt brinjal into India, which is the center of diversity for brinjal. GM corn is being introduced in Mexico, the center of the diversity of corn. The GM banana is being introduced in two countries where banana is a significant crop and has large diversity. One is India, and the other is Uganda, the only country where banana is a staple. The women of India succeeded in stopping the Gates GMO banana from being imposed on India, which falsely claimed it would save women's lives. It is still under field trials in Uganda after 10 years and millions of dollars to complete the research.[i]

Not only is the GM banana not the best choice for providing iron in our diet, but it also further threatens the biodiversity of bananas and iron-rich crops, and, as recognized by Harvest Plus, the corporate alliance pushing biofortification, there could be insurmountable problems with the biofortification of nutrients in foods as they:

> "[M]ay deliver toxic amounts of nutrients to an individual
> and also cause its associated side effects (and) the poten-
> tial that the fortified products will still not be a solution to
> nutrient deficiencies amongst low-income populations who
> may not be able to afford the new product and children who
> may not be able to consume adequate amounts."[ii]

SEED FREEDOM CAMPAIGN: "NO GMO BANANA"

The "No GMO Banana" international campaign was launched by Navdanya and partners Mantasa to stop the controversial project of Dr. James Dale of Queensland University of Technology, Australia, the beneficiary of 15 million dollars in investment from the Bill and Melinda Gates Foundation.

A petition was sent to the Prime Minister of India urging the cancelation of the project and the creation of an agreement between the Department of Biotechnology and University of Queensland in Australia to use the money in support of a national movement that creates access to community and kitchen gardens for women.[iii]

After a meeting with farmers in Kediri, Indonesia, who highlighted their yellow and red bananas, Navdanya and the Indonesian activists decided to form a joint project to research where the developers of the GMO bananas got the traits from, leading to the GMO banana biopiracy research and campaign.[iv] They found that the beta-carotene-rich traits had been pirated from an Indigenous Micronesian banana. This led to the international "Stop Banana Biopiracy" campaign and an open letter to Dr. James Dale at QUT, the Bill and Melinda Gates Foundation, and the Convention on Biological Diversity.[v]

News also spread of banana feeding trials using students from Iowa State University (ISU as guinea pigs, also funded by the Gates Foundation. In addition to the ethical violations involved in Biopiracy of Banana, these unapproved human trials also were clearly another serious ethical violation, prompting graduate students at Iowa State to stage a silent protest in October 2014, though the University refused to engage publicly or respond to issues raised by the students.[vi] The Alliance for Food Sovereignty in Africa (AFSA), Dr. Wendy White from Iowa State University, and the Human Institutional Review Board of Iowa State University subsequently submitted an open letter and petition to the Bill and Melinda Gates Foundation expressing fierce opposition to the trials while ISU graduate students dispatched a petition with 57,309 signatures[vii] to the College of Agriculture and Life Sciences with AGRA Watch members delivering the same petition to the headquarters of the

Bill and Melinda Gates Foundation in Seattle, Washington. In April 2016, the petition was delivered to Dr. Dale' at QUT in Australia by Dr. Vandana Shiva along with the Open Letter mentioned above by the Alliance for Food Sovereignty in Africa.

In addition to the success of stopping the Gates GMO banana from being imposed on India, these international campaigns against GMO Bananas served to address the issues of GMOs, biopiracy, and the ethical violations of human trials by connecting movements in Asia, Africa, Australia, and the US.[viii] It helped expose the colonialist mindset behind the project and the multiple human rights issues connected with it. The campaign also showed the absurdity of GMO bananas when there are so many more effective solutions to nutritional and iron deficiencies issues.

The "Super Banana": Biopiracy of a Traditional Crop in Papua New Guinea

MANTASA

THE GATES FOUNDATION has invested $15 million in Dr. James Dale's GMO so-called "super-bananas" developed at Queensland University of Technology (QUT) since approximately 2005. The project is being touted as philanthropy with a humanitarian purpose in combating micronutrient deficiency. The GMO bananas have gained considerable media attention for the project, but it is not at all clear that the GMO banana project is truly a charitable exercise. It is, however, a clear case of biopiracy.

Fe'i bananas (*Musa troglodytarum*) are a traditional food across the Asia-Pacific, found in an area ranging from Maluku in Indonesia to Tahiti and Hawaii in the Pacific. Until recently, local consumption of Fe'i bananas across the region was largely displaced by imported, unhealthy, colonial food cultures.

In the early 2000s, US researcher Lois Englberger, living in Micronesia after searching for sources of vitamin A in the traditional diet of Micronesia, found that Micronesian Karat bananas (named because of their orange "carrot-like" flesh) and subsequent high beta-carotene content had been traditionally used in Micronesia as an infant weaning food.[ix]

Based on Englberger's work, the Federated States of Micronesia has an ongoing program to bring back and encourage the cultivation and consumption of these local banana varieties.[x] Englberger's work with the Island Food Community of Pohnpei, Federated States of Micronesia, has seen the use of these varieties widely adopted in a campaign called "Let's Go Local!" The program has been so successful that the Karat banana has been adopted as the state emblem of Pohnpei.[xi]

Englberger's work, however, did include nutritional surveying of pacific banana cultivars in Australia held in a collection by the Queensland Department of Primary Industries[xii]:

> "What Dr. Dale has done is to take the high beta-carotene banana gene for his GMO 'super bananas from an existing Fe'i banana variety from Papua New Guinea, following a study that compared ten cultivars with yellow to orange fruit."[xiii]

The "winner" was the Asupina cultivar, which had the highest level of trans-beta-carotene—the most important provitamin A carotenoid—more than 25 times the level in the Cavendish cultivars that dominate the international banana trade.[1] The trouble is, this makes Dr. Dales' GMO super banana a clear case of biopiracy. The original Asupina, collected 25 years earlier from Papua New Guinea and held by the Queensland Department of Primary Industries (Q-DPI), is the rightful property of the nation and the communities that developed it."[2]

The Asupina is not a wild variety as Dr. Dale has claimed—it is a domesticated cultivar from PNG.[3] It is also not unpleasant to eat, as Dr. Dale has also claimed. As Englberger was at pains to point out, there are Fe'i banana varieties that are delicious when eaten raw, baked, or boiled.

Dr. Dale's globe-trotting GMO bananas are a globe-trotting case of biopiracy. The traditional knowledge they have used comes from Micronesia and Lois Englberger's work. The Q-DPI public collection from which Jeff Daniels sourced the Asupina variety should have

---

1 Ibid.

2 Breasley, Adam, and Oliver Tickell. "Why Is Bill Gates Backing GMO Red Banana 'Biopiracy'?" The Guardian, November 24, 2014. https://theecologist.org/2014/nov/24/why-bill-gates-backing-gmo-red-banana-biopiracy

3 Huizen, Jennifer. "'Super Bananas' Enter U.S. Market Trials." Scientific American, July 1, 2014. https://www.scientificamerican.com/article/super-bananas-enter-u-s-market-trials/

been a collection held in public trust. Their GMO "super banana" project, on which Dr. Dale holds multiple patents for "banana transformation," now proposes to sell these purloined treasures back to the world as their own patented product from which they can derive royalties, determine access, and is ironically being offered up as an act of charity. Rather this is an act of biocolonialism.

Moreover, the GMO super-bananas are an expensive distraction away from real solutions for vitamin A deficiency. We do not need to waste time and millions on GMOs when we have viable existing solutions that are based on biodiversity and available right now. Malnutrition is a complex problem that monocultural solutions cannot solve, whether of the mind or of the field, not by "Golden Rice" nor the cartoon solution of GMO "super-bananas."

Taking resources away from communities can only be done violently. The GMO banana project began violently, with the unacknowledged theft of traditional knowledge and cultural heritage of local communities and farmers in PNG and Micronesia, which has now been enclosed in patents for "banana transformation."

It continued violently with the Market Trials conducted on unsuspecting human subjects in Iowa—female students, who were being paid $900 to turn themselves into human guinea pigs, while no safety tests for human consumption of the GMO bananas have been done.

IV

GLOBAL AGRICULTURE

The Recolonization of Agriculture

❧

NAVDANYA

THE FACT THAT Ag One will be based in St. Louis, Missouri, home of Monsanto and other GMO and pesticide giants, is not a coincidence. Ag One claims to "empower smallholder farmers" by providing more accessible technology to help them face climate change. This sounds eerily like Bayer, who also claims to "empower 100 million smallholder farmers around the world by providing more access to sustainable farming solutions—all by the year 2030."

Through looking at examples of current and past co-investments, it is obvious what "private partnerships" will most likely emerge in Ag One's quest to "empower smallholder farmers to lift themselves out of poverty."

In 2010, a US financial website published the Gates foundation's annual investment portfolio, which showed it had bought 500,000 Monsanto shares of around $23 million.[i] More recently, publications of Gates' Annual investment portfolio, or "strategic investment fund," which is stated to allow the foundation to advance its "philanthropic goals" through investments in for-profit companies, showed a $7 million equity stake in AgBiome, a biotech start-up focused on developing synthetic biological products through CRISPR technology for the agricultural sector.[ii] AgBiome holds investments from agrochemical companies Monsanto and Syngenta and received a $20 million grant from the Gates Foundation to develop pesticides for Africa.[iii]

This shows just one of the numerous ventures where the Bill and Melinda Gates Foundation and Monsanto have invested together with a false narrative of "helping the poor in Africa." Pivot Bio, a biotech start-up focusing on making nitrogen-fixing microbes, is another Gates Foundation-funded start-up that received $70 million and holds investments from Monsanto Growth Ventures and the US Defense Advanced Research Projects Agency (DARPA).[iv]

More explicitly, with its launch of Ag Tech (the Latin American Ag One), the Inter-American Institute for Cooperation on Agriculture (IICA) has announced partnerships for its implementation with Microsoft,[v] Bayer,[vi] Corteva,[vii] and Syngenta,[viii] along, of course, with the Bill and Melinda Gates Foundation.

By looking at the outcomes of AGRA, we can start to see what pattern is to be repeated with all of these strategic alliances in the launching of Ag One. Through the Gates Foundation's promotion of chemical and genetically modified inputs, they have opened up previously hard-to-reach markets in Africa, South Asia, and Latin America to benefit private corporations. No one owns these patented "high-yield" seeds, and investments are very clearly made towards for-profit companies. The commercialization mentioned by Voorhies means private company profit.

To be specific, in 2008, the year AGRA was launched, South Africa was the only African country that had approved the use of genetically modified seeds. Subsequently, GM seeds were expanded to the previously GM-free Egypt, Burkina Faso, and Sudan. Other countries such as Ghana, Kenya, Tanzania, Uganda, Malawi, Mali, Zimbabwe, and Nigeria began researching GM crops. By 2017, some countries had even moved into implementing field trials.[ix]

This huge expansion of GM crop use, particularly corn, is a consequence of large-scale promotion directly aimed at increasing market share to the large agribusiness companies that own the patented seeds. Those patented GM seeds go along with their accouterments of chemical inputs, all promoted through alliances with agrochemical companies under the guise of AGRA.

In sum, roughly 10 years after the revival of the Green Revolution through AGRA, industrial agriculture grew in some form or another, from one country to eleven, showcasing a huge expansion in Big Ag business. In "The Gates Foundation's Green Revolution Fails Africa's Farmers," Timothy Wise explains that in a decade, productivity rates in these countries only increased due to these inputs being highly subsidized and were nowhere near enough to alleviate poverty and hunger.[x] This means that only big agrochemical companies directly benefited from Gates' push for "agricultural development."

This comes as no surprise, as in a video shot by the Gates Foundation to explain the necessity of development of agricultural innovation, Gates describes the Green Revolution as being "the most significant advancement in human history behind modern medicine, due to its ability to drastically increase yields."[xi] With just this one statement, which shows his full-scale support of industrial agriculture, we can almost guarantee this pattern will be repeated with the implementation of Ag One.

✳

UNVEILING THE RHETORIC OF AG ONE

After looking closely at the Ag One concept, one can quickly start to pick apart how its rhetoric is completely disconnected from any true lived experience of the impacts of the first Green Revolution and its unprecedented global ecological, social, economic, and cultural impacts. Contrary to what Bill Gates might think, agroecological food systems are more productive, resilient to climate change, and provide greater livelihood security.

Rhetoric "Yields on farms in regions like Sub-Saharan Africa and South Asia are already far below what farmers elsewhere in the world achieve and in the future the crop production will further worsen because of climate change." Hence, we need Ag One to accelerate new innovations that are needed to increase crop productivity.

Counter Contrary to the myth that small farmers and their agroecological systems are unproductive and that we should leave the future of our food in the hands of the Poison Cartel, small farmers are providing 80% of global food using just 25% of the land that goes into agriculture.[xii]

There have been countless studies proving that agroecology and organic agriculture, especially approaches based on biodiversity, are all around more resilient to climate change, economically viable, and lead to increases in crop productivity.[xiii] For example, biodiversity helps reduce agroecosystem diseases which improves the resilience of plants and inevitably leads to higher yields.

The diversity of knowledge embedded in agroecological and traditional farming systems provides a greater safety net for confronting extreme weather patterns and ecological shifts. As stated in a study on the climate resiliencies of agroecological systems, "Observations of agricultural performance after extreme climatic events (hurricanes and droughts) in the last two decades have revealed that resiliency to climate disasters is closely linked to farms with increased levels of biodiversity."[xiv]

Rhetoric 2 Ag One will "empower smallholder farmers with the affordable, high-quality tools, technologies, and resources they need to lift themselves out of poverty."

Counter Reliance on internal inputs and recycling resources leads to less cash strain for costly chemical inputs. Coupled with increased productivity, farmers can better meet their monetary needs and overall livelihoods. This fact was corroborated in a study presented at the 2nd International Conference on Global Food Security through looking at global comparative data. The study found that adopting agroecological farming practices generally led to increased crop yield and profitability compared to conventional practices.[xv]

This begs the question, does being lifted out of poverty mean being folded into the commodity market? Considering Gates' longstanding alliance with giant industrial agriculture companies, this is most likely the objective. While farmers have bred hundreds of thousands of varieties and species, the Green Revolution has reduced the agriculture and food base to a handful of globally traded commodities, with only 30 plants supplying 95% of global food demand.[xvi]

Genetic engineering has further narrowed the commercially planted crops to four plants—corn, soy, cotton, canola—with two traits: Bt and HT (herbicide tolerant). This reduction of marketable crops also creates flooding of commodity crops that keep prices low, making it more difficult for small-scale, non-organic farmers to make a living. Regardless, such a simplistic view of simply solving poverty with technological innovation reduces the multidimensionality of why certain populations remain poor.

Through this and similar rhetoric, Gates pushes the philanthropist ethic where the rich give to the poor, painting the rich as providing favors to the people they exploited to gain their wealth, making the poor even more dependent on the rich. Coupled with his development agenda, a chimera of charity development emerges that reinforces the power structures of inequality in the areas where they work, reiterating the trope of "white saviorism."

For example, Gates' chief scientist at Microsoft Azure Global, Ranveer Chandra, who is in charge of developing sensors for data gathering on farms through the FarmBeats project, has, along with Gates himself, readily admitted that they have no expertise in agronomy, biology, farming or related fields. But they still believe that computer and data science can solve complex, multifaceted ecological and social problems such as poverty.[xvii]

They are reiterating the trope of the technical expert who comes to bestow the poor with their knowledge. Never leading to empowerment but only to dependence. In the end, this reductionist way of implementing top-down technologies works to deepen global poverty by creating further dependence on centralized high-cost inputs.

Rhetoric 3 "Smallholder farmers are involved in unsustainable practices like grazing into forests which affects fragile ecosystems and will cause further damage to the environment and exacerbate the effects of climate change."

Counter Commodity-based, fossil fuel-intensive, monocultural industrial agriculture is far more responsible for the effects of climate change and ecosystem destruction.[xviii] Chemical pesticides are directly responsible for the mass killing of birds and insects.[xix] Fossil fuels are used in almost every step of the industrial food system, from the field through nitrogen fertilizers, diesel fuel for the myriad of industrial, agricultural equipment, to transportation of commodities in the international supply chain, their storage, and eventually their disposal.[xx] Nitrogen fertilizers also pollute water sources, dry out land, and destroy the soil.[xxi] Overall, they lead to more water being necessary for industrial agriculture, which furthers the global water strain.[xxii]

The true culprit of large-scale deforestation has been the industrial agriculture sector, whose search for the perpetual amplification of the agricultural frontier is responsible for between 70% to 90% of global deforestation.[xxiii] The land cleared is then used to produce chemically intensive monocultures of commodity crops like corn, soy, sugarcane, cotton, palm oil, and so on. These crops are then used in industrial food-making processes, biofuels, or animal feed, creating a vicious cycle of greenhouse gas emissions, and perpetuating the industrialized food system.[xxiv] Gates seems to completely disregard this, as in 2016, when he invested $14 million into the biofuel conversion company Renmatix. This company produces a technology to aid in the conversion of biomass to cellulose sugars for biofuels.[xxv] Biofuels, not small farmers, have been responsible for clearing rainforests worldwide, especially in the Amazon in Brazil.[xxvi]

By framing the narrative in a way that pins the responsibility of climate change on "smallholder farmers who are involved in unsustainable practices," the Gates foundation evades responsibility for the destruction it has been instrumental in causing. We cannot address climate change and its very real consequences without recognizing the central role of the industrial and globalized food system, actively supported by the Gates Foundation. The globalized food system contributes between 44% and 57% of all greenhouse gas emissions through deforestation, industrial inputs (such as chemical fertilizers, petrol, fertilizer, irrigation, etc.), animals in concentrated animal feeding operations (CAFOs), plastics and aluminum packaging, long-distance transport, and food waste.[xxvii]

We cannot solve climate change without small-scale, ecological agriculture based on biodiversity through living seeds, living soils, and living food systems. A proven way to decrease CO_2 emissions is exactly through local food economies that eliminate fossil fuel-intensive methods and global supply chains in favor of resource recycling, low-intensity inputs to heal the soil, and biodiversity. Slow, whole foods, organic diets increase nutrition and lessen climate impact in a multidimensional fashion.[xxviii]

Rhetoric 4 "Everyone has the right to live a healthy, productive life. But many of the world's poorest people—those who make their living through agriculture—will not have that opportunity unless they can access the innovations needed to adapt to the challenges caused by climate change" and we will "help smallholder farmers, the majority of whom are women, adapt to climate change."

Counter The BMGF makes it sound like farmers cannot live a healthy and productive life without technology. They also make it sound like the only way to face climate change is with the help of their "innovations," which they will profit massively from. Through this elevation of technological means to human ends, the corporate agenda is made the human agenda, and imposition is defined as "inclusion" and "democratization."

Corporations endow their tools with inevitability and rob societies of options and alternatives. However, there is no inevitability in the tools that humanity uses. Chemicals and the Green Revolution were not inevitable. They were imposed through conditionalities.[xxix] The failures of the Green Revolution and its "innovations" do not provide a solid base for the argument of new technological inno-vations.[xxx] Technology itself also greatly impacts climate change through the whole chain of its material extraction, production, dis-tribution, and waste processing.[xxxi] New technological fundamen-talism makes corporate tools a measure and indicator of human progress, immune to social and democratic assessments.

With the ecological emergency, climate emergency, and food emergency, the technologies needed must be participatory and evo-lutionary, with the focus on breeding for climate resilience, increas-ing nutrition, and making agriculture poison-free.

The urgency implied around the need for technological solu-tions to climate change provides the mask to push the universal adoption of a new series of data-reliant technologies. Since climate change is "new," there must also be a "new and innovative solution" to solve it.

"One Agriculture One Science" essentially means "one research and one knowledge."[xxxii] In a world of diversity, claiming to be the "one" is a design for imperialism. It is a design for epistemic coloni-zation. It is a denial of the richness of agroecological knowledge and practices that are resurging around the world.

TECHNOLOGICAL MYTHS TO COLONIZE OUR FOOD AND FARMING SYSTEMS

Corporations turn a blind eye to the knowledge, tools, and innova-tions farmers have evolved over millennia to breed seeds, renew soil fertility, manage pests and weeds ecologically and produce good food.

They elevate corporate tools to a new religion and new civilizing mission, which has been imposed to civilize the ecological, indepen-dent, knowledge-sovereign farmers who are seen as the new "bar-barians." New technological fundamentalism makes corporate tools a measure and indicator of human progress, immune to social and democratic assessments. Farmers have a fundamental democratic right to compare their agroecological tools with what the Poison Cartel has to offer with full knowledge and information to make a democratic choice. Through this elevation of technological means to human ends, the corporate agenda is made the human agenda, and imposition is defined as "inclusion" and "democratization."

Corporations endow their tools with inevitability and rob societies of options and alternatives. However, there is no inevitability in the tools that humanity uses. Chemicals and the Green Revolution were not inevitable. They were imposed through conditionalities. GMOs are not inevitable and are failing as tools of pest control and weed control, leading instead to the emergence of super pests and superweeds. There is multiple and diverse intelligence in nature and society. Artificial Intelligence or machine learning is not inevitable. It is being imposed through forced digitalization, making us forget the intelligence in nature and her diverse living beings, the intelligence in the soil food web, the ecological intelligence of farmers and women, the intelligence of the microbes in our gut, and the enteric nervous system—our second brain. When society develops and chooses technologies democratically, the questions we ask are:

- ► What does the technology do?
- ► What is the tool for? Who controls the tools?
- ► Do we have technological alternatives to address the same problem?
- ► Do we need them to improve human well-being and the well-being of all species?
- ► What are the ecological impacts of the tools on life and human health?
- ► What are the social impacts of the tools?

THE CASE STUDY OF THE ICRISAT DIGITAL FARMING TOOLS

One example of the digitalization of agriculture comes through a collaboration between ICRISAT and Microsoft in India. Used as a case study by Feed the Future and USAID, ICRISAT is looking to develop the tech initiatives shown below.

The ICRISAT case study on Digital Agriculture shows what Gates Ag One has been preparing for. But one flawed assumption made by such initiatives and, in particular, Gates is the continued use of "yield," a failed measure that hides more than it reveals.

Navdanya's research has shown that industrial agriculture is inefficient, unproductive, creates a dependency on corporations for eternal inputs, and dependency on global supply chains that impose uniformity on farms. We have shown that "yield" is an unscientific measure that does not reflect true biological productivity. It is a manipulated measure that promotes monocultures and commodification.

The Sowing App and the Intelligent Agricultural Systems Advisory Tool (ISAT) use predictive analytics, Cortana artificial intelligence, and machine learning from multiple weather, soil, and crop data points to predict sowing times for farmers and provide them with a series of possible decisions. These programs are reliant on mining farmer data while then portraying farmers as lacking in intelligence or skill. Farmers of forty centuries did not need an SMS through Microsoft software to know how to sow and farm. Not only is this a denial of farmer knowledge and intelligence, but it is also creating a new dependency on an external input—data. The objective is clearly to undermine food sovereignty and self-reliance by locking farmers into digital dependency. The ICISAT case study is a good example of how Gates is attempting to centralize farmers' knowledge, wealth, and value by turning all aspects of an agricultural environment into data points. All the business generated by this digitalization partnership is diverted to Microsoft.

AG ONE: SOWING THE SEEDS OF SURVEILLANCE

Although we have seen how the new Ag One initiative will line up with previous iterations of Gates' attempt to expand the classic, failed methods of the Green Revolution, Ag One also sees the unveiling of a new generation of external input technologies. The focus of Ag One is to transition small farmers to use "new digital tools and

Digital Agriculture Investment	Purpose of the Tool	Value Chain Stage
Sowing App and Intelligent Agricultural Systems Advisory Tool (ISAT)	To deliver targeted and timely SMS messages to farmers about sowing and other farm management practices	On-farm production
iHub	An incubator program and platform to catalyze technology innovations that can change the lives of farmers	Cross-cutting
Plantix	To provide extension officers with automated and targeted responses about diseases and pests through a mobile app	On-farm production
LeasyScan	To rapidly measure leaf surface area characteristics and water stress and accelerate the identification of promising new varieties	Planning
HarvestMaster	To record highly accurate measurements of grain weight and moisture characteristics for development of new varieties	Planning

technologies." Principally referenced are the "yield-enhancing or drought-tolerant seeds, which include old and new types of GMOs, as well as CRISPR technologies adopted on seeds and living plants.

Gates has been pushing CRISPR and gene editing for several years now. In 2016, an investment firm called BNGO headed by former science advisor to Gates, Boris Nikolic, provided a huge seed investment of $120 million to fund Cambridge's Editas Medicine, one of the first to research and develop CRISPR technology.[xxxiii]

Since then, he has publicly expressed his full-fledged support of CRISPR for its use in agriculture and medicine. The other most important aspect is the use of digital agricultural extension through sensors to gather data points on everything from soil moisture, and weather patterns to soil nutrient levels and individual plant health. The end purpose for using such sensors is to fill the "data gap" of the global south and provide data as a resource to build maps and predictive models of agricultural systems. Big data, data analytics, and machine learning are being incorporated into agriculture through electronic tracing systems, electronic weather data, smartphone mapping, and other remote sensing applications, all for AI and machine learning to be able to model such things as when to plant the next season of crops, when to water, when to fertilize or to predict pest outbreaks.

This new type of data-reliant agriculture is oriented toward the implementation of precision agriculture, which is essentially a "data-generating agriculture" as it is based on observing and measuring crops and environment variables using sensors and satellites to supposedly lower the use of chemical inputs. Precision agriculture is a double-edged sword. On the one hand, it is just a way to placate critiques of the high costs of chemical inputs. At the same time, on the other, it provides the means to reduce farmers to possible data sets used to generate artificial intelligence models. This, in turn, reduces the world's diversity to only an environment to improve predictive models through the complete disregard for—even the concept of—living systems.

A Treaty to Protect Our Agricultural Biodiversity

❧

JOSÉ ESQUINAS-ALCAZAR

FOR CENTURIES PEASANTS have stored, selected, and exchanged seeds by keeping them in an evolutionary relationship with the surrounding environment. This is a heritage of humanity that has suddenly been threatened by the regime of the Green Revolution and entrance of multinational corporations into the seed sector. Over thousands of years, humanity had more than 10,000 natural species available for their nutrition, while today we have just a little more than 150 commodities grown for commercial use. Among them, only 12 of those make up 80% of the global food supply and four of them alone—rice, wheat, corn, and potato—cover more than half of our consumption.

The damage to biodiversity has been so significant that the same FAO, starting from the 1970s, began negotiations to create a UN International Treaty on Plant Genetic Resources for Food and Agriculture to contain biodiversity erosion. To this day, the treaty, coming into force in 2004, is the only international instrument protecting local farmers' rights to save and exchange their seeds within biodiversity.[i]

The treaty provides for a global genetic resources reserve of 64 plant species representing 80% of our fruit and vegetable consumption. This treaty must be continuously strengthened and protected from economic interests in the awareness of its inestimable value for the future of humanity. In November 2019, the biennial meeting for the treaty took place in Rome, which, according to many observers, was a failure precisely because of the huge economic corporate interests present.

In terms of the hoped for and necessary advances for the protection of biodiversity, we must acknowledge that no agreement has been reached on what was considered by many to be the most important issue, namely the updating of the benefit-sharing mechanism whereby those who receive plant genetic resources included in the multilateral system are required to pay a fair share of the benefits generated by the marketing of those products. However, we should not consider it a failure. Since the treaty is constantly under definition, there are still many positive aspects. Firstly, there has been no criticism of the treaty as such. It has been consolidated and is regarded as a reference of fundamental importance by all—even by the seed industry, which would not be able to work without access to genetic resources.

Then there was the Rome meeting with the ratification of the USA and Japan, which took place in 2018, almost 15 years after the European countries. Progress has also been made on farmers' rights and the important initiative to monitor and study good practices, which will continue into 2022. The next phase is now being realized, that of interpretation of the treaty, especially on those parts where the text has become obsolete due to the introduction of new technologies. It is preferred to not reach an agreement rather than make a bad one. Therefore, as far as the benefit-sharing mechanism is concerned, it was decided to postpone the discussion. In the meantime, the huge issue of Digital Sequence Information (DSI) has opened up and presents several issues.[1]

DSI is about the digitalization of all genetic information related to seeds. In this way, it is possible to improve varieties without having access to the actual seed but by simply using genetic sequences. This

---

1 African Centre for Biodiversity, Third World Network, Prudence versus Pressure at the Seed Treaty, October 2019, https://www.acbio.org.za/sites/default/files/documents/Prudence_versus_Pressure_at_the_Seed_Tr eaty.pdf#_blank

new technological milestone has an immediate economic impact because some countries and seed companies when using DSI do not want to recognize the obligation of benefits distribution.

On the other hand, it is also true that the farmers who developed the original varieties in the first place and that without those seeds, there would be no information available. This is like agreeing to buy a printed book but refusing to pay the digital version of the same book, even though the copyrights are the same. We are facing a revolution in the way we conceptualize seeds. We cannot allow them to be defined as mere sequences of genetic information because they are real genetic resources. We must insist on establishing this principle. Within two years in Rome, an agreement will need to be reached. We cannot afford to lose further biodiversity in times of climate change when we will need resilient varieties to be available to everyone. The issue is so important that we have no right to pessimism.

In the early stages of the process, small producers and multinationals agreed to sit at the same table, and the latter accepted the idea that an agreement had to be reached. As in the second half of the 1970s, the loss of agroecological diversity became clear to everyone, including the FAO who had promoted the Green Revolution and even the multinationals. Every farmer had their own heterogeneous local varieties replaced with a few commercial homogeneous varieties, which became more productive only through fertilizers and pesticides. The increase in productivity was achieved at the price of biodiversity and local identity loss.

Everyone realized what the issue was and the importance of biodiversity. Uniformity equals vulnerability, and it is essential to preserve biological diversity to cope with both plant diseases and environmental changes. Ex situ germplasm banks do not solve the problem because they store frozen germplasm.[2] In this way, also the evolution of the plant freezes and no longer develops the ability to

---

2 "Ex-Situ Conservation Definition| Biodiversity A-Z." https://biodiversitya-z.org/content/ex-situ-Conservation

adapt to new conditions. Only in situ conservation guarantees the preservation of a living seed that has the ability to adapt.[3] The beginning of the negotiation was difficult, and we had to organize "secret meetings" to inform journalists and politicians about the facts. That was until we managed to convince the FAO to promote an international agreement.

The treaty is also crucial because of inter-country interdependence. For example, what happened in Ireland in the 1940s, when potato crops, which was the national staple food, were attacked by a fungus, the *Phytophthora infestans*. The famine that followed is considered one of the greatest catastrophes in European history as it caused the death of some two million people. But what was the underlying problem? Why was it impossible to cope with the disease? The answer is simple and brings us back to the dangerous concept of uniformity. At the end of the 1500s, a handful of uniform varieties of potatoes were introduced into Ireland. It is because of that uniformity that the *Phytophthora* fungus was able to spread easily. The conquistadors had only brought that one variety. At that point, how could this problem that threatened the rest of Europe be solved? European agronomists had to return to Latin America, and precisely to Peru, to find other diverse resistant varieties to eradicate the disease. But this is not an old story.

For example, in 1971, a corn disease attacked all American hybrid varieties and wiped them out. Confronted with evidence that commercial varieties could not adapt, agronomists searched and found resistant varieties in Africa. Diversity is what saved Europe and the United States. The only difference with the great Irish famine is that there were not millions of deaths but billions of dollars lost. This explains the inter-country interdependence, where small farmers of Latin America solve the problems of Europe and small farmers of Africa solve the problems of the USA. In times of climate change,

---

3 "In-Situ Conservation Definition| Biodiversity A-Z." https://biodiversitya-z.org/content/in-situ-\conservation

stability and uniformity are suicidal. These cases have recurred and continue to happen today.

Although inter-country interdependence is a fact, the dispute between developed and developing countries is always heated. At the last meeting in Rome, the chairmanship was entrusted to the USA, and the working groups were unbalanced in favor of the developed countries behind which the interests of seed companies lie. This great paradox already existed in the 1970s. As the greatest diversity resides in developing countries while the most important germplasm banks are located in developed countries, who do these genetic resources belong to?

According to the law, they belong to the country that preserves them. There was then a need to develop an agreement to ensure that these resources remained a patrimony of humanity. But even if they were declared a patrimony of humanity, who would use them? Still, the rich countries. That is why I speak of a paradox—the poorest countries, which were the actual suppliers of the raw material, had to pay royalties on the seeds afterward.

We have now lost the beautiful concept of the Patrimony of Humanity in the Treaty, but we have come to a fairly good agreement that includes the multilateral system of benefit sharing, which includes economic benefits. Profits from new varieties will be channeled into an international financial mechanism aimed at financing projects to benefit farmers in developing countries. This was not an easy objective to achieve. In the beginning, the US opposed the principle that multinationals should be required to pay a percentage of their revenues. I remember that during the deadlock, it was the multinationals themselves who declared that they would agree to pay a percentage. This episode tells us two things: the first is that it is vital for companies to have access to genetic material, and the second is that governments, in their efforts to defend multinationals, are often more royalist than the king.

But the multilateral system of benefit-sharing has to be improved because it's gathered very little revenue so far. It is a mechanism overloaded with bureaucracy. Moreover, having to trust the company that starts to calculate the percentages only after the commercialization of the new variety takes place, which often happens about eight years after the acquisition of the genetic resources. As a matter of fact, payment for access to resources is supposed to be guaranteed. In short, it is a self-regulating mechanism that has not worked that well so far to the point that it had to be supported by voluntary funds from countries.

Still, the treaty is considered binding, and it is important for farmers and consumers. Almost 150 countries have ratified it. All legislation must adapt to it. Of course, concrete implementation depends on the priorities of each country. In Italy, for example, some regions have decided to apply it in advance without waiting for a national law.

As far as farmers are concerned, the treaty is an instrument against the overwhelming power of multinationals. It recognizes the rights of farmers as guardians of agricultural biological diversity and traditional knowledge. Nothing must oppose the exchange of conservation and breeding of traditional varieties. As far as consumers are concerned, it is necessary to inform them that there is no diversity in their plates without biodiversity.

Nor do we have the right nourishment in industrial products whose production does not respect the environment, as territories are poisoned and biodiversity destroyed while products travel thousands of kilometers and are full of chemicals. In Europe, we are spending 700 million euros a year on diseases caused by junk food. The problem is that farmers are disappearing because they cannot compete with industrial agriculture that does not pay for externalities. And with what results? Much more than we need is being produced, but people are still dying of hunger or diseases caused by poor nutrition. A third of the food produced is also being thrown away. In Spain, each inhabitant throws away an average of 160 kilos of food per year. The employment factor is also affected. Today in Spain, only 2.5% of the population works in agriculture, and unemployment rates are sky high. The employment factor is also an externality of the agribusiness system.

In short, for every dollar we pay in the agribusiness market, we pay two dollars plus tax to reduce the negative effects. The real price of the food we buy is three times higher. We must reverse this situation, starting with the elimination of subsidies to industrial agriculture.

DIGITAL SEQUENCE INFORMATION (DSI) AND THE INTERNATIONAL TREATY ON GENETIC RESOURCES

When the International Treaty was being negotiated, there was a debate over what the treaty should be named. It was deliberately decided that the name should be referent to "genetic resources" and not "seeds" (as was proposed by some countries), since what is really considered valuable is not the seed understood as physical support, but the genetic resource or information contained in its genes.

In the same way that all the information contained in a book is coded in a 28-letter vocabulary (in the case of the Spanish language) which are repeated by changing the sequence of the letters, in the case of seeds, the information is "written," in their genes in a vocabulary of only four "letters" (bases): Adenine, Guanine, Thymine, and Cytosine. In both cases, it is the sequence or order in which the respective "letters" appear that allows all the different messages in the book or all the characteristics of the plant to be expressed.

When scientists can "read" the genetic code of a traditional seed or variety, it is possible to reproduce it with no other limits than those imposed by the available technology. Today, Digital Sequential Information (DSI) technology allows us to access these genetic resources, reproduce and use them without the need to have access to the physical or tangible seed.

For the reader of a book, it is the content, regardless of whether we have access to it physically or virtually, which is why the copyright is paid. Similarly, for the researcher or seed company, the value of a traditional variety or seed depends on its genes or genetic sequences regardless of whether we have access to them physically (seed) or virtually (DSI).

The crux of the matter is that the DSI is not only information, but the genetic resource in virtual form; therefore, its access, use, and benefit-sharing should be regulated as a genetic resource and not simply as information in the multilateral system of access and benefit sharing. If we were to allow access to the virtual genetic resource without the obligation to share benefits, we would have emptied the treaty of its content and thrown 30 years of difficult negotiations overboard in search of a balance between the interests of those who contribute their genetic resources and those who contribute the technology.

Ag Tech: Bill & Melinda Gates Agricultural Innovations in Argentina

♼

FERNANDO CABALEIRO

BILL GATES HAS landed in the Argentine agrifood system. He has done so at the hands of the Inter-American Institute for Cooperation on Agriculture (IICA), an international organization supported by the United States of America. The partnership has clearly blurred the line between the public and the private sectors. It is truly a covert entity of agribusiness through which the Bill & Melinda Gates "philanthrocapitalist" Foundation has been operating, since 2011, by making contributions and donations.

In 2018, IICA and Bill Gates' Microsoft built a strategic alliance called the Alliance for Digital Education in the Americas with the objective of implementing a complete digitalization of agriculture through a broad technological platform developed by Gates' computer company using the Internet of Things (IoT), Big Data and Artificial Intelligence (AI) tools, as well as the application of innovation, information technology, and communication in development projects.[i]

Previously, IICA and Microsoft had tested the development of prototypes using the IoT and AI to combat diseases that occur in coffee cultivation and create a platform to strengthen farmers' capacity to handle agricultural issues.

In addition to the celebrated strategic alliance with Microsoft, Gates was joined by the Global Hitss corporation, a subsidiary of

American Móvil (owned by billionaire Carlos Slim), to strengthen software applications, and the agro-biotechnology companies Bayer/Monsanto, Corteva (Dow, Dupont, and Pioneer) and Syngenta ChemChina.[ii]

The alliance's one objective is to carry out IICA's Medium-Term Plan (MTP) 2018-2022 for agriculture in the Americas, specifically targeting Argentina and Brazil first, to then implement the plan throughout the Latin American and Caribbean region. IICA's website states:

> "Pilot programs will be implemented in Brazil and Argentina, in accordance with the definition of priorities for implementing the agreement that the two organizations (IICA and Microsoft) signed in October to work for the benefit of the rural areas of the countries of Latin America and the Caribbean."[iii]

The plan is called Ag Tech and was presented in Argentina on June 30, 2020, by Manuel Otero, President of IICA, in the presence of the Ministers of Agriculture and Science of Argentina and other public officials in strategic positions.[iv]

Ag Tech is nothing other than the Ag One that Bill Gates designed and built from his philanthrocapitalism, developing, and investing in research and technology projects in Asia and Africa to be applied in the agrifood system and that have no other purpose than to generate processes of accumulation of capital, economic concentration, appropriation of genetic resources, and social domination.

IICA is also in partnership with Bill Gates, along with other foundations, in the formation of the System Reference Group (SRG), which submitted its recommendations in July 2019 calling for the unification of the 15 Consultative Group on International Agricultural Research (CGIAR) centers, with their respective seed banks, into one. The intentions of this group were set out in the report, "Feeding the World in a Changing Climate: An Adaptation Roadmap for Agriculture."[v] IICA boasts that with the excuse of accelerating adaptation to climate change, it proposes to transform the

world agricultural system, "With the task of feeding an ever-grow-
ing population and under more extreme climatic conditions...the
adaptation of the food production system is urgent in the Americas,
not only because of the high vulnerability of the sector to climate
change but also because the maintenance and increase of the continent's food supply to the world depend on it."[vi]

IICA, the Bill Gates Foundation, Bayer (Monsanto), Corteva
(Dow, Dupont & Pioneer), and Syngenta, without a doubt, make up
the most dangerous alliance for agriculture and food sovereignty for
each country in Latin America and the Caribbean.

The objectives of Ag Tech and Ag One cover all the productive
processes of the agrifood system, which are crossed by Bill Gates'
hegemonic and domination design. The gateway chosen was Argentina, just as Monsanto chose our country in 1996 to release its first
transgenic seed.

The cellular material to create ultra-processed synthetic meat
that tastes like chicken or fish and eggs, such as corn, soybean, and
sunflower seeds (as well as other fruits, vegetables, and greens),
are subjected to genetic editing using the CRISPR technique and
grown in unpopulated fields. These fields are overseen by remote-
controlled and programmable drones for planting, measuring, and
the application of new combinations of agrochemicals and synthetic
fertilizers. On top of this, the incorporation of precision software
for mapping collects all the information needed on biological and
genetic resources.

Some of the material presented by Ag Tech on June 30, 2020,
was the intention to automate the physical harvesting process at
all stages of intensive agriculture, meaning that machines replace
farmers. It was suggested that super cows, pigs, and chicks—resulting from biotechnology—should be applied to increase production
without any concern for human health risks. This is the complete
annulment of the knowledge that farmers have accumulated over
thousands of years.

This relaunch of the agro-industrial model in Argentina is about
the dehumanization of agriculture itself. It is a plan alienated
from reality and the consequences that the immunosuppressive

agro-industrial model has had as a pivotal co-author of the obligatory social confinement devastating the planet because of the COVID-19 pandemic.

The Ag Tech tests the call for a broad deregulatory framework as if the agro-industrial model did not know about it. It is enough to mention that, in Argentina, GMOs were never subject to any congressional law and that CRISPR crops and new biotechnology events are not even necessarily subject to a risk review if it is so determined by a consultative body. The members of CONABIA are not public officials but rather belong to the public and private entities that, in many cases, have serious conflicts of interest due to their agribusiness links.

IICA suggests that it would be valuable for Ag Tech to have performance legislation (as opposed to indicative legislation in key regulatory areas) to incentivize innovation-based solutions, according to specific technical parameters.

Such a requirement by IICA is intended to make the processes involving Ag Tech subject to open regulation. The indicative or prescriptive legislation that IICA opposes is based on the constitutional criterion that there are no absolute rights and the law must operate as a social controller. Of course, not from the perspective of capitalist persecution, but from the viewpoint of the "common good," which forms the basis of the Argentine legal order, as it is the end purpose of the State which, therefore, empowers it to regulate rights.

Likewise, the areas in which Ag Tech operates impose technological advances that open up significant uncertainties in such a sensitive area as food, a key determinant of health, where precaution is a legal criterion that cannot be ignored. IICA's approach is more in line with the need to speed up processes and take for granted that there are no risks whatsoever. The proposed deregulation of Ag Tech is based on Bill Gates' Ag One Biosafety Deregulation Program.

The rhetoric of Ag Tech, obviously the same as that of Bill Gates' Ag One, talks about the need to provide technological innovation to small and medium farmers to increase their production when they do not even have the right to access land. Most of the individuals in a family, peasant, Indigenous, or self-managed farm who produce the food consumed by the Argentine population do not own the land and are forced to pay high rents. Furthermore, there is talk of increasing key food production through actions to mitigate climate change. However, agriculture continues to be directed towards the production of monocultures such as soy, which is not food for humans but for animal consumption (mainly as exports to China), or biodiesel production for fuels whose climate impact is greater than that of fossil fuels.

Since the Green Revolution, the agro-industrial regime in Argentina has never been the scene of a democratic debate in the institutional and sovereign space of public policy, the National Congress. We are faced with an autocracy over agriculture that, as it has no diverse democratic content of ideas and opinions, favors, almost automatically, the monolithic and hegemonic influences of the large agribusiness corporations and Bill Gates (under the representation of IICA).

By twisting the will of some government officials and visiting the offices of directorates, deputy secretaries, and ministries, Gates can reach his goals to advance expeditious regulations made to the mold of his interests, without the need for congressional laws nor the parliamentary procedures with the due citizen participation. From their perspective, these procedures are obstacles to their inevitable, urgent, and immediate objectives.

Therefore, denouncing is the sovereign act of freedom that we exercise by making visible what is happening in Argentina. As if COVID-19 had nothing to do with the agro-industrial model, and naivete governs us into believing that Gates and the agribusiness corporations (now under the lying mantle of IICA) are part of the solution. But they are wrong; they are a big part of the problem. Fortunately, our critical gaze and skepticism did not enter quarantine.

V

THE THIRD "GREEN REVOLUTION"

The Golden Rice Hoax

ꕥ

VANDANA SHIVA

FIRST CONCEIVED OF in the 1980s, and a focus of research since 1992, genetically engineered vitamin A rice was heralded on the cover of Time magazine in 2000 as a genetically modified (GMO) crop with the potential to save millions of lives in the Third World and proclaimed as a miracle cure for blindness.[i]

According to the UN, more than two million children are at risk due to vitamin A deficiency, which can cause vision impairment and lead to blindness. Is this Golden Rice really a miracle cure and the only means for preventing blindness in Asia? Or will it instead threaten biodiversity across Asia and introduce new ecological problems just as the Green Revolution did?

Despite unlimited resources at political, institutional, financial, and corporate levels, no reliable and stable vitamin A rice that can significantly relieve the symptoms of vitamin A deficiency has been produced in over 20 years of research.[ii]

In 2018, according to an article by Allison Wilson, PhD and Jonathan Latham, PhD:

> "[T]he US Food and Drug Administration (FDA) has concluded its consultation process on Golden Rice by informing its current developers, the International Rice Research Institute (IRRI), that Golden Rice does not meet the nutritional requirements to make a health claim....In an attached memo, FDA notes the beta-carotene content

of unmilled Golden Rice GR2E ranged from 0.50-2.35ug/g (FDA 2018a).[iii] That is, beta-carotene levels in Golden Rice are both low and variable. This compares to beta-carotene levels measured in non-GMO foods such as fresh carrot (13.8-49.3ug/g),[iv] Asian greens (19.74-66.04 ug/g),[v] and spinach (111ug/g). FDA notes the mean value of beta-carotene for GR2E is 1.26ug/g. This is, paradoxically, less beta-carotene than the 1.6ug/ g measured for the original iteration of Golden Rice."

Moreover, when we consider the number of patents involved in this initiative, it becomes all too clear that the only beneficiaries of these supposedly people-led ventures are large companies operating for profit—not for people.[vi]

In 2011, the Bill & Melinda Gates Foundation resurrected this failed idea by donating some $10.3 million dollars to IRRI, which BMGF heavily funds as part of the CGIAR system, for the development of Golden Rice.[vii] When peasants started the Movement to Stop Golden Rice, Bill Gates gave free rein to the Gates-funded Cornell Alliance for Science journalist, Mark Lynas, to distort the reporting in favor of Golden Rice. Through Lynas and the Gates PR for Golden Rice, misleading reports were spread instead of what independent scientists and peasants actually had to say.[viii]

Subsequently, in 2016, the Biotech PR lobby organized Nobel Laureates to promote Golden Rice and attack any criticism[ix] from Civil Society Movements.[x] Despite strong opposition, a Golden Rice permit for Direct Use for Food, Feed, and Processing was issued by the Philippines' Dept. of Agriculture's Bureau of Plant Industry (DA-BPI) in December 2019. The Filipino Stop Golden Rice network immediately started a campaign,[xi] and on August 7, 2020—which is now celebrated as No to Golden Rice Day—released their statement "Why We Oppose Golden Rice."[xii]

In 2000, Navdanya also started a campaign in India showing that there were superior and safer alternatives to genetically engineering vitamin A into the rice.[1] Children under the age of seven require 450 units of retinol (vitamin A equivalents). This means children would, therefore, have to eat 300 grams of Golden Rice to get their daily requirement of vitamin A. In Indigenous food cultures, a child's diet normally contains less than 150 grams of rice but also contains a range of other nutritious foods grown by rural communities. In fact, Golden Rice is 350% less efficient in providing vitamin A than the biodiverse alternatives nature has to offer.

Table 1: Traditional Indian food Sources of Vitamin A and their β-carotene content. *Source: Nutritive Value of Indian foods*

Source	Hindi Name	Content (microgram/100mg)
Amaranth leaves	Chaulai Saag	266–1166
Coriander leaves	Dhania	1,166–1,333
Curry leaves	Curry patta	1,333
Drumstick leaves	Saian Patta	1,283
Cabbage	Bandh Gobhi	217
Fenugreek leaves	Methi- ka-saag	450
Radish leaves	Mooli-ka-saag	750
Mint	Pudina saag	300
Spinach	Palak saag	600
Carrot	Gajar	217–434
Pumpkin (yellow)	Kaddu	100–120
Mango (ripe)	Aam	500
Jackfruit	Kathal	54
Orange	Santra	35

1 Shiva, V., Singh, U., & Navdanya (Organization). (2002). Vitamin—A Deficiency: Green Solutions Vs Golden Rice. Diverse Women for Diversity. https://books.google.it/books?id=4gruNAAACAAJ

Source	Hindi Name	Content (microgram/100mg)
Tomato (ripe)	Tamatar	32
Milk (cow, buffalo)	Doodh	50–60
Butter	Makkhan	720–1,200
Egg (hen)	Anda	300–400
Liver (goat, sheep)	Kaleji	6,600–100,000
Cod liver oil	N/A	10,000–100,000

Not only do these Indigenous alternatives based on farmers' knowledge provide more vitamin A than Golden Rice at a lower cost, but they also provide other nutrients. Indeed, the first deficiency of genetic engineering rice to produce vitamin A is the eclipsing of alternative sources of vitamin A.

The lower-cost, accessible, and safer alternative to genetically engineered rice is to increase biodiversity in agriculture. Further, since those who suffer from vitamin A deficiency typically suffer from malnutrition too, increasing the diversity of crops and diets of people in poverty is the most reliable means for overcoming nutritional deficiencies.

Even the World Bank has admitted that rediscovering the use of local plants and conservation of vitamin A rich green leafy vegetables and fruits have dramatically reduced vitamin A deficiency. Women in Bengal use more than 200 varieties of field greens. Over 3 million people have benefited greatly from a food-based way of removing vitamin A deficiency by increasing vitamin A availability through home gardens. The higher the diversity of crops, the better the uptake of vitamin A.

ENVIRONMENTAL COSTS OF VITAMIN A RICE

Tragically, sources of vitamin A in the form of green leafy vegetables are being destroyed by the Green Revolution and genetic engineering, which promote the use of herbicides in agriculture. For example, bathua, a very popular leafy vegetable in North India, has been pushed to extinction in Green Revolution areas where intensive herbicide use is a part of the chemical package.

Vitamin A from native greens and fruits is produced without irrigation and wastage of scarce water resources. Introducing vitamin A in rice implies a shift to a water-intensive system of production since so-called high yielding rice varieties are highly water-demanding. Vitamin A rice will therefore lead to mining of groundwater or intensive irrigation from large dams with all the associated environmental problems of waterlogging and salinization.

Why We Oppose Golden Rice

✤

STOP GOLDEN RICE NETWORK (SGRN)

Originally Published on August 7, 2020, in Independent Science News.

THE PUSH FOR corporate-led solutions to hunger and malnutrition is alarming. In particular, Golden Rice is now being proposed as a solution to the worsening hunger and malnutrition associated with the pandemic. Agrochemical transnationals (TNCs) and collaborating institutions such as the International Rice Research Institute (IRRI) are using concerns over food security during the pandemic to push for an industrial agricultural system that is already discredited. To quote PAN Asia Pacific:

> "[I]n the webinar 'The future of food systems in Southeast Asia post-COVID19' organised by IRRI and the FAO, Jean Balie, IRRI's head of Agri-Food Policy, said that they are 'looking to increase the mineral and vitamin content in rice grains" as a response to the pandemic, alluding to renewed promotion of the genetically-modified Golden Rice, which has recently been approved for commercialization in Bangladesh and the Philippines.'[xiii]

Golden Rice projects and applications are currently underway in three countries. On December 10, 2019, the Philippines' Dept. of Agriculture's Bureau of Plant Industry (DA-BPI) issued a Golden Rice permit for Direct Use for Food, Feed and Processing. This was despite the standing challenge by farmers, scientists, and civil society groups regarding Golden Rice's unresolved safety and efficacy issues.[xiv]

In August 2019, it was confirmed that the Indonesian Center for Rice Research (BBPADI) had grown Golden Rice in their testing fields in Sukamandi, West Java. But BBPADI is still awaiting permission from Indonesia's biosafety clearinghouse for confined field testing in selected areas.

In Bangladesh, rumors have circulated that Golden Rice would be approved by the Biosafety Core Committee under the environment ministry last November 15, 2019. While there have been no specifics yet, proponents are optimistic that approval in Bangladesh will occur.

We, the Stop Golden Rice Network (SGRN), believe that Golden Rice is an unnecessary and unwanted technology being peddled by corporations purely for their profit-making agenda. Golden Rice will only strengthen the grip of corporations over rice and agriculture and will endanger agrobiodiversity and peoples' health. Therefore, farmers, consumers, and basic sectors have been campaigning against the propagation and commercialization of Golden Rice since the mid-2000s, utilizing various forms and actions, including the historical uprooting of Golden Rice field trials back in 2013.

WHY IS THERE INTENSE OPPOSITION TOWARDS GOLDEN RICE?

The importance of rice in Asian countries cannot be understated—90% of rice is produced and consumed in Asia. Rice is at the center of the social, cultural, and economic activities of peoples across Asia. It is also a political commodity as rice is the staple food for a majority of the Asian population. Asian countries such as the Philippines, Indonesia, and India are centers of origin of more than 100,000 varieties of rice. Also considered as among the most biodiverse countries in the world—a wide array of vegetables, fruits, root crops, and cereals abound in the farms and forests of these countries—ensuring a dependable source of nutrition for the families and the communities.

Yet, malnutrition is prevalent, particularly among children and women. This is not simply because of the absence of an important nutrient or vitamin. It is caused by the "lack of access to sufficient, nutritious and safe food" due to poverty and changing food production and consumption patterns.

This impact is seen in IRRI's Green Revolution wherein many farmers across Asia have become bound to the expensive inputs and seeds peddled by huge agrochemical TNCs who promote a single-crop diet. As a result of the Green Revolution, white rice has become dominant in once very diverse Asian diets, but white rice has a high glycemic index which causes diabetes, and 60% of global diabetes cases are in Asia. Packing more nutrients, like vitamin A, in rice, which requires more rice consumption, would make this worse. Especially with the new pandemic for which diabetes is considered a risk factor for the severity of COVID-19.

The United Nations Food and Agriculture Organization (UN FAO) identifies the dominance of large corporations over food systems as among the factors that contribute to food insecurity and malnutrition. In developing countries, large tracts of agricultural lands are being converted either to industrial and commercial land uses or to large-scale mono-cropped plantations of cash crops such as pineapples, palm oil, and bananas that hardly serve the nutrition needs of the people. The FAO further acknowledges that the changes in food systems and diets, such as the prevalence of highly processed foods and displacement of traditional foods and eating habits also contributes to the worsening trend of food insecurity and malnutrition.

Given this context, we assert that Golden Rice is simply a band-aid solution to the gaping wound of hunger and poverty. Worse, the issues that continue to hound Golden Rice further prove the point that it is unnecessary and unwanted.

1. *Negligible beta carotene content* – The current version of the Golden Rice, GR2E, contains a negligible amount of beta-

carotene (from 3.57 ug/g to 22 ug/g), which the United States Food and Drug Administration (US FDA) also acknowledged, making the product useless in addressing vitamin A deficiency (VAD) in contrast to existing and readily available food sources. Already minimal, Golden Rice's beta-carotene was also found to degrade quickly after harvesting, storing, and processing, such as milling and even cooking, unless the farmers vacuum-pack and refrigerate the GM rice. Farmers from developing countries, however, do not seal or store the paddy rice in vacuum packs, which will make the product more expensive. Electricity also remains scarce in remote farming communities, so refrigerating the harvest is unrealistic, bordering on the absurd.

2. *No meaningful safety tests have been done* – Even as the Golden Rice has been approved in the Philippines, there has been no testing done to ascertain if it is safe for human consumption.[xv] Meanwhile, the aforementioned beta-carotene degradation may result in toxic compounds causing oxidative stress damage, which might lead to cancer. Dr. David Schubert of the Salk Institute for Biological Studies, USA, and Dr. Michael Antoniou of King's College London state that "there have never been short nor, more importantly, long-term safety testing in laboratory animals (of Golden Rice) and this must be done for several generations in rats to determine if it causes birth defects, which we consider a serious possibility."

3. *Contamination of other rice varieties and wild relatives of rice* – Field trials conducted so far have only looked at the agronomic traits of Golden Rice and not its long-term effects on the environment, including its possible effects on the genetic diversity of the thousands of rice varieties being cared for by small scale farmers and Indigenous peoples. While rice is a self-pollinating crop, cross-contaminationis still inevitable. Contamination can also occur through seed mixing. Such contamination has already happened in the US

with the Liberty Link rice scandal back in 2006 that caused US farmers millions of dollars in losses because of the inadvertent contamination of the yet unapproved GM rice.

4. *Safer sources of beta-carotene* – Being some of the mega-diverse countries, vegetables and fruits that are high in beta-carotene are found in abundance in the Philippines, Indonesia, Bangladesh, India, and other target countries for Golden Rice. These foods are available and accessible for people and contain much higher levels of beta-carotene than Golden Rice.

The worsening land-grabbing and land conversion cases, liberalization of agricultural commodities, and increasing control of corporations over agriculture and food, however, are preventing farmers and their communities from having access to these safe and nutritious foods. In developing countries, the challenges described above remain the main culprit of food insecurity and malnutrition. Both the development of biofortified crops like Golden Rice for solving health issues and corporate-led projects in agriculture as ways to ensure food security represents a worrisome push for top-down and anti-diversity approaches to food and health that will ultimately undermine people's capacities to strengthen their local food systems. By emphasizing dependence on just a few market-based crops, biofortification actually promotes a poor diet with little nutritional diversity.

Golden Rice is a failed and useless product and that is why we continue to resist and oppose it. Time and time again, huge agrochemical companies, philanthrocapitalists, and pseudo-public agencies have done everything in their power to deny the people's right to participate in decisions about their food and agriculture. Already, zinc and iron GM rice and 30 other GM rice are in the pipeline, with Golden Rice serving as the Trojan horse to lure the people into social acceptance and false security.

More than resisting the release of Golden Rice, however, we are pushing for safer, better, and healthier alternatives to addressing

VAD and other malnutrition issues. VAD and other malnutrition problems can be mitigated and addressed by having a diverse diet. Nutrition does not need to be an expensive commodity nor rely on advanced technology. We believe that instead of pushing Golden Rice and biofortifying crops through genetic modification, governments should promote biodiversity in farms and on tables by supporting safe, healthy, and sustainable food production. We are also calling on governments to pay attention to the needs of our food producers, including facilitating access to lands to till, appropriate technologies, and an agriculture policy that will promote and uphold the people's right to food and the nation's right to food sovereignty.

The Dystopia of
the Green Revolution in Africa

🌱

NICOLETTA DENTICO

IN 2006, JUST one year before food prices skyrocketed, the Gates
Foundation launched the Global Development Program, whose
primary focus was agriculture. The funds for the operation came
from the giant and unexpected mountain of money given to Gates by
Warren Buffet, who in turn had been flooded with cash by activities
engaged in during the speculative bubble that would soon burst in
the United States. It was enough to cross the sensitivity of the Rockefeller Foundation and launch together an invincible proposal—the
gospel of the Green Revolution (Rockefeller's old warhorse) and
bring it to the underdeveloped African continent.

This is how the Alliance for Green Revolution in Africa (AGRA)
was born.[i] The basic concept is always the same. Hunger in Africa
results from the lack of modernization of agriculture and the absence
of functioning markets. AGRA must fill this gap; it must develop
synergistic action with the private sector and promote access to
markets by disseminating agricultural innovation as a propellant
capable of increasing rural productivity. Gates and Rockefeller are
AGRA's primary sources of funding. As such, they are the ones who
identify the problem, direct its solution, place their staff in key positions, and establish the entire approach to the work.

As early as 2001, Gates had already tackled nutrition through
seminal funding to the Global Alliance for Improved Nutrition
(GAIN), the first in a series of new public-private alliances on food.[ii]

GAIN had just been born when it could obtain a hasty blessing from the United Nations Assembly meeting in a special session dedicated to children in 2002.[iii]

The Gates' decision to fund this new reality was a desire "to champion the concept of a major new push for improved nutrition on a global scale, initially through food fortification, working closely together with the private sector and leveraging partnerships to achieve the maximum possible scale of impact."[1]

Not only did support for GAIN never stop, from 2002 to 2014, the alliance received $251 million from the Gates Foundation out of a total spending budget of $284 million,[iv] but in 2003, Gates also began funding research on the Golden Rice project, a genetically modified rice that "can save the lives of millions of children."[2] The project is of great value to Gates because it experiments with the idea of a "humanitarian license," granted by Syngenta, as a donation to public institutions and farmers to cultivate this rice. This was the first instance of humanitarianization of the right to food, which serves to institutionally redefine practices around access to proprietary knowledge to enhance the industrial "donor" role as a benefactor while completely redefining the terms of the GMO debate.[v]

AGRA points in the same direction.[vi] AGRA's roots can be traced to a 2006 Rockefeller Foundation document that launched the concept of a dynamic, African-led alliance to help small producers and their families fight poverty and hunger.[vii]

AGRA defines Africa's agricultural problem as an issue arising from poor seed varieties, inadequate access to technology, and poor country infrastructure. Reproducing the mechanistic model that had already inspired the first Green Revolution in Asia and Latin America, AGRA was born in September 2006 to fulfill the vision that "Africa can feed itself and the world, transforming agriculture from a

---

1 Ibid.em, p. 375.

2 Brooks S., "Investing in Food Security? Philanthrocapitalism, Biotechnology and Development", in Science and Technology Policy Research, Working Papers Series, SWPS 2013-12, University of Sussex, November 2013.

solitary struggle to survive to a business that thrives."[viii] The purpose is to promote this market ideology as a solution to the productivity deficit of African crops, which philanthropists consider to be the reason why there is a lack of food to feed the growing population of the continent, which is obviously their definition of the problem.

AGRA claims to be the largest entity dedicated to eradicating hunger in Africa. The Gates Foundation considers it an "African face and voice of our work." Indeed, it is a subsidiary of the foundation on the continent, given the amount of money invested—about $630 million—since its establishment. Its faith in genetic engineering is associated with the plan to develop an intensive industrialized system for Africa involving seed companies and small farmers through agro-dealer platforms. These platforms interact with small- and medium-sized companies to supply the main AGRA hybrid seeds (maize, sorghum, cassava, soy, bananas, rice, sweet potatoes, beans), chemical pesticides, herbicides, and fertilizers to farmers.

The case of Malawi offers an eloquent example. With $4.3 million, AGRA financed the Malawi Agro-Dealer Strengthening Programme (MASP), conceived by the American organization Cultivating New Frontiers in Agriculture (CNFA), which is in turn financed by Gates.[ix] It is an entity that promotes the private sector, from large corporations to small local entrepreneurs, as a strategy of choice for the spread and development of agricultural markets and the adoption of market-oriented solutions in agriculture.[x] The giant Monsanto is one of the main beneficiaries of this program—if not the main beneficiary. Monsanto's own country manager in Malawi has admitted that all of their herbicide and seed sales are channeled through the platform, with an 85% increase in 2007.[3] Through its network of agricultural dealers, these giants become the only channel of training and information for African farmers who, absurdly enough, cease to be food producers and become consumers of goods, engines of

3 Curtis M., e Hilary J., The Hunger Games: How DFID support for agribusiness is fuelling poverty in Africa, edited by War on Want, 2012, pp. 4-7; https://waronwant. org/sites/default/files/The%20Hunger%20Games%202012.pdf.

a powerful agrochemical machine imposed, as in a new civilizing mission, by the private sector.[xi]

About 75% of seed supply in Africa comes from recycling and exchange between millions of small farmers from one year to the next, but, as the African Centre for Biodiversity (ABC) reports, "a battle against the African seed system is underway."[4] A concern shared by the NGO Action Aid. In a 2009 report, the NGO warns against AGRA's overly technical orientation, which completely ignores the complex social system of agricultural production on the continent. The report considers that there is a dangerous asymmetry in the field between small producers (with their seeds) and the multinationals involved in AGRA, with their monopolistic control over seed technology. Finally, it points out the decisive issue of intellectual property rights of seeds, and the transfer of local seeds to private individuals, as was the case in Zambia and Zimbabwe.[xii]

That, in a nutshell, is the black box of philanthropy. While preaching about "boosting the productivity and income of smallholder farmers across the continent,"[xiii] it is spreading opportunities for major economic interests while undermining any in-depth analysis of African agriculture and respect for local practices and knowledge. AGRA declares on its website that it embraces a model of participatory and self-determined development, calling itself an "alliance led by Africans with roots in farming communities across the continent."[5] Too bad that there is no trace of Indigenous participation at all.

The Gates Foundation provides subsidies to biotechnological research programs and uses this economic leverage to finance research circuits that have little or no local participation. Farmers are merely recipients of technologies developed in laboratories and sold to them by large companies.

The critical voices on the continent were not long-awaited,[xiv] however taking advantage of the World Social Forum in Nairobi in 2007,

---

4 "Crunch Time for the Seed Treaty." African Centre for Biodiversity (ACBIO), October 8, 2019. https://www.acbio.org.za/en/crunch-time-seed-treaty

5 "Our Story." AGRA. https://agra.org/our-story/

a composite platform of African associations, immediately manifested their collective dissent against AGRA, the continent's largest industrial agricultural war machine.[xv]

The GMO case is, in fact, the other tricky issue.[xvi] In 2007, AGRA released an official announcement saying that GMOs are not currently part of its programs but that they could become part of a long-term strategy if African governments would welcome the use of GMOs in their countries. The Rockefeller Foundation had already taken early action to clear the ground with governments, organizing Biotech, Breeding and Seed Systems for African Crops, an initiatory meeting, where participants were given a substantial dose of presentations on GMO research in Africa and experiments already underway in the continent. A small consortium of very powerful corporations—Monsanto, Dupont, and Syngenta—promptly engaged AGRA to promote this agenda and enter into agreements with several national research centers to establish their activity in Africa with the irrefutable humanitarian excuse. It takes nothing to seduce African scientists by funding their research, convincing decision-makers by glorifying the benefits of GMOs, and then imposing them on farmers, who will undoubtedly have no say in the matter. AGRA recruits several research centers, more or less well-known. Among them is the famous Kenya Agricultural Research Institute (KARI), now practically a subsidiary of Syngenta.

According to Bill Gates, GMOs are important innovations in the fight against hunger. Already in 2009, during a famous World Food Prize speech, he admitted that "some of our grants [in Africa] do include transgenic approaches because we believe they have the potential to address farmers' challenges more efficiently than conventional techniques."[6]

On this basis, the foundation continues with relentless activism in financing the creation of new institutions. The African Agricultural Technology Foundation (AATF), with $169 million in funding

---

6 Philpott T., "Bill Gates reveals support for GMO", in Grist, 22 October 2009, https://grist.org/article/2009-10-21-bill-gates-reveals-support-for-gmo-ag/.

over the last ten years, was created to instigate the illusion of African demand for GMOs.[xvii] AATF acts as a broker between seed multinationals and the scientific communities of these countries to facilitate experiments aimed at developing GM monocultures, sold in the context of humanitarian programs such as Water Efficient Maize of Africa (Wema), and has a negotiating mandate on the management of corporate patents. It promotes food bio-fortification and the digitization of agriculture to bring "prosperity through technology" in the One Agriculture, One Science initiative framework.[xviii] This involves 42 African universities working closely with the giants of the computer industry, starting with Microsoft. In just a few years, AATF has gained enormous importance. It is designed to expand the freedom of maneuver of companies, which actually have control over it, and at the same time, it is accredited to participate in regional policies.[xix]

It, therefore, lobbies governments to persuade them to adopt biosafety laws as a prerequisite for the marketing of genetically modified products. Not surprisingly, the number of countries that have undertaken GMO research or cultivation has risen from 2 to 9 in less than a decade.[xx]

New institutions, new programs that intersect and belong to the same core of monopolies.[xxi] The thread of these processes develops through the classical patterns of the most invincible colonialist interference. AGRA has all the room for maneuver it needs in the domestication of governments, starting with financial lubrication. Through its policy and advocacy program, AGRA provides African governments with data collection and analysis on agricultural policies. It unleashes consultants and officials to formulate or reform national policies under the pretext of shaping "home-grown agricultural policies that provide comprehensive support to smallholder farmers."[7]

---

7 In October 2009, the Gates Foundation announced the release of $15 million in funding for the definition of new agricultural policies in Ethiopia, Ghana, Mali, Mozambique and Tanzania, with activities aimed at training policy analysts in the agricultural sector, creating think tanks, building databases to support evidence-based policy development, etc: https://www.gatesfoundation.org/Media-Center/ Press-Releases/2009/10/AGRA-Launches-Policy- Initiative-to-Empower-Africa-To-Shape-Agricultural-Policies

In this way, AGRA avoids the risk of regulatory barriers in advance and adapts the laws of individual countries to its own objectives on issues like seeds, soil quality, market access, land ownership rights, environmental regulations, and digitization of processes. An interesting case in this respect is the reform of seed policies in Ghana in 2011, which allowed the introduction of GMOs and genetic research into agriculture.[xxii] Similar pathways have been conducted in Egypt, Burkina Faso, and South Africa, all countries that have already completed GMO approval processes. In a network of synergies with other foundations and the corporate sector, the Gates Foundation's goal is to establish GMOs throughout Africa, with the blessing of multilateral institutions and national governments, in the name of food security by 2030.[xxiii] It is no coincidence that Gates is one of the main financiers of the International Finance Corporation (IFC), the right arm of the private sector within the World Bank, which commits 6% of its portfolio to support the agribusiness agenda. It calls for Sub-Saharan Africa to "accelerate change on the continent."[8] AGRA is the powerful apparatus that consolidates this agenda. A rather irresistible form of market domination. Every scientific thought based on the recognition of Earth as living nature is relegated to the rank of "a tradition to be emancipated," not science, if not even downright considered anti-science, to be fought in the name of innovation.

Yet, contrary to the notion that it is industrial agriculture that feeds the planet, even today, only 30% of the food comes from megafarms, and 75% of the corn and soy produced with monocultures are used for fossil fuels and animal feed. 70% is instead the result of the complex knowledge, the ancient and always new work of small farmers who cultivate biodiversity, develop better varieties, in a constant discipline of the relationship between soil and food.

The scientific alternative to genetic engineering that inoculates toxic genes in food is agroecology, as recognized by the

---

8 International Financial Corporation (IFC),) Investing for Impact, IFC Annual Report 2019, p. 50. https://www.ifc.org/wps/wcm/connect/4ffd985d-c160-4b5b-8fbe-3ad2d642bbad/IFC-AR19-Full- Report.pdf?MOD=AJPERES&CVID=mV2uYFU

International Assessment of Agricultural Knowledge, Science, and Technology for Development (IAASTD) study.[xxiv] Food sovereignty and freedom from hunger passes through this route, creating the path towards justice.

The Gates Foundation's Green Revolution Fails Africa's Farmers

❧

TIMOTHY WISE

In 2006, the world's largest private foundation, the Bill and Melinda Gates Foundation, endowed by the fortunes of technology monopolist Bill Gates, got lucky. Barely one year before the food-price spikes in 2007, the foundation launched a new agricultural development initiative to supplement its global health and education programs. Much of the initial funding came from investor Warren Buffett, awash in cash from the speculative bubble that would burst the following year. The Gates Foundation joined the Rockefeller Foundation to launch the Alliance for a Green Revolution in Africa (AGRA), which would prove to be their ready-made answer to the coming question: "How can Africa grow more food?"

AGRA's goals to double productivity and incomes by 2020 for 30 million small-scale farming households while reducing food insecurity by half in 20 countries were ambitious. As with other BMGF initiatives, Western technologies would save the poor.

How is that Green Revolution going? AGRA has published no overall evaluation of the impacts of its programs on the number of smallholder households reached, the improvements in their yields and household incomes, or their food security. It does not even refer to those goals or progress in achieving them. Neither has the Gates Foundation, which has provided two-thirds of AGRA's roughly $1 billion in funding. This lack of accountability represents a serious oversight problem for a program that has consumed so much in the way of resources and driven the region's agricultural development policies with its narrative of technology-driven, input-intensive agricultural development.

My research shows that AGRA is failing on its own terms. There has been no productivity surge. Many climate-resilient, nutritious crops have been displaced by the expansion of supported crops such as maize. Even where maize production has increased, incomes and food security have scarcely improved for small-scale farming house-holds—AGRA's supposed beneficiaries. The number of undernour-ished in AGRA's 13 focus countries has increased 30% during the organization's well-funded Green Revolution campaign.

The Gates Foundation prides itself on its science-guided, data-driven, results-oriented philanthropy. On AGRA, it has spent two-thirds of a billion dollars. The results have been poor, which is all the more remarkable given that African governments have been per-suaded to subsidize the purchases of Green Revolution seeds and fertilizers with up to $1 billion per year in support. The Gates model for agricultural development is clearly flawed. Will the foundation recognize its failures and change course?

FAILURE TO YIELD

As I document in my recent paper, "Failing Africa's Farmers: An Impact Assessment of the Alliance for a Green Revolution in Africa,"[i] and the related report, "False Promises: The Alliance for a Green Revolution in Africa,"[ii] AGRA has received nearly $1 billion in contributions and made over $500 million in grants. I set out to fill the accountability gap as AGRA reached its self-declared 2020 deadline. Not surprisingly, AGRA declined my request to provide data from its own internal monitoring and evaluation of progress. That has been my experience with both BMGF and AGRA. They are more image-conscious than results-oriented, more concerned with protecting a carefully crafted reputation than they are with openly sharing and reflecting on their impacts. As a researcher, I have never spoken with anyone past the Communications Department at either institution.

Table 1: AGRA: Limited Signs of the Green Revolution
% Growth, selected crops, 2004/2006 to 2016/2018

	Production (MT/year)	Area (hectares)	Yield (MT/hectare)
Maize	87	45	29
Rice (paddy)	163	87	41
Wheat*	93	28	51
Millet	-24	-5	-21
Sorghum	17	13	3
All cereals	55	22	27
Cassava	42	51	-6
Roots/tubers (all)	42	51	-7
Pulses (all)	80	19	51
Groundnuts	17	52	-23
Soybean**	58	35	18

Sources: Author's calculations using data from FAOSTAT.

*excluding Burkina Faso and Ghana.
**excluding Ghana, Mozambique, and Niger.

In the absence of data on AGRA's direct beneficiaries and impacts, we used national-level data from 13 AGRA countries through 2018. We tracked trends in production, yield, and area harvested for most of the region's important food crops to assess the extent to which Green Revolution programs are significantly raising productivity. We also examined data on poverty and hunger to gauge whether there were signs that smallholder farmers' incomes and food security are improving across the region at levels commensurate with AGRA's goals of improved farmer welfare.

As Table 1 shows, we found no evidence that productivity, incomes, or food security increased significantly for smallholder households. Specifically, we found:

- ► Little evidence AGRA was reaching a significant number of farmers. Its last progress report says that AGRA had trained 5.3 million farmers in modern practices with only "1.86 million farmers using" such practices. This is vague and far short of the stated goal of doubling productivity and incomes for nine million farmers directly and another 21 million indirectly.
- ► No evidence of significant increases in smallholder incomes or food security. For AGRA countries as a whole, there has been a 30% increase in the number of people suffering extreme hunger since AGRA began, a condition affecting 130 million people in AGRA countries. Kenya, home to AGRA's headquarters, saw an increase in the share of its people suffering undernourishment in the AGRA years.
- ► No evidence of large productivity increases. For staple crops as a whole, yields are up only 18% over 12 years for AGRA's 13 countries. Even maize, heavily promoted by Green Revolution programs, showed just 29% yield growth, well short of AGRA's goal of doubling productivity, which would be a 100% increase.
- ► Where technology adoption has taken place, input subsidies provided by African governments seem far more influential than AGRA's programs. It is difficult to find evidence that AGRA's programs would have any significant impacts in the absence of such large subsidies from African governments.
- ► Even where production increased, as in Zambia, a near-tripling of maize production did not result in reductions in rural poverty or hunger. Small-scale farmers were not benefiting as poverty and hunger remained staggeringly high, with 78% of rural Zambians in extreme poverty.

▸ Green Revolution incentives for priority crops such as maize drove land into single crop production and out of more nutritious, climate-resilient traditional crops such as millet and sorghum, eroding food security and nutrition for poor farmers. Millet production declined 24%, with yields falling 21% in the AGRA years.

▸ No signs of "sustainable intensification," the goal of sustainably increasing production on existing farmland. Environmental impacts are negative, including acidification of soils under monoculture cultivation with fossil-fuel-based fertilizers.

▸ Production increases have come more from farmers bringing new land under cultivation "extensification" than from productivity increases. Subsidies and other support programs encourage farmers to expand the cultivation of supported crops such as maize. This has implications for climate change mitigation and adaptation.

RWANDA: "AFRICA'S HUNGRY POSTER CHILD"

Rwanda, widely considered an AGRA success story thanks to rising maize production and yields, illustrates AGRA's failings. As Table 2 shows, Rwanda's relative success in increasing maize yields 66%, with heavy subsidies and pressure from the government, came at the expense of sorghum, sweet potato, and other more nutritious crops. Area expansion was more responsible for production increases than were improved yields, as promised by the Green Revolution. Our more comprehensive measure of yield improvements for a basket of staple crops shows mediocre yield gains of just 24% over 12 years.

TIME TO CHANGE COURSE

Table 2: Rwanda Under AGRA
% Growth, selected crops, 2004/2006 to 2016/2018

Crop	Production	Area (hectare)	Yield (MT/hectare)
Maize	305	146	66

Rice (paddy)	98	147	-19
Wheat	-46	-60	46
Millet	28	132	-45
Sorghum	-18	-17	0
All cereals	82	43	27
Cassava	30	-16	55
Roots/tubers (all)	3	-3	6
Groundnuts	76	129	-24
Soybean	1	26	-19
Pulses (all)	89	54	23
Staple Yield Index			24

Source: Author's calculations using data from FAOSTAT.

More telling, the increased production of maize has done little to improve the lives of Rwanda's small-scale farmers. The number of undernourished has increased 15% in the AGRA years. The national rate of extreme poverty has barely moved, from 63% before AGRA to 60% in 2018.

Most other AGRA countries have done even worse. Only Ethiopia and Ghana show any sign of dynamism in productivity growth while reducing the number of undernourished. As Table 3 shows, most AGRA countries have seen only small productivity increases with rising numbers of malnourished people. AGRA's home country, Kenya, has seen a 7% decline in staple yields with a 43% increase in undernourishment.

Table 3: AGRA: Productivity & Undernourishment
% Change 2004/2006 to 2016/2018

Location	Staple Yields Index (%)	Number Undernourished (%)
AGRA Total	18	31
Burkina Faso	-10	15
Ethiopia	73	-29
Ghana	39	-20

Location	Staple Yields Index (%)	Number Undernourished (%)
Kenya	-7	43
Malawi	50	-3
Mali	19	-14
Mozambique	30	6
Niger	36	71
Nigeria	-8	181
Rwanda	24	13
Tanzania	22	29
Uganda	0	155
Zambia	20	29

Source: Author's calculations using data from FAOSTAT.
Staple Yield Index: weighted yield increases for maize, millet, sorghum roots/tubars. For AGRA total, Ethiopia, Nigeria, and Tanzania (cereals plus roots/tubers).

Rwanda's former Agriculture Minister, Agnes Kalibata, now heads AGRA. In a controversial move, the UN Secretary General named his Special Envoy to lead a planned UN World Food Systems Summit in 2021.

She is likely to bring her narrow Green Revolution perspectives to a discussion meant to address systemic failures in our food systems. The World Food Summit should instead actively consider agroecology and other low-cost, low-input approaches, which have shown far better short and long-term prospects than high-input Green Revolution practices. One University of Essex study surveyed nearly 300 large ecological agriculture projects across more than 50 poor countries and documented an average 79% increase in productivity with decreasing costs and rising incomes.[iii] Such results far surpass AGRA's.

AGRA and the Gates Foundation have had their chance to show that they could bring a Green Revolution of agricultural productivity and rising incomes to Africa's small-scale farmers. They have failed even with the unprecedented levels of subsidies from African governments to entice farmers into buying Green Revolution seeds and fertilizers.

Many farmers' groups in Africa actively opposed AGRA from the start, pointing to the negative environmental and social impacts of the first Green Revolution in Asia and Latin America. They have been proven right. Now it is time for the Gates Foundation, donors, and African governments to listen to farmers and shift their support to agroecology and other farmer-led, climate-resilient efforts to transform our food systems.

Seeds of Surveillance Capitalism

❦

NAVDANYA

THERE IS AN illusion that running faster on the chemical and Poison Cartel treadmill, now equipped with artificial intelligence and robots, will be more effective in producing more food and feeding the hungry. On the contrary, the tools and technologies of the Poison Cartel have brought the planet and the lives of farmers to the brink with climate havoc, species extinction, water crises, farmer incomes collapsing to zero, and food-related diseases killing larger numbers of people.

As Shoshana Zuboff, Professor Emerita at Harvard Business School, writes, "Surveillance capitalism is not a technology; it is a logic that imbues technology and commands it into action." Additionally, John Hamer, Managing Director of Monsanto Growth Ventures (Monsanto's venture capital arm), says: "If you think about it, there are only two people on earth that need to know a lot about remote sensing technology—Monsanto and the CIA."[1]

When technology is seen as a religion, a civilizing mission to be forced undemocratically on people, and a means for money-making elevated to human ends, it goes beyond ethical, social, ecological, and democratic assessment. Instead of being chosen, adopted, or rejected, we see technology as a forced recolonization in modern garb.

Similar to how it has been perpetuated throughout history, the diversity of life, culture, knowledge, sovereignty, and democracy are being exterminated through violence for economic gain and political power. Zuboff reiterates this in her book when she says:

"Surveillance capitalism is a rogue force driven by novel economic imperatives that disregards social norms and nullifies the elemental rights associated with individual autonomy that are essential to the very possibility of a democratic society."[ii]

Surveillance capitalism refers to an economic system centered around the commodification of personal data with the core purpose of profit-making. Since personal data can be commodified, it has become one of the most valuable resources on Earth. It is a new mutant form of capitalism that uses tech for its purposes.

The propaganda for surveillance capitalism is exactly the same that was used in the failed Green Revolution: "To feed the 9.7 billion people in the world in 2050, agriculture efficiency must increase by 35%-70% and technology is the key. India's rich mix of farming practices and small landholdings provide a massive data set to inform our models."[iii] Smallholders and their farming practices have been reduced to a "data set" for surveillance capitalism that will "provide valuable insights for the agri-industry, financial institutions, growers and policymakers."[iv]

SURVEILLANCE CAPITALISM ENTERS INDIAN AGRICULTURE

CropIn Technology Pvt. Ltd., a Bengaluru-based company, has raised $12 million in funding. It is funded by the Poison Cartel, venture capital firms, and Ag Tech companies, including Chiratae Ventures, the Gates Foundation, Strategic Investment Fund, Seeders Ventures Fund, Syngenta, Bayer, and BASF. Its clientele includes PepsiCo, Mahindra & Mahindra, ITC, Field Fresh, and McCain.

CropIn claims to use big data analytics, artificial intelligence, and remote sensing to "analyze data" for 265 crops for agriculture processors, distributors, inputs providers, lenders, and insurers. The start-up claims to be building an "agri-information dataset" to detect patterns and "predict the future" of a variety of crops.

The company has a tie-up with the Department of Agriculture (DOA), the Government of Karnataka, to "help" farmers create "more value" for their crops. The project aims to "assist" 415,000 farmers across 30 districts of Karnataka in digitizing 340,000 acres of farmland.

In 2017, CropIn started a project in collaboration with the Department of Horticulture (DOH) in Andhra Pradesh to digitize farms under two Farmer PRODUCTION Organizations (FPOs) in the districts of Chittoor and Krishna. It also works with the Bihar State Government and is part of the Jeevika project that uses "smart technologies" for climate resilient agriculture.[v] Additionally, the World Bank has chosen CropIn as the technology partner in the public-private partnership project of the Government of India and World Bank. CropIn is also partnering with the Government of Punjab's department of agriculture and welfare to plan the certification and traceability of seed potatoes. Punjab Agri Export Corporation (PAGREXCO) has been reported to deploy blockchain technology with the help of barcode, QR code, and geo-tagging to undertake certification and traceability of seed potato right from the nucleus to seed level (harvest).

Furthermore, it has been reported that India's agriculture ministry is working with National Informatics Centre on a 50-million-rupee project which involves rolling out software that will barcode all seeds. This has been justified on the grounds of making everything "more transparent" and "more traceable" to "weed out poor quality seeds."

The seeds will be "tracked" throughout the supply chain. There are also discussions with state governments to adopt the same software. What is even more troubling is that 5,000 private seed companies have already come on board with this, profits being their motivation, of course. The goal of this initiative, within two years, is to know how much of what seeds are sold in which areas.

However, it must be reiterated that the community seed exchange of farmers' varieties has total reliability and transparency; there is no need for surveillance technologies to monitor and deny their sense of quality and freedom.

It was recently reported that the 18,000-crore (180,000 million) seed industry has called for the introduction of a National Agricultural Policy and expedition of the 2019 Seed Bill and Biotech Regulatory Authority of India (BRAI) Bill to "ensure policy direction and predictability."

The paradigm of seeds of surveillance is one of the combinations of digital agriculture, data science, and genetic engineering, creating a higher level of integration of abstractions and instruments for control. This is also why we see that the old toxic cartel is recombining as a new one through mergers, and it is moving beyond the convergence of seeds, pesticides, and fertilizers to farm equipment, information technology, climate data, soil data, and insurance.

Seeds of surveillance transform the knowledge and knowing from a participatory process of co-creation with the Earth, her biodiversity, her soils to take better care of the soil and the seed, based on seed and knowledge sovereignty into "data" for increased control over farming by the Poison Cartel, a continuation of the industrial food system, and the basis of an attempt at epistemic imperialism. We must resist these seeds of surveillance and defend the seeds of freedom.

VI

BIOTECHNOLOGY &
GEOENGINEERING

The Problems with Lab Made Food

❧

VANDANA SHIVA

TECHNOLOGIES ARE TOOLS and need to be assessed on ethical, social, and ecological criteria as well as in the context of contributing to the well-being of all. The biodiversity of the soil, plants, and our gut microbiome is one continuum.

Today, most people are now aware that what you eat directly affects the state of your health. As countless studies have shown, industrial chemical-based food is a major contributor to ill health and a root cause of disease.[i]

Despite this, rather than shifting to ecological food and agriculture—which works in alignment with the laws of nature and the ecology of our bodies—Big Tech and the billionaires, with Bill Gates leading the way, are now investing in hyper-industrial food developed in laboratories, beginning with breast milk.

Our first food is milk from the breast. Breast feeding is a living relationship, it is an ecological, biological activity, which deepens the bond between the mother and baby. Breast milk contains all the nutrients for neural development and creates immunity to many diseases. Nutrients and antibodies are passed to the baby, while hormones are released into the mother's body.[ii]

Breast milk is not a product which can be substituted with industrial products, artificially made in factories and laboratories. Artificially created milk lacks the many natural benefits found in breast milk. UNICEF estimates that a formula-fed child living in disease-ridden and unhygienic conditions is between six to 25 times more likely to die of diarrhea and four times more likely to die of pneumonia than a breastfed child.[iii]

The mechanized and industrialized vision of society promoted by big business and the industrial baby food industry has eroded the culture of breast feeding, particularly in the Western world. The International Breast Feeding Action Network was created primarily aimed at Nestlé, the world's leading producer of food for infants.[iv]

Concern that the dramatic increase in mortality, malnutrition, and diarrhea in very young infants in the developing world was associated with the aggressive marketing of formula for breast milk substitutes. In May 1981, the WHO International Code of Marketing Breast Milk Substitutes passed by 118 votes to 1, the US casting the sole negative vote.[v]

Despite the known hazards caused by breast milk substitutes and notwithstanding regulations, the race for developing substitutes for breast milk has intensified.

Bill Gates' climate change investment firm, Breakthrough Energy Ventures, has invested $3.5 million into "Biomilq" which is targeting infant nutrition by attempting to reproduce mother's breast milk in a laboratory as a solution to climate change.[vi] It comes with no surprise that there is a patent pending for Biomilq.[vii]

The explosion of chronic diseases with the increase in factory farming and industrial food production and processing has already shown that artificially produced food is neither good for people's health nor good for the planet's health. Those who are contributing to the collapse of the planet and of our well-being have joined hands in creating hyper-industrial toxic diets in the name of protecting our health and saving the planet.

The creation of the Impossible Burger is a case in point. The Impossible Burger, based on vast monocultures of GMO Roundup-sprayed soy cannot be considered a "safe" option, both for its high levels of glyphosate, recognized as being carcinogenic to humans, and for its effect on our gut microbiome.[viii]

Roundup-sprayed GMO soy has already caused massive ecological devastation[ix] as well as chronic worldwide health problems.[x]

Promoting GMO soy "plant-based meat" as healthy is misleading the eater both in terms of the origins of the burger and, most importantly, on claims of its safety. The Impossible Burger is marketed promoting the myth that protein comes essentially from animals and now from "meat" produced in a lab using GMO soy, manipulating people into forgetting that we have been getting our protein down the ages from a diversity of plants.

As Zen Honeycutt of Moms Across America states: "The levels of glyphosate detected in the Impossible Burger by Health Research Institute Laboratories were 11 times higher than the Beyond Meat Burger. This new product is being marketed as a solution for "healthy" eating, when in fact 11 ppb of glyphosate herbicide consumption can be highly dangerous."[xi]

Roundup Ready crops, which have led to an increase of 1,500% in Roundup spraying in the US, failed in their primary objective of weed control.[xii] Weeds evolved resistance to Roundup and have become "superweeds," requiring more and more lethal herbicides. Beneficial plants like amaranth have turned into superweeds. Bill Gates and DARPA are even calling for the use of gene drives to exterminate amaranth, a sacred and nutritious food in India, since the Palmer Amaranth became a superweed in the Roundup Ready maize fields of the US.[xiii]

The following statement by Pat Brown, CEO amd Founder of Impossible Foods, is quite revealing.[xiv] He states, "If there's one thing that we know, it's that when an ancient unimprovable technology counters a better technology that is continuously improvable, it's just a matter of time before the game is over....I think our investors see this as a $3 trillion opportunity." Here is a perfect example of the mechanistic and profit-based mindset governing the extractive global food system. For Brown, food that nourishes our health is an "unimprovable technology."

The production of fake food is clearly about patents, profits, and control with no regard or concept of the essence of life, the web of life and the vital role of living food in our health and that of the environment. Patents are instruments for extracting royalties and rents by creating an artificial system to displace natural systems that are affordable, biodiverse, renewable, and healthy. Such is the case of Monsanto trying to patent seeds to profit from farmers.[xv] Today, the Impossible Burger has no less than 15 patents for the processes of making artificial food.[xvi]

The sudden awakening to "plant-based diets" based on hyper-industrialized processing, including use of GMO soy, is an onto-logical violation of food as a living system that connects us to the ecosystem and other beings. It also indicates ignorance of the diversity of cultures that have always used a diversity of plants in their diets. Artificial lab food reduces real food to industrial raw material and promotes large scale monocultures of industrial farming for the supply of raw material. As Bob Reiter, Bayer's Head of Research & Development (R&D), said in reference to plant-based meat companies: "They are sourcing different types of crops, and that also could create opportunity for us, being a company that is a plant-breeding company."[xvii]

Oblivious of the clearly growing shift to agroecology and organic food with more and more communities creating local, diversity-based, ecological, systems of growing food, the Poison Cartel continues to manipulate and promote new industrially-based markets. Through fake food, health, Indigenous food cultures, evolution, biodiversity, and the web of life are being disparaged as "ancient unimprovable technologies," totally ignorant of the sophisticated knowledges that have evolved in diverse agricultural and food cultures, in diverse climate and ecosystems to sustain and renew the biodiversity, the ecosystems, and the health of people and of the planet which have so far allowed humanity to survive.[xviii] Our knowledge of food for health is being erased.

At a time when movements across the world are growing and getting stronger for a GMO and chemical-poison-free future and independent scientists are establishing the links between cancer and vital organ failure and chemicals such as glyphosate (Roundup), which go hand in hand with GMOs, these destructive tools are being given a new lease on life through artificial lab food as Big Tech, Big Food, and Big Pharma become one in the Gates Empire.[xix]

Artificial, ultra-processed food will further spread chronic diseases. The "market" of sickness and disease will continue to grow. With an expanding market of ill-health, so too profits for the 1% will keep growing. By now the reality should be clear; industrial food is the basis of disease, whereas organic biodiversity-based food is the basis of health.[xx]

A recent study has shown that a week of eating organic food reduces glyphosate levels by 70%.[xxi] Fake food is building on a century and a half of food imperialism and food colonization of our diverse food knowledges and cultures. Decolonization of food is at the heart of protecting the health of the planet and people. Food is the basis of life and freedom. In the times of digital dictatorship, freedom begins with food; and food freedom is an inviolable right.

THE WORLD'S TECH FOUNDERS ARE INVESTING IN SYNTHETIC BIOLOGY

The industry of synthetic biology is booming. It has reached a worth of $12 billion over the past decade, of which $3.8 billion make up only last year and is expected to double by 2025. In the last twenty years, the number of companies specializing in this field has increased from less than 100 in 2000 to over 600 this year.

Synthetic Biology involves reconfiguring the DNA of an organism to create something entirely new, allowing for limitless applications in multiple fields such as fake meat and other fake foods in agriculture to new engineered raw materials in pharmaceuticals.

Among the largest investors in this sector is Microsoft founder Bill Gates. His early investments include Beyond Meat and Ginkgo Bioworks which is developing custom-built microbes as well as Pivot Bio, a biotech startup that focuses on making nitrogen-fixing microbes.

Co-founder of Google, Eric Schmidt, has invested in several synthetic biology companies through the venture capital firm Innovation Endeavours. His synthetic biology portfolio includes Zymergen, Bolt Threads, GRO Biosciences, and Ukko.

Peter Thiel, co-founder of PayPal, Palantir Technologies, and Founders Fund, a world-renowned VC firm and, also, the first investor in Facebook, has invested along with Schmidt in Bolt Threads, and is also backing Synthego and Emerald Cloud Lab. Marc Andreessen, founder of Netscape and Andreessen Horowitz, invested in Benchling, a company that offers tools to engineer DNA digitally. Other high-profile investors in synthetic biology include Vinod Khosla (Sun Microsystems), Jerry Yang (Yahoo!), Bryan Johnson (Venmo), and Max Levchin (PayPal).

Software To Swallow: Intellectual Property Model of Food Detracts from Regenerative Agriculture

❧

SETH ITZKAN

Impossible Foods should really be called Impossible Patents. It's not food, it's software—intellectual property with 14 patents. In fact, each bite of Impossible Burger has over 100 additional patents pending for animal proxies ranging from chicken to fish. It's iFood, the next killer app. Just download your flavor. This is likely the appeal for Bill Gates, their über investor. It's a food operating system (FOS), a predecessor, perhaps, to a merger with Microsoft, MS-FOOD. The business model is already etched in Silicon Valley: license core technology (protein synthesis) while seeking vertical integration of supply chains, not from coders to users, but from genetic engineers to protein seekers.

In this software-as-food scenario, there is no place for nature. Manufacturing of Impossible Burger starts with glyphosate-sprayed soy grown on what was once healthy prairie. It is then infused with heme molecules produce by patented yeast in high-tech labs for the blood-like upgrade. Finally, it ends its journey as a plastic-wrapped puck that some are brave enough to ingest. Just fry with canola oil and the illusion of a meal is complete. As Pat Brown, Impossible Foods founder and CEO openly states: "[A]nimals have just been the technology we have used up until now to produce meat....What consumers value about meat has nothing to do with how it's made. They just live with the fact that it's made from animals."

The pretense that this wealth-concentrating march of the software industry into the food sector is in any way good for people or the environment is predicated on a comparison with only the worst aspects of animal agriculture. It ignores, entirely, the rapidly growing regenerative movement that is offering so much hope for the planet at this key time, healing landscapes, replenishing aquifers, and mitigating fires. Because of its reliance on grains, tillage, pesticides and fertilizers, fake meat of scale exacerbates depletion of grasslands and undermines more legitimate solutions. As soon as there is a price on soil carbon, this misdirection will become evident. Will Impossible Foods stand against healthy soils legislation? That will reveal what their appetite is for.

PATENTS ASSIGNED TO IMPOSSIBLE FOODS INC.

Patent number 10287568: Methods for extracting and purifying non-denatured proteins

Patent number 10273492: Expression constructs and methods of genetically engineering methylotrophic yeast

Patent number 10172380: Ground meat replicas

Patent number 10172381: Methods and compositions for consumables

Patent number 10093913: Methods for extracting and purifying non-denatured proteins

Patent number 10039306: Methods and compositions for consumables

Patent number 10087434: Methods for extracting and purifying non-denatured proteins

Patent number 9943096: Methods and compositions for affecting the flavor and aroma profile of consumables

Patent number 9938327: Expression constructs and methods of genetically engineering methylotrophic yeast

Patent number 9833768: Affinity reagents for protein purification

Patent number 9826772: Methods and compositions for affecting the flavor and aroma profile of consumables

Patent number 9808029: Methods and compositions for affecting the flavor and aroma profile of consumables

Patent number 9737875: Affinity reagents for protein purification

Patent number 9700067: Methods and compositions for affecting the flavor and aroma profile of consumables

Patent number 9011949: Methods and compositions for consumables

Bill Gates' Climate "Solutions": Funding for Geoengineering

❦

DRU JAY AND SILVIA RIBEIRO, ETC. GROUP

B ILL GATES' APPROACH to our planet's climate is designed to appear sensible, even handed, and evidence based. A closer look, however, reveals a powerful billionaire with a deep attachment to techno-solutions that don't interfere with the normal functioning of capitalism—and a large financial stake in the continued extraction of fossil fuels.

In a 2010 TED talk, Gates outlined, in carefully crafted messages, what he considered the most effective solutions to climate change.[i] His approach, titled "Innovating to Zero," centered on five "energy miracles" he believes the earth needs to avoid catastrophic temperature increases. In Gates' view, those technologies are carbon capture and storage, nuclear energy, wind power, solar power, and solar thermal.

Gates presents the technologies, noting the drawbacks and potential of each one. He makes a show of deferring to evidence and science in each case. This is typical of Gates' rhetoric. A posture of disinterested curiosity shows up in all his public appearances; it is effective and disarming.

As a sort of afterthought to the TED talk, Gates answers a question about solar geoengineering—the idea that engineers could block enough sunlight to offset global temperature increases—with a carefully-prepared answer and an elaborate metaphor: "If this doesn't work, then what? Do we have to start taking emergency measures to keep the temperature of the earth stable? Yeah, if you get into that situation—it's like, if you've been overeating and you're about to have a heart attack, then where do you go? You may need heart surgery or something. There is a line of research on what's called geoengineering, which are various techniques that would delay the heating to buy us 20 or 30 years to get our act together. Now that's just an insurance policy, you hope that you don't need to do that. Some people say you shouldn't even work on the insurance policy because it might make you lazy, that you'll keep eating because you know heart surgery will be there to save you. I'm not sure that's wise, given the importance of the problem. But now that the geoengineering discussion about should that be in the back pocket in case things happen faster or this innovation goes a lot slower than we expect..."

Perhaps disingenuously, Gates leaves the last sentence unfinished. At the time of the talk, Gates had already been funding geoengineering research with millions of dollars for several years.[ii] Geoengineering refers, essentially, to attempts to stop global temperature increases by blocking the sun or sucking carbon out of the air on a massive, global scale instead of reducing carbon emissions to zero. The potential risks run the gamut from unexpected feedback effects that destabilize the global climate, to droughts and floods in Africa and South America, to land grabs, ecological destabilization, ocean acidification, pollution, and the growing political and financial power of the fossil fuel industry. This is a high-risk strategy; the consequences we know about are massive and the ones that are unknown could be more so. The process could alter weather patterns locally, regionally, and globally, with destabilizing geopolitical impacts as well.

In fact, Gates has, through personal funding and investments, been one of the major backers of the most extreme forms of geoengineering research for more than a decade. Prominent geoengineers like Ken Caldeira and David Keith are among his close advisors, and his donations are supporting some of the most controversial proposed experiments.

Gates' heart attack metaphor is flawed in a number of ways. Unlike heart surgery, geoengineering has never been done before, and there is only one patient to try it out on—the planet. Geoengineering is more akin to administering a massive dose of a hypothetical, untested medication that one is certain will have permanent negative effects. In this metaphor, one is uncertain which effects will happen, but there is potential for organ failure, psychosis, or death. In the same way, geoengineering—if implemented—will have global effects covering a range of severity from destructive to fatal, including unanticipated climate destabilization to continental crop failures. The problem is that we don't know which one will happen and the only way to properly "research" the question is to take that one shot.

Gates' engineering-for-everything mentality and his preference for purely technological solutions are well-known. And like many billionaires, Gates has a blind spot when it comes to questioning the logic of capitalism. Nearly every solution Gates proposes for the climate centers on "innovation" by entrepreneurs, driven by the promise of profits.

But hidden behind Gates' carefully cultivated persona of detached curiosity on climate solutions are significant financial interests in fossil fuel extraction. For example, at the time of his 2010 TED Talk, Gates had already been a major shareholder in Canadian National (CN) Railroads for at least four years. CN was making—and continues to make—big profits by shipping crude oil from Canada's tar sands to market. Rapidly expanding tar sands extraction has been stymied by a number of campaigns led by Indigenous communities and climate activists to stop construction and expansion of pipelines. In this context, Canada's railroads (of which CN is one of two major operators) have become an alternative oil pipeline, shipping over 400,000 barrels per day in January 2020.[iiiiv] For comparison purposes, the Trans-Mountain Pipeline that Canada's government is attempting to expand currently has a capacity of 300,000 barrels per day.

Tar sands operations are among the dirtiest and most environmentally destructive forms of fossil fuel extraction. In some cases, the land is strip mined to remove the bituminous sand below. The 2013 explosion of an oil train killed 42 people in Quebec.[v] In the aftermath, despite posting record profits, CN has pushed its workers to work longer hours and dismissed safety concerns from union representatives.[vi]

Since 2011, Gates has been the single largest shareholder in CN and his holdings have increased over time. Through Cascadia Investment Fund,[vii] which he controls, and through the Bill and Melinda Gates Foundation, he has gradually increased his holdings of CN stock to 16.7% of the company.[viii] That means that in 2019, Gates' Cascadia and the Foundation received around $190 million in dividends alone.[ix] Steep growth in oil-by-rail exports has accounted for the company's record-high profits and steady profit growth.[x]

Although Gates has sold a lot of his holdings in Microsoft, he still owns about $70 billion in stock of the now $1 trillion company. Microsoft has invested heavily in pursuing oil giants, signing deals with Exxon Mobil, Chevron, Shell, and BP.[xi] Despite a recent pledge to be "carbon negative by 2030," the company's cloud services web site advertises "oil and gas solutions" that will "increase drilling hit rates," "improve reservoir production" and "extend asset life cycles."[xii] In other words, they're helping oil companies extract more oil, at a time when we should be doing anything but that. Finally, according to a former employee, Microsoft allegedly also helped oil companies to conduct surveillance of their workers.[xiii]

Gates is not a disinterested observer seeking solutions to the climate crisis. In addition to being a billionaire who made his fortune skirting government regulations and dominating competitors with monopolistic practices, he holds a very significant financial stake in the continued expansion of the fossil fuel industry. His shares in CN Rail alone are worth $10.9 billion.[xiv]

If the planet stays within what scientists say is our maximum "carbon budget," oil companies will see vast assets disappear from their balance sheets—estimated at between $1 trillion and $4 trillion. This is the "carbon bubble."[xv] Geoengineering is the fossil fuel industry's final escape hatch. It is the only way to keep on extracting and burning in order to recuperate some of those $1.6 trillion in soon-to-be stranded assets. According to a report from CIEL, since the 1970s, oil companies have been investing in and supporting geoengineering.[xvi] However, they have kept a lower profile when it comes to more extreme forms of solar geoengineering such as blocking sunlight.

Into this void has stepped Bill Gates, whose carefully cultivated philanthropic image appears to be a relative public relations coup for the fossil fuel players who would like to drive geoengineering but can't show their faces. Climate geoengineering refers to large-scale human intervention in the climate, and it includes projects that could alter marine and terrestrial ecosystems and atmosphere. Geoengineers have divided projects into two major categories: carbon dioxide removal (the idea of removing CO_2 from the air on a massive, global scale) and solar geoengineering (the idea of blocking a portion of sunlight to temporarily cool the planet).

Carbon Dioxide Removal (CDR) proposals are the more mainstream of the two; there are dozens of research projects running around the world but so far, they either haven't proven that they can remove any CO_2, or only that they remove currently tiny amounts of CO_2 from the air while being too energy-intensive and expensive to make sense. Their proponents speculate, however, that they will eventually remove billions of tons per year from the atmosphere, either storing it underground or using it to produce synthetic fuels (in which case it ends up in the atmosphere again).

Direct Air Capture (DAC) is a form of CDR where fans suck in vast amounts of air, push it through substances that absorb carbon dioxide molecules, and then process the substances to remove the carbon. The process of removing the carbon requires high heat and thus large amounts of energy.

Bio-Energy with Carbon Capture and Storage (BECCS) is another form of CDR. It involves growing biomass (e.g., wood), burning it in a power plant, capturing the carbon (using a similar process to DAC) before it enters the atmosphere, and then storing it underground. In theory, carbon is thus removed from the atmosphere by plant growth and kept out when it is buried. However, many questions have been raised about the full life cycle impacts of BECCS, as it would demand millions of hectares of land (by one estimate the equivalent of the entire landmass of India). Its land and water needs would severely compete with food production and devastate ecosystems. Though it has been discredited in many climate circles, it persists as a policy idea and has been prominently featured by the Intergovernmental Panel on Climate Change (IPCC) in its Fifth Assessment Report.

Carbon Capture and Storage (which generally refers to capturing carbon before it is emitted) is on Gates' list of "miracle" technologies that need to be developed. It's also at the top of oil companies' wish lists. The top investors in CCS technologies have been oil companies, who own much of the intellectual property around related techniques. Microsoft's plan to achieve "net zero" emissions leans heavily on unidentified carbon removal techniques to offset the company's fossil fuel use.[xvii]

Along with tar sands billionaire N. Murray Edwards, and Chevron, Gates is a major investor in Carbon Engineering, a Canada-based Direct Air Capture firm. CE's founder and chief scientist David Keith, a Gates advisor since the mid-2000s, is at the center of what journalist Eli Kintisch called the "geoclique"—a small group of people who are driving geoengineering.[xviii]

There are some, including the IPCC, who don't consider carbon dioxide removal to be geoengineering. If, however, these projects were to reach the proposed scale, in order to really influence the climate, the impacts would be global and profoundly negative. Many CDR proposals require massive amounts of energy to function, and its rapid growth could slow the climate transition. It also requires massive infrastructure, and some forms (e.g., Bio-Energy with

Carbon Capture and Storage, or BECCS) require land covering the equivalent of several countries. Storage of billions of tons of carbon raises major questions about leaks, pollution, and the massive infrastructure required.

Keith is also the most well-known advocate for solar geoengineering, a term that covers various efforts to block sunlight from reaching earth or reflect it back into space on a massive scale. Along with Ken Caldeira, he manages the Fund for Innovative Climate and Energy Research (FICER).[xix] Gates had given FICER at least $4.6 million as of 2012, and further donations are unknown, though the website notes that research grants come from "Bill Gates from his personal funds" (i.e., not the Bill and Melinda Gates Foundation).

For years, FICER was the main source of financing for research related to solar geoengineering. Two of the North American solar geoengineering projects that are closest to testing—Keith's Stratospheric Controlled Perturbation Experiment (SCoPEx), and the California-based Marine Cloud Brightening Project—have received funding from FICER. According to a 2012 Guardian report,[xx] about half of FICER's funding was then going to Caldeira and Keith's projects, but it had also funded an initiative to advance governance of solar geoengineering (SRMGI),[xxi] and contributed to a Novim report on geoengineering, which was convened by Dr. Steven E. Koonin, Chief Scientist for multinational oil and gas company BP.[xxii]

Keith's current research project is the SCoPEx, an attempt to conduct an open-air test of solar geoengineering technology by spraying various substances into the stratosphere from a balloon. The experiment has been repeatedly delayed, but if it moves forward, it would be a violation of the provisions of the moratorium on geoengineering passed by the 196 countries who are party to the United Nations Convention on Biodiversity.

In his book *The Planet Remade*, journalist Oliver Morton calls Gates the "sugar daddy" of geoengineering and concludes that "Keith and Caldeira would have been leaders in the field based on their work but having this fund at their disposal gave them extra heft. It has allowed them to support work that would otherwise not have been supported and create space for discussions that might otherwise not have taken place."[xxiii]

Because changing the amount of sunlight that reaches Earth is so dangerous and difficult to understand without doing it at scale and over a long period of time, solar geoengineering has received less mainstream discussion, for now. Few open-air tests of solar geoengineering have been announced. Of those announced, most have been cancelled or delayed after opposition and protests. David Keith's favored proposal is to spray tens of thousands of tons of aerosols, potentially sulfur dioxide (SO_2), into the stratosphere, blocking sunlight before it reaches the Earth. Keith, who, according to the same Guardian report, received direct annual funding from Gates around 2012, wrote a book advocating for solar geoengineering. He took a strategy of embracing the shocking nature of spraying tens of thousands of tons of sulfuric acid into the stratosphere, defending the position that "we need to talk about it." He even allowed himself to be the butt of several cruel jokes on the satirical show the Colbert Report in order to convey his ideas, which he describes as a last resort if other climate strategies fall through.[xxiv]

Another one of Gates' connections to geoengineering stretches back to 1986, when Nathan Myrhvold joined Microsoft after his company was acquired by Gates' software giant. Myhrvold was a close collaborator for 14 years: "I don't know anyone I would say is smarter than Nathan," Gates told a reporter in the 1990s. "He stands out even in the Microsoft environment." Myhrvold is also a geoengineering enthusiast and a proponent of injecting the stratosphere with sulfuric dioxide.

Myhrvold reportedly took Bill Gates and Warren Buffet on a tour of Canada's tar sands mining operations.[xxv] One of the byproducts of tar sands processing is vast quantities of sulfur, which is stored in giant yellow pyramids outside of the Syncrude refinery, viewable from the highway. Myhrvold marveled at the possibilities of burning that sulfur to make sulfur dioxide and pumping it into the stratosphere via a hose suspended from a series of balloons: "So you can put one little pumping facility up there," Myrhvold enthused, "and with one corner of one of those sulfur Mountains, you control the whole global warming problem for the Northern Hemisphere." That idea forms the basis for "Stratoshield," a project of Myhrvold's Intellectual Ventures, an investment fund that seeks to profit from inventions that anticipate trends and future developments. The Stratoshield consists of a very long hose (30 kilometers long) stretching from the ground to the stratosphere with balloons, each of which houses a small pumping station that would keep a steady stream of sulfur dioxide flowing into the sky. A "string of pearls," in Myhrvold's words, that would "spritz the stratosphere with a fine mist," a veil of 100,000 tons per year of sulfuric dioxide that would encircle the planet.

Who is behind the Stratoshield? It's unclear, but FICER co-director Ken Caldeira works as an "inventor" for Intellectual Ventures and has co-authored a paper with Myhrvold.[xxvi] Caldeira has also speculated publicly that a government of a "vulnerable country" like Bangladesh could unilaterally implement solar geoengineering.[xxvii] In addition to the stratospheric shield, Intellectual Ventures has also proposed weather modification technology using ocean cooling.[xxviii]

In a chapter of the book *SuperFreakonomics: Global Cooling, Patriotic Prostitutes, and Why Suicide Bombers Should Buy Life Insurance*, which sold over 7 million copies, Myrhvold discusses climate at length with the authors and makes the case for injecting sulfur into the stratosphere. After quoting Myhrvold for several pages, the authors reach the conclusion that reducing carbon emissions doesn't make sense.[xxix] Spending money on "anti-carbon initiatives, without thinking things through" would be "a huge drag on the world economy." Then what would work? The authors say about Myhrvold's Stratoshield plan that "Once you eliminate the moralism and the angst the task of reversing global warming boils down to a straightforward engineering problem."

Gates, who is still close with Myhrvold, has invested in Intellectual Ventures, which includes Stratoshield under its umbrella of inventions. He and Myhrvold appear to share the view that capitalism is the main force that will lift—and has lifted—the poor people of the world out of poverty.[xxx]

Myhrvold later backtracked and denied portraying solar geoengineering as a solution. He now opts for the more politically correct "it's a last resort" approach. The "last resort" rhetoric echoes how Gates talks on the rare occasions when he speaks about his support for geoengineering. But the facts outlines here—the much more aggressive pro-geoengineering stance portrayed in *SuperFreakonomics*, coupled with Myhrvold's proximity to Gates, and Gates' investments in transportation of tar sands oil—raise significant questions about Gates' real privately-held views about geoengineering technologies, and what is driving his investments in them.

VII

GENE DRIVES & THE SIXTH MASS EXTINCTION

Driven to Exterminate:
How Bill Gates Brought Gene Drive
Extinction Technology Into the World

❦

ZAHRA MOLOO AND JIM THOMAS (ETC GROUP)

I N 2016, AT the Forbes 400 Summit on Philanthropy in New York, Bill Gates was asked to give his opinion on gene drives, a risky and controversial new technology that could—by design—lead to the complete extermination of the malaria-carrying mosquito species, Anopheles gambiae. If it were his decision to wipe out this mosquito once and for all, given the risks and benefits being considered, would he be ready to do it? "I would deploy it two years from now," he replied confidently. However, he added, "How we get approval is pretty open ended."

Gates' "let's deploy it" response may not seem out of character, but it was an unusually gung ho response given how risky the technology is widely acknowledged to be. Gene drives have been dubbed an "extinction technology" and with good reason: gene drive organisms are created by genetically engineering a living organism with a particular trait, and then modifying the organism's reproductive system in order to always force the modified gene onto future generations, spreading the trait throughout the entire population.

In the case of the Anopheles gambiae project (that Gates bankrolls), a gene drive is designed to interfere with the fertility of the mosquito; essential genes for fertility would be removed, preventing the mosquitoes from having female offspring or from having offspring altogether.[i] These modified mosquitoes would then pass on their genes to a high percentage of their offspring, spreading auto-extinction genes throughout the population. In time, the entire species would in effect be completely eliminated.[ii]

Although still new and unproven, gene drives have provoked significant alarm among ecologists, biosafety experts and civil society, many of whom have backed a call for a complete moratorium on the technology. By deliberately harnessing the spread of engineered genes to alter entire populations, gene drives turn the usual imperative to try to contain and prevent engineered genes from contaminating and disrupting ecosystems on its head. The underlying genetic engineering technology is unpredictable and may provoke spread of intended traits. The notion that a species can be removed from an ecosystem without provoking a set of negative impacts on food webs and ecosystem functions is wishful thinking. Even taking out a carrier of an unpleasant parasite does not mean the parasite won't just jump to a different host. Moreover, the implicit power in being able to re-model or delete entire species and ecosystems from the genetic level up is attracting the interest of militaries and agribusiness alike and runs counter to the idea of working with nature to manage conservation and agriculture.

That Gates is so enthusiastic about releasing this powerful genetic technology is not so surprising when one scratches the surface of the myriad institutions that have been researching and promoting gene drives for years. To date, the Bill and Melinda Gates Foundation (BMGF) is either the first or second largest funder of gene drive research alongside the shadowy US Defense Advanced Research Projects Agency (DARPA) whose exact level of investment is disputed.[iii] Gates is not just another tech optimist standing on a business stage calling for gene drive release to be allowed—his foundation has poured millions of dollars into gene drive research for over a decade. Yet, direct research funding is not the only way in which the BMGF has accelerated the development of this technology. They have also funded and influenced lobbyists, regulators, and public narratives around gene drives in an attempt to push this dangerous sci-fi sounding technology into real world use, shifting research priorities on industrial agriculture, conservation, and health strategies along the way.

FUNDING THE RESEARCH

While the controversy around gene drives is recent, promoters like to emphasize that research towards creating gene drive technology has been in the works for many years. From its inception, much of this research has received direct funding from the BMGF, funneled through different academic institutions. The beginning of current research into genetically modified extinction technology can be traced back to 2003 when Austin Burt, a professor of Evolutionary Genetics at Imperial College in London, was working with yeast enzymes, noting how "selfish genes" were able to reproduce with a greater probability than the usual 50/50 ratio that occurs in normal sexual reproduction. In a paper, he explained how these genes could be adapted for other uses, such as in mosquitoes, where the destruction of the insects could be embedded directly into their genes. Burt, along with Andrea Crisanti, another biologist at Imperial College, applied for a $8.5 million grant from the Bill and Melinda Gates Foundation (which they received in 2005) to take forward their theories and apply them in a lab, eventually creating an international project called "Target Malaria." In an interview with Wired magazine, Crisanti explained how this funding and the relationship with the BMGF was instrumental in the further development of gene drives technology: "If you need a resource, you get it, if you need a technology, you get it, if you need equipment, you get it. We were left with the notion that success is only up to us," he said.[iv]

At the same time, in 2005, the BMGF was also channeling money into the Foundation for the National Institutes of Health (FNIH), as part of a larger $436 million grant for a project called the Grand Challenges in Global Health Initiative. Through the FNIH, a biologist at UC Irvine, Anthony James, was injecting DNA into mosquito embryos to create transgenic mosquitoes resistant to dengue fever.

These mosquitoes were able to reproduce which meant that normal mosquito populations could possibly be replaced by GM mosquitoes if only a way could be found to drive the engineered genes into populations. In 2011, James' lab genetically engineered the mosquito species Anopheles stephensi with genes that made it resistant to malaria.

All these developments were significant, but they had not yet led to the creation of gene drives. That moment came in 2015, when two scientists at UC San Diego, California, Ethan Bier and Valentino Gantz, created a gene-construct that could spread a trait through fruit flies, turning the entire population yellow. The technology they had developed used a new genetic engineering tool called CRISPR-Cas9 that could cut DNA and enable genes to be inserted, replaced or deleted from DNA sequences.[v] In effect, they built the genetic engineering tool directly into the flies' genome so each generation genetically engineered its offspring. CRISPR technology was instrumental in the creation of the gene drive and in late 2015, functional gene drive modified mosquitoes were created. This is what the Gates Foundation was waiting for. In 2016, an official with the Gates Foundation said in an interview that malaria could not be wiped out without a gene drive; all of a sudden this "extinction technology" was considered not just desirable but "necessary" in the fight to end malaria.

Since then, the push for further research and deployment of gene drives has gained considerable momentum—mostly propelled by Gates dollars. The BMGF has funneled even more funding into taking gene drive research forward. In 2017, UC Irvine received another $2 million directly from the BMGF for Anthony James to genetically engineer the malaria-carrying mosquito species Anopheles gambiae, with a view to eventually releasing them in a trial.[vi] Meanwhile, Target Malaria, the flagship research consortium that came from Burt and Crisanti's work, has received $75 million from the foundation.[vii] This has been used to create labs in Burkina Faso, Mali and Uganda in order to begin experimenting with gene drives in Africa, and in 2019 Target Malaria released 4,000 genetically modified (not gene drive) mosquitoes in Burkina Faso as a first step in their experiment. Their goal is to release the gene drive mosquitoes in Burkina Faso in 2024. BMGF has also bankrolled further gene drive research in Siena, Italy, Jerusalem, and Boston.[viii]

SYNTHETIC BIOLOGY AND AGRICULTURAL INTERESTS

Although mainstream media coverage of gene drive developments emphasizes Gates' grandiose philanthropic intentions in eliminating malaria and saving lives in Africa, there is more than meets the eye when it comes to Gates' direct funding of gene drive research.

Gene drives are classified as part of a controversial field of extreme genetic engineering known as synthetic biology (SynBio) or "GMO 2.0" in which living organisms can be redesigned in the lab to have new abilities.[ix] Synthetic biology aims to redesign and fabricate biological components and systems that do not exist in the natural world.[x] Today, it is a multi-billion dollar industry that creates compounds like synthetic ingredients (synthetic versions of saffron, vanilla etc.), medicines, and lab-grown food products. Gates' ambitions for this radical biotech field extend beyond gene drives and malaria research and into the field of SynBio. In an interview, he said that if he were a teenager today, he would be hacking biology: "If you want to change the world in some big way, that's where you should start—biological molecules."[xi]

The Gates Foundation has had a substantial influence on the synthetic biology industry since its inception. In 2005, when the field was still relatively new, the BMGF gave a grant of $42.5 million (and later more) to the University of California, Berkeley, and Amyris, a startup SynBio company, in order to produce the antimalarial drug artemisinin in a laboratory with genetically engineered microbes.[xii] The aim of this grant was not only to create the antimalarial drug, but also to create new biofuels, medicines and high value chemicals. The founder of Amyris, Jay Keasling, has told ETC Group that the Gates funds were contingent on finding other more profitable lines of business in addition to artemisinin and so initially the technology was simultaneously applied to biofuel production. Jack Newman, a scientist at Amyris, explained that, "the very same pathways" used in artemisinin "can be used for anticancer (drugs), antivirals, antioxidants."[xiii]

While using philanthropic funds to bankroll a private biofuel business might seem ethically questionable, the supposedly beneficial target of making an antimalarial molecule may not have been so positive either. In 2013, after many years of research by the UC Berkeley laboratory and Amyris, it was announced that the French pharmaceutical company, Sanofi, would launch the production of synthetic artemisinin.[xiv] Commercial production of the compound was hailed as more affordable than naturally grown artemisinin, which is farmed in countries like Kenya, Tanzania, Madagascar, Mozambique, India, Vietnam, and China. However, what was not mentioned during all the hype around the synthetic production of the compound was that artemisinin farmers in these countries would lose their livelihoods as a result of the sale of the SynBio version.[xv] In the hype and supported by philanthropic money, prices for artemisinin crashed and some natural artemisinin extractors were shuttered. Eventually, even the synthetic product proved too expensive to sell.[xvi]

The BMGF investments in SynBio go further still. The Foundation invested in a number of other SynBio companies including Editas Medicine, a genome editing company that controls the CRISPR-Cas9 technology behind gene drives, and Ginkgo Bioworks, which creates microbes for application in fashion and medicine industries.[xvii]19 Gates is also keen on the "cellular food revolution," which grows food from cells in a lab. His investments in the sector include Memphis Meat, a company that creates cell-based meat without animals, Pivot Bio, which creates engineered microbes for use in agriculture, and Impossible Foods, which makes processed meat-like burgers from a synthetic biology-derived blood substitute.

That Gates is pouring money into an industry oriented toward shifting agriculture toward technology is no accident, given how influential BGMF is in global health and agriculture policy generally, and in promoting industrial agriculture in the Global South and especially Africa. In the case of gene drives, while most international debate has focused on their application in malaria and conservation, the industrial farm is where gene drives may first make their impact; the very foundational patents for gene drives have been written with agricultural applications in mind.[xviii] In 2017, a secretive group of military advisors known as the JASON Group produced a classified study on gene drives commissioned by the US government which was tasked to address "what might be realizable in the next 3–10 years, especially with regard to agricultural applications." The JASON Group was also informed by gene drive researchers who were present during a presentation on crop science and gene drives delivered by someone from Bayer-Monsanto. Other groups involved in gene drive discussions behind the scenes include Cibus, an agricultural biotech firm, as well as agribusiness majors including Syngenta and Corteva Agriscience.

The startup Agragene, whose co-founders are none other than the gene drive researchers Ethan Bier and Valentino Gantz of University of California at San Diego, "intends to alter plants and insects" using gene drives. The JASON Group and others have also raised the flag that gene drives have biowarfare potential—in part explaining the strong interest of US and other militaries in the technology.

SHAPING THE NARRATIVE AROUND GENE DRIVES

Not only has the Gates Foundation funded the underlying tools of the SynBio industry and molded gene drive research for years, but it has also been working behind the scenes to influence the adoption of these technologies. The way in which policy and public relations about gene drives research has been shaped by the Foundation becomes clear when one examines what happened immediately after the creation of the first functional gene drives with CRISPR technology in late 2014.

In early 2015, the US National Academies of Science, Engineering and Medicine announced that they would have a major inquiry into gene drives—an unprecedented move for such a brand new (only months old) technology. The study did not explore just the science of gene drives, but also aimed to frame issues around policy, ethics, risk assessment, governance, and public engagement around gene drives.[xix] It was sponsored by the Defense Advanced Research Projects Agency (DARPA) and The Bill & Melinda Gates Foundation, through the National Institutes of Health (NIH) and the Foundation for the National Institutes of Health (FNIH). Several panel members were recipients of Gates funds.

The Foundation has also channeled money into the MIT Media Lab, home to Kevin Esvelt, who directs a group called Sculpting Evolution and was among the first people to identify the potential of CRISPR to alter wild populations.[xx] Last year, the MIT Media Lab was embroiled in a controversy when it was revealed that it had received donations from the convicted sex offender Jeffrey Epstein. Through Epstein, the media lab secured $2 million from Gates although it is not clear for which project.[xxi]

One of the most controversial findings that illustrates the extent to which the Gates Foundation is invested in influencing the uptake of gene drive technology was made in 2017 by civil society organizations following a Freedom of Information request. That process led to the release of a trove of emails revealing that a private PR firm called Emerging Ag, was paid $1.6 million by BMGF.[xxii] Part of their work involved coordinating the "fight back against gene drive moratorium proponents" as well as running a covert advocacy coalition to exert influence on the UN Convention on Biological Diversity (CBD), the key body for gene drive governance. After calls in 2016 for a global moratorium on the use of gene drive technology, the CBD sought input from scientists and experts in an online forum.[xxiii] Emerging Ag recruited and coordinated over 65 experts, including a Gates Foundation senior official, a DARPA official, and government and university scientists, in an attempt to flood the official UN process with their coordinated inputs.

EMERGING AG INC.

Emerging Ag Inc.	2020	Malaria	Global Health	$2,509,762
Emerging Ag Inc.	2017	Malaria	Global Health	$1,603,405

Emerging Ag now manages an overt advocacy network also funded by BMGF called the Outreach Network for Gene Drive Research whose stated intention is to "raise awareness of the value of gene drive research for the public good."[xxiv] Its members include researchers and organizations that work on gene drive research, stakeholder engagement, outreach and even funders. Almost all of its members are separately funded by the Gates Foundation. In 2020, Emerging Ag received another grant from the Foundation for $2.5 million.

GOVERNANCE AND LOBBYING

During the international negotiations of the Convention on Biological Diversity (CBD) COP14 in Sharm El-Sheikh in 2018, the influence of the Gates machinery was on clear display. The multiple initiatives in which the Foundation had invested beforehand ended up having important consequences. Not only had the Foundation sought to influence the expert panels that inform the Convention before the actual negotiations took place, but they had also managed to ensure that political support for gene drives in Africa— where the first gene drive mosquitoes are due to be released—was established well before the official negotiations by countering civil society concerns and resistance to this highly risky technology.

About six months prior to COP14, the African Union's technical arm, the New Partnership for Africa's Development (NEPAD), released a report in support of gene drive mosquitoes for malaria eradication. A year prior to the report, NEPAD was awarded $2.35 million from the Open Philanthropy Project, a major funder of Target Malaria alongside BMGF, to support the evaluation, preparation, and possible deployment of gene drives. Open Philanthropy's funding priorities often move in lockstep with BMGF priorities, and they are part of the same "effective altruism" movement of techno-cratic billionaires. Additionally, a new crop of African negotiators, new to the CBD, arrived at the Sharm El-Sheikh negotiations vocally arguing in favor of gene drives. Many of this new cohort were drawn from ABNE, the African Network on Biosafety Expertise—a Gates funded biotech policy network on the African continent that is at the heart of BGMF influence on African biotech policy. It was no surprise then when, at the CBD, the consensus position of the Afri-can group of delegates was one that was in favor of gene drives, and they blocked a moratorium on the release of gene drive organisms that was requested by African civil society groups.[xxv]

So embedded were the individuals from institutions funded by the BMGF in the official negotiations that even certain people serv-ing as official government delegates were found to have been paid or employed by Target Malaria. On the sidelines, lobbyists from other Gates funded outfits, such as the Cornell Alliance for Science also railed against the moratorium proposal.[xxvi]

From bankrolling the technology development and creating the underlying tools, to shaping the narrative, picking the policy nego-tiators, and even paying the lobbyists, Bill Gates and his foundation have been tightly interwoven into every part of the story of gene drive extinction technology so far. However, although the foun-dation has been highly successful in influencing the technology's future deployment, they have not been able to suppress the global movements that have sprung up in resistance to gene drive technol-ogy. And just as health activists and food sovereignty activists have pushed back against the white savior complex of philanthrocapital-ists, movements in West Africa have been quick to point out the racism and injustice of Gates-backed groups such as Target Malaria, who are using African people and ecosystems as experimental sub-jects for gene drive technology.

In June 2018, over 1,000 farmers and activists protested against gene drive technology in the streets of Ouagadougou. Many are con-cerned about the eventual agricultural applications of gene drives and, in the case of malaria, they believe that Indigenous medicine and existing methods are better suited to fight the disease, particularly given the increasing number of countries that have completely eradicated it.[xxvii] In the words of food sovereignty activist Ali Tapsoba, with the organization Terre à Vie, "The best way to fight against malaria remains to put in place a good sanitation policy for our habitats and our environment. It is out of the question for us to let these scientists continue to conduct dangerous experiments outside their laboratories." It is perhaps at its intended point of experimentation, in Burkina Faso, that the Gates machinery will finally be forced to grind to a halt.

Gates Foundation Hired a Public Relations Firm to Manipulate the UN Over Gene Drives

❧

JONATHAN LATHAM

THE BILL AND Melinda Gates Foundation paid a PR firm called Emerging Ag[i] $1.6 million to recruit a covert coalition of academics to manipulate a UN decision-making process over gene drives, according to emails obtained through Freedom of Information requests. Gene drives are a highly controversial new genetic extinction technology. They have been proposed as potentially able to eradicate malarial mosquitoes, agricultural pests, invasive species, as well as having potential military uses.[ii] Emerging Ag calls itself "a boutique international consulting firm providing communications and public affairs services." Its president and founder is Robynne Anderson, a former international communications director of CropLife, the global lobby group for the biotechnology, seed, and pesticide industries.[iii]

The FOIA emails reveal that the project coordinated by Emerging Ag was dubbed the "Gene Drive Research Sponsors and Supporters coalition." It consisted of three members of a UN committee called the Ad Hoc Technical Expert Group on Synthetic Biology (AHTEG) plus a larger group of 65 covertly recruited, but seemingly independent, scientists and officials, all coordinated by a still larger number of government officials (mainly from English-speaking countries),

PR advisors, academics, and members of various Gates-funded projects. The AHTEG on Synthetic Biology is part of the UN Convention on Biological Diversity (CBD). This AHTEG is tasked with creating a formal set of regulatory recommendations to help governments avoid negative impacts on biodiversity. Its recommendations are supposed to draw from the discussions of an online forum of experts called The UN CBD Online Forum on Synthetic Biology. The three AHTEG members who coordinated with Emerging Ag are Dr. Todd Kuiken of North Carolina State University, Robert Friedman of the J Craig Venter Institute,[iv] and Professor Paul Freemont of Imperial College, London. The first and last represent teams and institutions that have received at least $99 million between them from the US military and US foundations, including Gates, to develop and test gene drive systems.

THE CBD ONLINE FORUM ON SYNTHETIC BIOLOGY

According to the emails,[v] which were obtained from the University of North Carolina by Edward Hammond of Prickly Research,[vi] the Gates funding for Emerging Ag was obtained to co-ordinate a "fight back against gene drive moratorium proponents." Funding for Emerging Ag first began after the last full meeting of the UN Convention on Biological Diversity, held in Cancún, Mexico in December 2016, which witnessed calls from southern countries and over 170 international organizations for a UN moratorium on gene drives.[vii] Adding to the pressure was a letter titled "A Call for Conservation with a Conscience: No Place for Gene Drives in Conservation" signed by 30 environmental leaders, including Jane Goodall. The letter asked for a "halt to all proposals for the use of gene drive technologies, but especially in conservation."[viii] A primary function of Emerging Ag was to recruit academics. The primary task of the covertly recruited academics (those who were not on the inner circle of the AHTEG itself) was thus to stack the UN's CBD Online Forum on Synthetic Biology. This forum was expected to discuss the wide scientific concerns about gene drives.[ix] The UN CBD process is the only multilateral process currently addressing gene drives. Recruited academics received daily briefings and instructions from Emerging Ag on how to influence the discussion:

> "My name is Ben Robinson, I work with Isabelle Coche & Delphine Thizy, and I will be sending you regular updates on the discussions taking place in the context of the CBD's Open-Ended Online Forum on synthetic biology. I will monitor contributions and provide you with brief summaries of the content and tenor of conversations, while highlighting topics and posts you may wish to address. Should you feel that a topic needs to be addressed but you do not have the relevant resources or expertise, I can also help identify and coordinate those best suited among the group to respond to particular issues."

THE KEY ROLE OF THE GATES FOUNDATION

Delphine Thizy,[x] cited in the email above, works at Target Malaria in London, England. Target Malaria is a Gates-funded project to use gene drives against mosquitoes.[xi] Emerging Ag's activities were overseen by Jeff Chertack who is Senior Program Officer of Global Policy and Advocacy at the Bill and Melinda Gates Foundation. He is a former public affairs executive from Ogilvy PR who previously represented biotech and pharma giants in Brussels. Chertack sat on the coordination team of Emerging Ag's "Gene Drive Research Sponsors and Supporters coalition"[xii] and is copied on several strategy calls and coordination phone calls.[xiii] This is also not the first time that the Gates Foundation has used academics to influence public and private opinion on genetic engineering technologies, as witnessed by its funding of the Cornell Alliance for Science.[xiv]

PUBLIC RESEARCH AND REGULATION INITIATIVE

The FOIA emails reveal that Emerging Ag also collaborated with a lobby group called the Public Research and Regulation Initiative (PRRI)[xv] that is little known outside the Convention on Biological Diversity. PRRI has a related influence operation which predates the efforts of Emerging Ag. Its history of lobbying the UN Convention on Biological Diversity over GMOs is mentioned in emails sent to a Canadian official on the UN AHTEG.[xvi] In them, a PRRI member, Piet Vander Meer,[xvii] boasts about its 24/7 "backup operation" for "like-minded" government and industry experts who sit on the AHTEG. The emails suggest that national government representatives of Canada, the US, the UK, Brazil, and the Netherlands were being remotely assisted by PRRI during closed door discussions. To help PRRI the Gene Drive Research Sponsors and Supporters coalition offered to approach US Department of Agriculture (USDA) contacts to find additional funding for PRRI's activities. The current funding sources of PRRI are not known but former funders include CropLife International, Monsanto, and the US Grains Council.

Targeting Palmer Amaranth: A Traditionally Nutritious and Culturally Significant Crop

🌿

VANDANA SHIVA

A 2016 REPORT FROM the National Academy of Science of the United States, titled "Gene Drives on the Horizon: Advancing Science, Navigating Uncertainty, and Aligning Research with Public Values"[i] warns: "One possible goal of release of a gene-drive modified organism is to cause the extinction of the target species or a drastic reduction in its abundance." Gene drives have been called "mutagenic chain reactions" and are to the biological world what chain reactions are to the nuclear world. The Guardian describes gene drives as the "gene bomb."[ii] Kevin Esvelt of MIT exclaims, "a release anywhere is likely to be a release everywhere," and asks, "Do you really have the right to run an experiment where if you screw up, it affects the whole world?"[iii] The NAS report cites the case of wiping out amaranth as an example of "potential benefit." The problem is that "Palmer amaranth infests agricultural fields throughout the American South. It has evolved resistance to the herbicide glyphosate, the world's most-used herbicide (Powles, 2008), and this resistance has become geographically widespread."[iv] Industrial agriculture—promoted by the United States Foreign Policy—treats amaranth greens as "weeds," and first tried to exterminate them with herbicides. Then came Monsanto, with Roundup Ready crops, genetically engineered to resist the spraying of Roundup so that the GMO crop would survive the otherwise lethal chemical, while everything else that was green perished. But not Palmer Amaranth, the superweed.

A QUICK FIX INVOLVING POTENTIAL IRREPARABLE DAMAGE

Instead of seeing the emergence of Palmer Amaranth as a superweed as a result of the failure of the misguided approach of herbicide resistant GMOs, Monsanto & Co— which includes investors, scientists, corporations, DARPA, and Gateses—are now rushing to drive the Amaranth species to extinction through the deployment of an untested tool. The tool of gene editing and gene drives. A "DARPA-Mind" report casually states potential harm: "Gene drives developed for agricultural purposes could also have adverse effects on human well-being. Transfer of a suppression drive to a non-target wild species could have both adverse environmental outcomes and harmful effects on vegetable crops, for example. Palmer amaranth in Case Study 6 is a damaging weed in the United States, but related Amaranthus species are cultivated for food in Mexico, South America, India, and China."[v] A scientific assessment would tell us that plants evolve resistance to herbicides that are supposed to kill them because they have intelligence, they evolve, and simply by the law of natural selection, they develop resistance. Denial of the intelligence in life and denial of evolution is unscientific.

AMARANTH IS A WEB OF LIFE IN ITSELF

Amaranth's root, the word *amara*—meaning "eternal" and "deathless" in both Greek and Sanskrit—connects two formidable houses of the ancient world. From the high slopes of the Himalayas, through the plains of north, central and south India, to the coastlines of the east, west and the south, amaranth is a web of life in itself. Numerous varieties are found throughout the country. In fact, the Himalayan region is one of the "centers of diversity" for amaranth. Amaranth, amaranto, love-lies-bleeding, tassel flower, Joseph's coat, or ramdana (god's own grain) is the grain of well-being. It is rich in names, nutrition, history, and meaning. There are records of amaranth cultivation in south and meso-America as far back as 5000 BCE. The sacred amaranth criss-crosses the ancient world, nourishing cultures from the Andes to the Himalayas. Amaranth is a sacred grain for the Indian civilization as much as it is for the Aztec civilization, civilizations in the shadow of time, yet very much alive.

The leaves of the amaranth contain more iron than spinach and have a much more delicate taste. Besides rice bran, the grain of the amaranth has the highest content of iron amongst cereals. Adding to 1 kilogram of refined wheat flour to 1 kilogram of amaranth flour increases its iron content from 25 milligrams to 245 milligrams. Adding amaranth flour to wheat or rice flour is a cheaper and healthier way to prevent nutritional anemia rather than buying expensive tablets, tonics, health drinks, or branded or bio-fortified flour. The amaranth is extremely rich in complex carbohydrates and proteins. It has 12–18% more protein than other cereals, particularly lysine—a critical amino acid.[vi] It also differs from other cereals in that 65% is found in the germ and 35% in the endosperm, as compared to an average of 15% in the germ and 85% in the endosperm for other cereals. When amaranth flour is mixed 30:70 with either rice flour or wheat flour, protein quality rises from 72 to 90 and 32 to 52, respectively. The amaranth grain is about the richest source of calcium, other than milk. It has 390 grams of calcium compared to 10 grams in rice, and 23 grams in refined flour.[vii] The diversity of amaranth greens is incredible, edibles that grow uncultivated in our fields. They are a major source of nutrition. Per 100 grams, amaranth greens can give us 5.9 grams of protein, 530 milligrams of calcium, 83 milligrams of phosphorus, 38.5 milligrams of iron, 14,190 micrograms of carotene, 68 micrograms of vitamin C, and 122 milligrams of magnesium.[viii]

Amaranth is a superior alternative as a carotene source to GMO Golden Rice—which is being promoted as a future miracle for addressing vitamin A deficiency. The poorest, landless woman and her children have access to nutrition through the generous gift of the amaranth plant.

CONCLUSIONS

The paradigm of genetic engineering is based on genetic determinism and genetic reductionism. It is based on a denial of the self-organized, evolutionary potential of living organisms. It treats living organisms as a play Lego set. But it is not, life is complex, self-organized, dynamic evolution—autopoietic.

The right to food and nutrition of the people outside the US, and the right of amaranth to continue to grow and evolve and nourish people, can be extinguished by powerful men in the US because they messed up their agriculture with Roundup Ready crops. Now they want to mess up the planet, its biodiversity, and the food and agriculture systems of the world with the tool of gene drives to push species to extinction.

The rush for gene drives and CRISPR-based gene editing are linked to patents. Bill Gates is financing the research that is leading to these patents. He with other billionaires have invested $120 million in a company Editas to promote these technologies.[ix] Bayer, the new face of Monsanto, has invested $35 million in the new technologies, and committed over $300 million over the next five years.[x]

"Biofortification" has been given the World Food Prize of 2016, yet biofortification is inferior to the nutrition provided by biodiversity and Indigenous knowledge. The same forces promoting biofortification are also promoting the extermination of nutritious crops like amaranth, as well as rich Indigenous cultures of food. The project of deliberately exterminating species is a crime against nature and humanity. We are members of an Earth family. Every species, every race is a member of one Earth community. We cannot allow some members of our Earth family to allocate to themselves the power and hubris to decide who will live and who will be exterminated. The DARPA-Mind is obsolete.

Global Resistance to Genetic Extinction Technology

❧

NAVDANYA

BESIDES CONSTANTLY EXPOSING the dangers of releasing the untested technology of gene editing and gene drives in the environment, as well as the lack of transparency in the decision process, independent scientists, Indigenous peoples, and civil society movements across the world have constantly been carrying out actions of resistance.[i]

In December 2016, over 160 civil society organizations from six continents called for a "Moratorium on New Genetic Extinction Technology" at the 2016 UN Convention on Biological Diversity (CBD) in Cancun, Mexico.[ii] This moratorium call included both lab research and field trials, because of the potentially devastating effects that synthetic biology can have on entire ecosystems.[iii]

Even though the moratorium found support among some countries, the final agreement merely urged caution in field-testing the products of synthetic biology, including gene drives, while supporting better risk-assessment of the products' potential effects.[iv]

There has been no lack of attempts by the industry, through a Gates-funded lobby firm, to manipulate the UN decision making process over gene drives, as emerged from a set of documents released in December 2017, revealing how external actors with interest in the development of gene drives coordinated among themselves to influence the work of the relevant UN expert group.[v]

In July 2018, The European Court of Justice ruled that organisms obtained by mutagenesis plant breeding techniques are GMOs and should fall under the GMO Directive.[vi] The court ruling was seen as a victory for environmentalists while the agrifood industry and farmers organizations started a lobbying campaign to roll-back the ruling in favor of a new EU legislation.[vii]

Independent scientists publicly demanded precaution, stating that gene-edited products must be strictly regulated with full recognition of the uncertainties of the gene editing process—and that they must be labeled to enable farmer and consumer choice.[viii]

In October 2018, in view of the 2018 CBD Conference of the Parties (COP), a broad alliance of Indigenous peoples and civil society organizations published a "Call to Protect Food Systems from Genetic Extinction Technology." All the while, a coalition of European movements called upon the European Commission to support an international moratorium on the release of organisms modified by gene drive technology into the environment.[ix]

The global decision passed at the 2018 CBD COP, did not issue any moratorium, but set further barriers to the release of gene drives by reinforcing as a priority the need to seek free, prior, and informed consent or approval from all potentially impacted communities and Indigenous peoples before even considering environmental release of gene drive organisms.[x]

Along the same lines, in 2020, a similar coalition of European movements has requested that the EU Commission fully support the EU Parliament's call for a global moratorium on the release of Gene Drive Organisms, in view of the EU preparation for the upcoming Conference of the Parties (COP15) to the Convention on Biological Diversity (CBD) and the Cartagena Protocol on Biosafety (COP-MOP10).[xi]

In the UK, Beyond GM, GM Freeze, and GM Watch started a mobilization campaign in July 2020[xii] in response to a proposed amendment[xiii] to the Agriculture Bill, that would give the Secretary of State for the Environment, Food and Rural Affairs (currently George Eustice) the power to change the definition of a genetically modified organism (GMO) and re-classify many forms of genome editing as non-GM, meaning that gene-editing and genetic modification techniques would no longer be regulated and could be used on farms and in food without public knowledge or consent.

In its last meeting before the summer recess, the UK House of Lords finally withdrew the amendment, but only after the government renewed its commitment to push, promote, and facilitate the wide use of genome editing in the future of UK farming and food.[xiv]

The Bill and Melinda Gates Foundation paid a PR firm called Emerging Ag[xv] $1.6 million to recruit a covert coalition of academics to manipulate a UN decision-making process over gene drives, according to emails obtained through Freedom of Information requests. Gene drives are a highly controversial new genetic extinction technology. They have been proposed as potentially able to eradicate malarial mosquitoes, agricultural pests, invasive species, as well as having potential military uses.[xvi]

✳

TARGET MALARIA PROJECT: GENETICALLY MODIFIED MOSQUITOES IN BURKINA FASO
TAPSOBA ALI DE GOAMMA

After the failed adventure of genetically modified cotton,[xvii] a future programmed drama is underway in Burkina Faso.[xviii] Indeed, under the fallacious pretext of helping to fight malaria, Burkina has become an open-air laboratory where populations are used as guinea pigs for the hazardous experience; we are talking about the genetic manipulation of mosquitoes under the leadership of the Target Malaria Project.[xix]

Genetically modified mosquito eggs were imported from the Imperial College of London to Burkina Faso in November 2016. The Burkina Faso Institute for Health Science Research (IRSS) is the project leader in Burkina.[xx] This project is a concentration of lies:

1. *Problem of informed population consent:* In the work with the populations of the Bana and Souroukoudingan villages, the Target Malaria Project used the fight against malaria as an argument to convince these populations to accept the experimental release in their villages of GM mosquitoes resulting from classical transgenesis (GM non-gene drive organism (GDO) mosquitoes) in 2019 (phase 1 of the project). There was no real free and informed consent but rather an abuse of the ignorance and illiteracy of local communities, the term GMO was never mentioned, nor explained.

2. *Absence of clear experimental conception:* According to the Target Malaria Project, "The purpose of the small-scale release is to collect scientific data on the longevity and dispersal of released mosquitoes, and it will serve also to strengthen the capacities and operational experience of our teams."[xxi] The first release took place in July 2019; 6,400 GM mosquitoes were released into the wild.[xxii] Up until now, no impact study of this release and no risk assessment has been made, creating a situation that is contrary to the elementary ethics of medical experimentation.

3. *Absence of correct population information:* The Target Malaria Project expects three phases. The first two concern the releases of classical type GMO mosquitoes resulting from transgenesis (a genetic manipulation based on the transfer of genes between the very different species that do not normally cross in nature) and the third, the release of GDO mosquitoes or GMOs resulting from a gene drive. This third phase is scheduled for 2024, but the local communities know nothing about the health and ecological hazards of what will happen, they know nothing about the real nature

of the experimentation that will take place in their villages.

Gene drives are a new technology that cause the extermination of the entire species, and it is this operation of extermination which is aimed at the *Anopheles gambiae* species which, according to Target Malaria, must be done to eliminate malaria. The populations are neither informed of the third phase of the project, nor of the technology of species extermination that will be used. Moreover, the Anopheles gambiae is not the only mosquito species that transmits malaria in Burkina, such as *Anopheles arabiensis* and *Anopheles funestus.*[xxiii] The impact of the removal of one among several mosquito species is uncertain.

Target Malaria offers the inhabitants of the villages a small income under conditions qualified as the basic ethical violation—be paid for accepting to be bitten by mosquitoes is an absence of respect for Indigenous people, which is contrary to the Declaration of Helsinki of the World Medical Association that governs medical research.

Since the announcement of the Target Malaria project, the civil society has mobilized to reject this dangerous project and is determined to remove it from Burkina Faso, as they had already done with Monsanto.[xxiv]

VIII

MEDIA, HEALTH,
AND EDUCATION

Digital Dictators

✹

SATISH KUMAR

TECHNOLOGY IS SEDUCTIVE and a double-edged sword. It can be a useful tool to connect, or it can be a brutal weapon to control. If technology is the servant, and if it is used with wisdom to enhance human relationships without polluting the environment and without wasting natural resources, then technology can be good. But if the technology becomes the master, and human creativity and ecological integrity are sacrificed at the altar of technology, then technology becomes a curse.

Recently, New York Governor Andrew Cuomo, Bill Gates of Microsoft, and former Google CEO, Eric Schmidt, have been promoting the idea of transforming face-to-face learning into a system of education rooted in internet technology and operated by remote control, thereby integrating digital technology, fully and permanently, into the educational process. And, by doing so, getting away from the need for personal relationships and intimate interactions between students and teachers. Cuomo, Gates, and Schmidt come from a school of thought that subscribes to the theory that technology is the solution—*what is your problem?*

Unfortunately, these highly "educated" people do not seem to know the meaning of "education." The word is derived from the Latin word "educare." It means to bring forth, lead out, or draw out what is potentially already there. Every human person comes into this world with their own unique potential. The work of a true teacher is to observe and spot that special quality in a child, then help to nurture and enhance it with care, attention, and empathy. Thus, the beautiful idea of education is to maintain human diversity, cultural diversity, and diversity of talents through decentralized, democratic, human-scale, and personalized systems of schooling.

A good school is a community of learners where education is not pre-determined by remote authorities. Rather, it is a journey of exploration where students, teachers, and parents work together to discover the right ways to relate to the world and to find meaningful ways of living in the world.

The idea of digital learning through remote control and pre-determined curriculum moves away from the rich and holistic philosophy of education. Digital teaching looks at children as if they were empty vessels in need of being filled with external information. The quality of information or knowledge given to the child remotely and digitally is determined centrally by people who have a vested interest in a particular outcome. That outcome is largely to turn humans into instruments to run the money machine and increase the profitability of big corporations.

Such centralized and impersonalized systems of digital education will destroy diversity and impose uniformity, destroy community culture and impose corporate culture, destroy multiple cultures and impose monoculture.

When teachers teach remotely, they tend to think as if the children have no body, no hands, and no heart—they have only a head. The information taught digitally is almost entirely of an intellectual nature. Thus, digitally educated children are less than half-educated. Eating half baked bread gives you indigestion. The life of a half-educated person lacks coherence and integrity. Proper education should include the education of the head, education of the heart, and education of the hands. In an ideal school community, children learn math with music, science with spirituality, and history with a human touch. Academic knowledge is complemented by the learning of the arts and crafts.

A computer cannot teach kindness. Only in a real learning community can children learn how to be kind, how to be compassionate, and how to be respectful. In a school community, children learn together, play together, eat together, and laugh together. They produce plays, perform concerts, and go on field trips together. It is through these shared human activities that children gain a deep appreciation of life. Education is more than the acquisition of information and facts—education is a living experience. Sitting in front of a computer for hours is no way to learn social skills.

Placing the future of our children in the hands of a few digital giants like Google, Microsoft, and Amazon and putting them in charge of educational systems is a recipe for digital dictatorship and opens the doors to disaster. If democratic societies are opposed to military dictatorship, then why should they embrace corporate dictatorship? Through smart technologies, these giant corporations will trace and exploit every activity of children and adults through data manipulation and control. Who wants to embrace such a "dystopia"?

Rather than investing in top-down, artificial, sedative, and virtual technology, democratic societies should be investing in people. We should be investing in more teachers in smaller schools, with smaller class sizes and bottom-up, imaginative, benign, and appropriate technology.

We have already experienced the way algorithms, artificial intelligence, biotechnology, nanotechnology, and other forms of "smart technologies" have been used to control, manipulate, and undermine democratic values. The tech giants who consider humans as "biohazards" cannot be trusted with the future of our children. We should be embracing the Green New Deal and not what Naomi Klein rightly condemns as the "Screen New Deal," screen-based technologies that do not require human interaction.

We need the greening of education rather than the screening of education. Our children need to learn not only about nature but from nature. They need to learn from forests and farming, permaculture and agriculture, agroecology and organic gardening, marine life, and wildlife. Such knowledge and skills cannot be learned by looking at computer screens. A computer is a box; it teaches you to think within the box. If you want to think outside of the box, you need to go out into your community and out into the natural world.

Children need to go out in nature with experienced teachers. Nature herself is the best and the greatest teacher. With the combination of a human teacher and a nature teacher, assisted by a limited amount of internet, children will gain a much more well-rounded education than through a digitally controlled and centralized system proposed by the tech giants.

Technology has a place in education, but let us keep it in its place and not allow technology to dominate our lives and the lives of our children. Technology is a good servant but a bad master.

PEDAGOGY OF FREEDOM

As mentioned earlier, education doesn't mean teaching, schooling, giving of knowledge, or even acquisition of knowledge. Education simply means the development of the qualities which are already there. Socrates compared a teacher with a midwife who just helps to bring forth the child. I compare a teacher with a gardener or an orchard keeper. The tree is already in the seed. The seed knows what kind of tree it is. The gardener doesn't put a tree in the seed; they only help the seed become a tree. The gardener may find a piece of good soil to plant the seed, add good organic compost to nourish the seed, put a fence to protect the seed, and give water to nurture the seed, but a gardener never tries to change an apple seed into a pear tree.

Parents and teachers need to be like gardeners. They need to observe their children, understand them, help them to become who they are, support them on their way to self-realization. But never try to impose on them their idea of an "educated person."

In our modern industrial age, education has become confused with training, schooling, or acquisition of facts—information and knowledge in order to get a job. Rather than a teacher helping a pupil become who he or she truly is and realize their true potential, a teacher has become a technician or a trainer, or even an agent to meet the needs of the market. The teacher is paid to mold the child so that they are fit to make a success of the economy. In this kind of educational system, the market and the economy become the masters, and the human beings become servants.

This corruption of education worried J. Krishnamurti. When I first met him on the banks of River Ganga in Varanasi in 1960, he said to me, "I want to recover the original and actual meaning of the noble word 'education.' I want schools and teachers to return to the true meaning of the word and dedicate themselves to the cause of helping young people to discover their vocation." Krishnamurti further said to me, "There is nothing wrong with the market or with the economy. As long as they serve the needs of humans, they have a place in the world. But when humans are required to serve the needs of the market and the economy, then we are in real trouble. Unfortunately, that is the problem at this moment in the world. This is why we need a total revolution in our idea of education."

"I understand the etymological meaning of the word education," I said, "but do you have something more to say about it?"

"Yes, I do. I want to say that we need to liberate ourselves from the idea that education takes place only within the four walls of a school. It is not that you read a book, go to a classroom for your lessons, or pass an examination, and then you have finished with your education. Education is a life-long process. From the moment you are born to the moment you die, you are in the journey of learning," said Krishnamurti.

"What exactly are we trying to learn during this journey of life?" I asked.

"We are learning to be free! Learning is all about liberation. We need to learn to be free from fear, free from anxiety, free from dogmas and doctrines. We need to discover and rediscover that we are born free, and freedom is our birthright! Fear is a conditioning of the mind—from our family, from our religious belief, from our media, and even from our educational systems, we are conditioned to fear. The purpose of true education is to free us from all kinds of fear.

For me, this was a new Pedagogy of Freedom! But our educational system at present is totally unaware of the fact that it is based on the Pedagogy of Fear. Since that meeting with Krishnamurti, I have keenly observed and realized that schools and universities around the world seem to look at their students and think of them as if they have only brains. No wonder that many of our young people feel inadequate, incompetent, and fearful. They have never developed their heart qualities. They don't know how to relate to other people and to the natural world. This lack of emotional and spiritual intelligence is a major cause of fear. The usual educational curriculum includes almost nothing about compassion, a sense of service, courage, or love! These qualities should be cultivated during the time we are being educated.

Most educated people not only lack this spiritual and emotional intelligence, but they also lack body intelligence. The curriculum also ignores all practical or physical skills. Most undergraduates or postgraduates coming out of universities know nothing about growing food, building a house, mending or repairing, and almost nothing about cooking. They have highly trained heads superbly capable of complaining, comparing, criticizing, and strong desires to control and consume. They have little or no capacity for making, producing, building, or creating. There is very little in our educational philosophy or practice that promotes self-reliance and self-confidence.

On top of this deficit in emotional intelligence and body intelligence, the current educational system is more or less indifferent to the development of the imagination. Music, art, dance, plays, poetry, and philosophy are relegated to some distant and specialized corners. Instead of the arts being an integral part of everyday life, they have been exiled to museums and art galleries to be pursued by a small minority of celebrities and marketed as commercialized commodities or practiced by a small number of struggling idealists who can hardly make a living.

The educational system produces millions upon millions of young people to serve the needs of machines, markets, and money. All of these young people are struggling to compete and succeed and are often afraid of not succeeding. This fear of failure is one of the most detrimental aspects of the current pedagogy.

To compensate for this fear of failure, young people seek success for themselves, bigger salaries, cars, houses, and higher positions with higher expectations. Some succeed, but many fail. This ego-centric rat race results in family breakdown, mental breakdown, discontentment, depression, and disappointment.

J. Krishnamurti was pained to see such a state of degradation in education. He called education a noble word that is misunderstood and misused. Therefore, instead of just criticizing the present paradigm, he established a number of exemplary schools where learning, living, and loving are integrated. In these schools, we can witness the education of the head, heart, and hands. I have had the privilege of visiting them and found that teenage girls and boys there are enjoying a holistic approach to learning based on a Pedagogy of Freedom. I wish these schools would provide a university level of education so that the students don't have to enter into the Pedagogy of Fear after they leave Krishnamurti schools.

The Philanthropic Monopoly of Bill & Melinda Gates

✿

NICOLETTA DENTICO

THE GATES FOUNDATION provides more global health funding than any major donor country. Influential newspapers praise Bill and Melinda for the fact that the two have revolutionized public health and the lives of billions of people on the planet.[i] In short, when we talk about Bill Gates as a philanthropist, we are dealing with a story of monopolistic vocation comparable only to the story of Bill Gates as Microsoft's founder. The style and culture of the company are identical. It is no coincidence that the two have always been intimately linked. Jeff Raikes, Microsoft's key man after Bill Gates, was the head of the Foundation. So was Microsoft co-founder Paul Allen, CEO of the foundation until 2013.[ii]

In the logic of philanthrocapitalism, doing business and doing benevolence are two sides of the same coin. It is reasonable to think that the Foundation—in so far as it promotes the development of the Global South inspired by information technology and supported by the intervention of large companies—helps Microsoft. The Foundation helps Microsoft when it puts pressure on national governments to open doors to the big companies with which it has privileged relationships, including Cargill, Monsanto, Nestlè, Mars, DuPont Pioneer, Syngenta, and Bayer.

There is no development area in which the foundation does not act as a superpower. This subjugation no longer applies only to the constellation of organizations that depend on it for funding but to a growing number of governments, not only among middle and low-income countries.

For 25 years, the Gates Foundation has held a position of undisputed hegemony with 1,541 employees (as of 2017) comprised of its headquarters in Seattle and seven offices around the world (Washington, London, New Delhi, Beijing, Addis Ababa, Johannesburg, and Abuja), and an endowment of $50.7 billion (as of December 31, 2017).[iii] The assets include a donation by Bill Gates of about $35.8 billion in Microsoft shares (as of December 2019) the mega-donation of $30.7 billion that was announced at the end of June 2006 by Warren Buffet, owner of the holding company Berkshire Hathaway.[iv]

83% of the patrimony of the second richest man in the world (Buffet) was destined to the charitable activities of the first billionaire on the planet (Gates)[v]—an ingenious move that would incorporate the Berkshire Hathaway holding company into the Foundation's investment apparatus. It was clearly a historic step for Seattle, with Buffet's entry into the foundation and Bill Gates' subsequent decision to leave Microsoft to devote himself full time to philanthropy.

Since then, the Foundation has been structured into two separate entities: the actual Bill & Melinda Gates Foundation, which selects strategic priorities, projects to be funded and allocates funds, and the Bill & Melinda Gates Foundation Trust, which is managed by Buffet and is responsible for managing the Foundation's assets, taking care of investments so as to finance the Foundation's ability to donate—and here's the best part.[vi]

From the records, it emerges that the Gates Foundation Trust's direct investments include the following:[vii]

- $466 million in Coca-Cola factories operating south of the US.
- $837 million in Walmart, the largest food, pharmaceutical, and alcohol chain in the US.

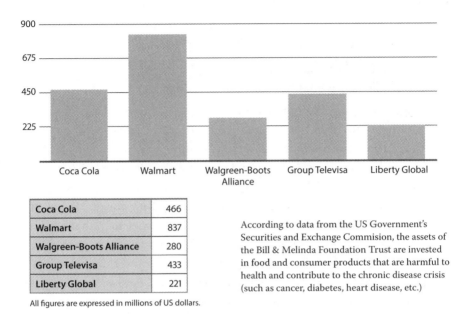

Coca Cola	466
Walmart	837
Walgreen-Boots Alliance	280
Group Televisa	433
Liberty Global	221

All figures are expressed in millions of US dollars.

According to data from the US Government's Securities and Exchange Commision, the assets of the Bill & Melinda Foundation Trust are invested in food and consumer products that are harmful to health and contribute to the chronic disease crisis (such as cancer, diabetes, heart disease, etc.)

> ▸ $280 million in the Walgreen-Boots Alliance, a large multi-national retail drug company.
> ▸ $650 million in two television production giants: GroupTelevisa ($433m) and Liberty Global PLC ($221m).

Furthermore, through Warren Buffet, a quarter of the Foundation's assets are invested in his own holding company Berkshire Hathaway Inc., which holds $17 billion of shares in the Coca-Cola Company in the US and $29 billion in funds invested in Kraft Heinz Inc., one of the top ten companies in the food industry. As pointed out in a letter from civil society to the WHO, and concerned about the company's dangerous liaisons with the Seattle philanthropist, the Bill & Melinda Gates Foundation is a beneficiary of the sale of products that are subjected to WHO standards and regulations, as well as government policies on nutrition, drugs, and health. Bill Gates, Melinda Gates, and Warren Buffet form an impregnable trinity that has governed the Foundation since 2006. Those who own wealth are the real dominant subjects, and they wield the hegemony of a class that has freed itself of any counterweight.

FINANCIALIZATION OF DEVELOPMENT: PHILANTHROPIC FINANCE AND CREATION OF NEW MARKETS FOR THE POOR

We do not have the opportunity to verify the fates of the "human promises" sown in the different communities across the planet, as foundations are not particularly fond of independent external evaluations. However, we do have evidence of a promise that the foundation "catalyzes" with increasing vigor.

A twofold promise—first, that of expanding the horizons of investors, drawing them into unknown territories of global health such as forgotten diseases or the health markets of the poor, with promises of substantial returns on investment and risk reductions (also a profit can be drawn from these markets). And second, that of making direct investments in multinational corporations, with the aim of involving them in responding to the needs of the poor while enhancing the companies' need for market expansion.

With an agenda that we could define as evolutionary, Gates perfectly captures the passage of the new phase of capital building, which differs from previous rounds of privatization and reforms because it aims straight at the financialization of social dynamics and public services. It is the international institutions themselves, with the World Bank in the lead, that is paving the way for attractive investment routes and inaugurating the operational trajectories of this acceleration. They aim to provide private individuals with technical assistance for co-investment initiatives, loans, and guarantees.[viii] They also test new classes of strictly investor-friendly financial instruments aimed at reducing the risk of investment with the use of public funds capable of attracting private financial capital.

This has led to the germination of thematic bonds and new investment categories that include, for example, health bonds (GAVI's International Financial Facility for Immunization),[ix] pandemic bonds (such as Ebola Bond)[x] , or the more recent forms of impact bonds (such as Cameroon Cataract Performance Bond).[xi]

The International Finance Corporation (IFC), the World Bank's private equity investment arm, plays a central role in this scenario and a recognized leading role, especially in Africa, India, and China, to channel private finance into health insurance, medical training, and digital technology.[xii] According to the IFC specialists themselves, health is one of the most promising areas in terms of investment return.[xiii] As the representative of a South African fund quoted by Bloomberg explains: "The economic management of HIV/Aids can be very profitable because the treatment involves not only medicines but also nutritional support, and opportunities are guaranteed throughout the entire value chain, from wholesalers to distribution."[xiv]

The Gates Foundation is one of the most accredited partners of IFC and has considerable influence both in the direction and in the selection of projects. Gates is in the Business of Health in Africa Group, has invested substantial capital in Africa Health System Management's Investment Fund for Health in Africa, and has undisputed leadership in the controversial Global Health Investment Fund.[xv]

This provides the foundation with an unrivaled capacity of acting as a broker of public-private alliances that can transform the sector's financial markets through intermediary investment funds often registered in tax havens such as Mauritius and the Cayman Islands.[xvi] The foundation also manages to intervene at the regulatory level in the countries involved so that companies can operate under legal, as well as fiscal, laissez-faire systems while having little or no transparency.[xvii] The aim is to mobilize the involvement of large companies to design new products or engineer new market models aimed at poor countries. Gates is convinced that market mechanisms can be put in a position to work well for populations that have no purchasing power. And that, in order to face the problems of the world, it is necessary to intercept the creativity, efficiency, and innovative potential of the private sector.[xviii]

TAKING OVER GLOBAL HEALTH

At the time of Bill's first trip to India in 1997, with direct experience of an anti-polio vaccination program, his interest in the field of health grew, and the creation of the Bill & Melinda Gates Children's Vaccine Program in 1998 to accelerate access to vaccines for children in low-income countries, took shape. The first donation amounted to $100 million.[xix] From there came the activism in the field of global health, as well as the approaches that will characterize the work of the Foundation. This was also the starting point for the financial pressure aimed at directing international political consensus towards technical solutions.[xx]

The Global Alliance for Vaccine Immunizations (GAVI) was announced with great fanfare at the World Economic Forum in 2000. With an investment of $750 million over five years, the Seattle-based couple gave birth to a health start-up that would quickly catalyze governments, other major donors, and multilateral institutions. GAVI is the first major creature of Gates philanthropy, of which they are still the largest private investors to date with $4.1 billion.[xxi] The birth of GAVI marks the first deviation in global health governance and heralds the launch of a model of institutional hybridization that will be unquestionably successful because of the political impetus and resources it will receive from the Gates Foundation. Collaboration with other foundations and with new initiatives that came into being formed a thick and practically impenetrable embroidery. To the point of unraveling, one piece at a time, the old fabric of classical multilateralism, which arose on the ashes of two world wars and on the human rights value framework.

THE GLOBAL ALLIANCE FOR VACCINE IMMUNIZATION: DEBUT OF THE PUBLIC-PRIVATE MODEL IN HEALTH

The Global Alliance for Vaccine Immunizations (GAVI) is an independent public-private partnership that aims to "save the lives of children and protect people's health by increasing vaccination coverage programs in poor countries."[xxii] Established in 1999, GAVI was launched in Davos in January 2000 with the adhesion of multilateral entities such as the WHO, UNICEF, and the World Bank. Its headquarters is located in Geneva. Since 2000, $ 16 billion has been invested in 76 low and middle-income countries to strengthen vaccination campaigns, with the aim of increasing the sustainability of national programs and, above all, conforming national markets to the relaunch of vaccines and other immunization products. GAVI has received a total of $18 billion from funders (as of June 2019) and 79% of the funds came from a core group of northern donor governments: the United States, the United Kingdom, Norway, Germany, Canada, Sweden, Italy, and the Netherlands, recently followed by Greece.

The largest private donor remains the Gates Foundation, which alone covers 20.8% of the budget. For the five-year period from 2021 to 2025, GAVI had planned to raise $7.4 billion.[xxiii]

But on the basis of COVID-19, the refinancing conference held in London at the beginning of June 2020 mobilized a much higher amount; $8.8 billion, with which GAVI, it was declared, will be able to immunize 300 million children against 17 infectious diseases in over 50 more fragile and developing countries.[xxiv]

Despite the result of an objective and significant increase in the number of children with vaccine coverage. Between 2000 and 2020, according to institutional communication, GAVI and its partners have immunized more than 760 million children and saved 13 million lives. GAVI has been criticized by accredited scholars and civil society researchers as the most accomplished expression of the so-called "Gates approach" to health challenges. What exactly does that mean? We are referring to the choice to fund vertical programs for specific diseases, with individual interventions (vaccines) that are not supported by actions to strengthen health systems. In 2005, in response to these criticisms, GAVI inserted an operational window dedicated to health systems, a move that did not fully convince the analysts considering the scarcity of funds (only 10.6%) addressed to this purpose.[xxv] In addition, by "health system," GAVI mostly means the creation of health markets to stimulate the purchase and inclusion of new vaccines, with a preference for adjustments imposed from above that are easily measurable.[xxvi]

Through GAVI, the Bill & Melinda Gates Foundation strongly promotes the financialization of health. In its 20 years of operation, GAVI has been the conceptual cradle of new financial incentives for the pharmaceutical industry to research and develop new vaccines for people living in low and middle-income countries. GAVI's programs exclude middle-income countries, which is a major concern. Among the main financial mechanisms put in place are the vaccine bonds of the International Financial Facility for Immunization (IFFIM) and the Advanced Market Commitment mechanism, an incentive that has given rise to a number of bellyaches because of the massive subsidy of public development aid investments to pharmaceutical multinationals (Pfizer and GlaxoSmithKline) for the production of anti-pneumococcal vaccines, with a final price negotiated without any transparency. This is definitely a high price for low and middle-income countries.[xxvii]

THE PHILANTHROPIC EPIDEMIC:
DONATING TO CONTROL GLOBAL HEALTH

With the ability to invest great personal wealth and enjoy maximum media visibility in the global circuits that matter, the Gates Foundation wisely handles the tools of consensus in the world of global health. Beyond the insistent narrative about Bill and Melinda and their common principles and the obstinate personalization of the battle for the health of the poor, one cannot overlook the juncture of opportunities which, like a propitious wind, swells the sails of the Seattle couple. The financial disengagement of Western governments towards the United Nations, in the aftermath of the Cold War, opened up boundless maneuvering space for the Gates' optimistic activism in the field of international health.[xxviii] The finances of the WHO were increasingly uncertain. In the two-year period of 1990–1991 when, for the first time, voluntary funds exceeded the regular payment due from the compulsory quotas of the member countries, and several countries suspended payment altogether (the United States, for example, refused to pay its accumulated debts).[xxix]

Following the merciless plans to cut social spending, which were imposed as a condition for lending to poor countries, the World Bank decreed a health reform strategy aimed at promoting the private sector and generating markets.[xxx] In the meantime, the international negotiations that resulted in the World Trade Organization (WTO) had definitively fenced off health as a variable of the economy. In the ascending phase of globalization, the countries of the Global South had to cope with the onset of a number of infectious diseases including the HIV/Aids virus.

Bill and Melinda Gates fit into this gap and filled the void left by governments' civil services.[xxxi] Their intervention, whether we like it or not, brought health back onto the international political agenda thanks to an injection of funds that first sprinkled the non-profit world, then think tanks and political analysis institutes, universities, and public institutions (including, as we shall see, the World Health Organization).[xxxii]

Bill Gates had no difficulty in establishing himself as the pied piper of global health.[xxxiii] He created an increasingly complex and diversified constellation of public-private initiatives[xxxiv] to "harness advances in science and technology to save lives in developing countries,"[xxxv] which allowed him to interface comprehensively with the scientific community, non-governmental organizations, and international institutions.[xxxvi] He then invented new management systems for the health alliances he created and new financing mechanisms for the initiatives in which he participates as a major or almost exclusive funder.

The public-private alliances represent Bill Gates' Trojan horse, the influence area where the operating methods open the floodgates to the corporate sector (which Gates personifies) in the field of health and global development.[xxxvii]

With its new and central role, the Gates Foundation has overtaken even the Rockefeller Foundation. With this change of scene, proceeding swiftly to the privatization of health with the blessing of the international financial organizations, as well as the protection of patents on pharmaceuticals for poverty-related diseases.

The Global Fund against HIV/Aids, Tuberculosis and Malaria, launched at the G8 in Genoa in 2001 and inaugurated as a private law entity in Switzerland in 2002, is the most disruptive of these new initiatives. It was created to accelerate efforts to combat the three pandemics that drew the attention of the international community. The Global Fund took its first steps by making use of the expertise, logistical and administrative structures of the WHO, which were essential to launch programs in the countries of intervention,[xxxviii] but its intended aim was to bypass the fossilized procedures of the United Nations.[xxxix] Its creation served, among other things, to channel (if not divert) the transnational civil society movement which, since the Seattle summit in 1999,[xl] had vigorously contested the intellectual property regime produced by the WTO agreements, which represented an insurmountable obstacle to access to life-saving medicines in low and middle-income countries.[xli]

The withdrawal of 39 pharmaceutical companies that had taken legal action against Nelson Mandela's South Africa,[xlii] after the mobilization of African patients, was a first resounding victory against the abuse of big pharma, but it was also a wake-up call for the private sector and the Western countries that supported it. Non-governmental organizations had to be involved and financed, as they promised a technical solution to the problem.[xliii]

It cannot be said that this clever strategy did not work and that it did not succeed in generating the adhesion to the Global Fund by large segments of international civil society. The new financial flow was aimed at organizing health programs that were increasingly separate from those of the WHO around biomedical solutions in the fight against disease. Solutions that bring a substantial handful of industry representatives into the governance structures of new health initiatives, as well as the tendency to propose substantial subsidies to companies, incentives for the development and procurement of essential medicines, and the stipulation of private contracts, which are by their very nature not easily accessible.[xliv]

As a result of pushing vaccines as a solution to the problems of the poor, perhaps the most important question that arises is the chain of public responsibility in health, and in particular, the autonomy of the WHO.[xlv]

Under pressure by Gates' activism and competition from private-public health alliances that had never been seen before, the WHO, already weakened at the beginning of the new millennium, found itself operating in the field of health policies as an old tool of 20th-century multilateralism. In a scenario dominated by fierce competition for visibility in the international community, the WHO soon had to deal with the prospect of gradual marginalization, preliminary to its occupation as a public body. While traditional billionaires only need to buy an island to be happy, Bill Gates aimed to buy an entire UN agency. He is succeeding, but what is even more severe is that the international community is allowing him to do so.

The disruptive effect of the Gates Foundation on a budget of the WHO is mainly due to the unwillingness of the member states to finance the institution, leaving it with freedom of maneuver on the use of money, which could be allocated to long-term programs of the agency, whether on prevention or on important but neglected areas of intervention—because of the reduction in government funds, further aggravated by the financial crisis of 2008, the WHO had to make cuts, laying off almost a third of its most qualified staff in 2009. While in subsequent years, halving the number of funds allocated to health emergencies, just when the Ebola virus was spreading along the caravan routes of Africa, devastating four countries on Africa's west coast.

Between 2010–2011, the Gates Foundation paid over $446 million to the WHO, which was more than any other government contributor after the United States: a figure 24 times higher than the contributions made by Brazil, Russia, India, China, and South Africa (the BRICS countries) combined.[xlvi] In 2013, it settled as the first absolute donor (in front of all governments) and as the first voluntary donor in 2015.[xlvii] At the end of 2017, it is in the second position with over $600 million (11% of the total budget), not counting the flow of funds to the WHO from Seattle through GAVI and other public-private entities.[xlviii]

To sum them all up, it is to be suspected with some reasonableness that Gates has held the golden share of the organization's funding for nearly a decade now. That's why it should come as no surprise that the Gates Foundation's priorities have gradually become the priorities of the WHO. Against all scientific evidence, the polio eradication program—which has always been a US priority and is widely supported by the Gates Foundation—is the lion's share of the 2016-2017 budget of the WHO (35.2%). This item has been boosted in the 2019-2023 budget,[xlix] with the effect of diverting even more funds from more pressing health priorities. In 2017, there were 22 polio cases worldwide[l], as well as triggering poor management at the WHO, which is forced to use the polio program to pay nearly 20% of WHO staff at about 1,300 people.[li]

THE GATES FOUNDATION AND THE PRODUCTION OF SCIENTIFIC KNOWLEDGE

Another critical issue concerns the interference of Gates funds in the production of scientific knowledge and literature. The subjection of the research community to the Foundation's priorities in the health sector—a syndrome that reproduces itself in the selection of funding areas in the field of agriculture—is now an established fact. We know that several members of the scientific community, when the microphones are off, criticize Bill Gates harshly for his obsession to impose the Silicon Valley business model on health care and his unconditional preference for technology.[lii]

When the Gates Foundation swoops in on a disease, it has no difficulty in soliciting the commitment of governments and other philanthropic entities to the cause and in redesigning the world's research agenda. This is what happened with polio in 1988. The WHO had undertaken a commitment to eradicate polio by the year

2000, thereby drastically reducing the number of cases but missing the target. Sensing the opportunity, Bill Gates invested more than $3 billion since 2003 on polio to become the largest funder of eradication programs. This included the WHO, UNICEF, and the Centre for Disease Control (CDC) in Atlanta.

This process enabled him to relaunch the elimination approach on other diseases as well. Malaria is a typical case. Gates began to take an interest in malaria and to fund research projects, first by revitalizing activities against the disease and then with the precise intention of changing the strategy of the international community. At the Foundation's forum in 2007, Melinda Gates left the scientific community working on malaria astonished, challenging the control strategy and launching the commitment to eradicate the disease.[liii]

Despite the skepticism of many researchers, convinced that the elimination of malaria was a project destined to fail, Gates began to inject so much money, a billion dollars in research projects by 2007, into this goal so as to silence the scientific community, with few exceptions.

Without consulting her experts, WHO director Margaret Chan immediately adhered to the Gates strategy, but at the beginning of 2008, the authoritative voice of Kochi Arata, head of the malaria program at WHO, expressed his disagreement in a note to Chan. Arata complained about the growing domination of the Gates Foundation in malaria research, a dominion that, according to him, was challenging the necessary diversity of approaches and opinions of the scientific community and threatened to undermine the role of the WHO.[liv] This bold stance was intended to alert the WHO about the fact that the flow of money from the Gates Foundation, "though crucial, could have long-range, largely undesirable consequences" because it ended up "capturing the world's best malaria scientists in a single 'cartel,'" so that "everyone has a vested interest in safeguarding each other's research [...] and the result is that independent review of the scientific evidence is becoming increasingly difficult." In this way, the creativity of research was damaged, something that "could have dangerous consequences for decision-making on global

health policies."[lv] Margaret Chan, unfortunately, decided to liqui-
date Arata shortly after this episode, and at the WHO, there have
been no more explicit voices of criticism of the Gates Foundation's
role in the field of malaria since Arata's removal. Bill and Melinda
are thus given a technical role.

But they are also granted an almost salvific profile in institutional
bodies. In ten years, the WHO has invited Bill & Melinda Gates three
times to open the World Assembly in Geneva (in 2005, 2011, and
2014).[lvi] A symbolic repetition that contributes to validating the model
of public-private initiatives conceived in Seattle as the only way to
stay with some entitlement on the scene and not be marginalized.[lvii]

Not everyone got adjusted to this. In the same period of the
malaria quarrel, two South African researchers published in the
prestigious journal Science an article that explicitly spoke of the "scientific imperialism" of public-private initiatives, which are designed
according to a Western cosmology that completely conditions the
strategy of intervention on infectious diseases, aimed at eradicating
in the most radical disregard of the scientific knowledge and skills
of the Global South.[lviii]

THE POWER OF PROPAGANDA AND
THE LANGUAGE OF PERSUASION

Beyond the recent conspiracy theories, on a planetary scale, the icon
of philanthropist Bill Gates corresponds to the image of generosity.
The optimistic and positive language in which he encloses problems
and hurries to administer solutions is an advanced form of magic
used to enchant his global audience and even himself.

Clearly, Bill and Melinda believe that aid storytelling needs to be
improved with more success stories and telling progress in some
areas of development. It's not for nothing that their philanthropy
blog, Impatient Optimists.[1]

---

1 Bill & Melinda Gates Foundation. "Impatient Optimist" website, http://www.
impatientoptimists.org/

This skillful, symbolic construct is one of the areas of investment that the Bill & Melinda Gates Foundation manages most carefully, funding international news sources such as NBC Universal, Al Jazeera, BBC, Viacom, to name but the most famous. Less known to the public, is the function of the Gates couple as a behind-the-scenes influencer of international magazines and media, something certainly not secondary.[lix]

Clearly, the public cannot fully grasp the collaborations that the Gates Foundation has consolidated with the media and the press through its advocacy and policy programs.[lx] No trace of them can be seen by the public, despite their substantial influence.

The Foundation does not spare resources devoted to the world of information. Almost a billion dollars are allocated to fuel this powerful consensus machine, which moves in unison with field programs (health, agriculture, education) and educational and scientific research initiatives. The two scholars, Alanna Shaik and Laura Freschi, gave an effective representation of this when they wrote that we are in a situation where we might find ourselves, "reading a story about a Gates-funded health project, written up in a newspaper that gets its health coverage underwritten by Gates, reported by a journalist who attended a Gates-funded journalism training program, citing data collected and analyzed by scientists with grants from Gates."

In particular, the Foundation is interested in promoting partnerships with journalists and newspapers on global health and development agenda issues. The Guardian, El Pais, National Public Radio, Public Broadcasting Service, and African Media Initiative are just some of the media outlets that have most focused their editorial choices on international issues, the priorities of which the Foundation operates, and act as a sounding board for Seattle's activities.

An interesting case is the disbursement of $1 million to Harvard University for the Nieman Fellowship on Global Health Reportage and the HIV Prevention Reporting Fellowship Fund in Sub-Saharan Africa.[lxi] This type of funding allocated to the press is associated with an impact award. The flagship initiative, Innovation in

Development Reporting (IDR), defines the grid for reading reality and the transformative horizon towards which to set the project to be funded. Including the need for specific and measurable objectives to be achieved through media action (articles, radio reports, videos, social media, etc.), the Gates Foundation operates according to the perspective of "solution" journalism, which aims to catalyze the media focus towards activities that solve problems, with the intention of depolarizing public dialogue and relaunching the Western version of human progress.[lxii]

So far, IDR has funded 185 projects.[lxiii] The result has been a marked increase in the focus on global poverty and public health issues. The narrative threads of this journalistic production follow the priorities and the cognitive approach of the Gates Foundation, which generally leads to positive publicity. While journalism, especially in the wake of the wave against racism that rightly pervades the world, needs more diversity and less white supremacy, the Gates Foundation's strategy is, on the contrary, focused on investing in the training of new generations of journalists, particularly in Africa. The pervasiveness of Gates in journalistic production (increasingly in crisis) is a phenomenon which, because of its problematic nature and conflicts of interest, has repeatedly attracted the attention of the Fairness and Accuracy in Reporting (FAIR) observatory.[lxiv]

How the Cornell Alliance Spreads Disinformation and Discredits Agroecology

❧

COMMUNITY ALLIANCE FOR GLOBAL JUSTICE / AGRA WATCH

THE BILL AND Melinda Gates Foundation (BMGF) has emerged over the past decade as an extremely influential actor in an ever-intensifying battle over the future of food and agriculture, pumping major funding into industrial agriculture while participating in powerful alliances seeking to reshape the trajectory of global governance of the food system. While some of these activities are drawing increasing scrutiny and analysis, this study examines a lesser-known aspect of BMGF's strategy by framing the debates and shaping how issues are communicated, as well as fostering a new generation of leadership to carry forward its mission. Funded by BMGF, the Cornell Alliance for Science (CAS) uses its affiliation with the only Ivy League institution that is a land-grant college to claim scientific neutrality while assiduously promoting communications aligned with agribusiness in its use of fellows, especially those from Africa.

Housed in Cornell University's College of Agriculture and Life Sciences in Ithaca, New York, the Cornell Alliance for Science (CAS) was launched in 2014 through a $5.6 million endowment by the Gates Foundation "to promote access to scientific innovation as a means of enhancing food security, improving environmental sustainability and raising the quality of life globally."[i] According to CAS director Sarah Evanega, CAS aims to "depolarize the GMO debate and engage with potential partners who may share common values around poverty reduction and sustainable agriculture, but may not be well informed about the potential biotechnology has for solving major agricultural challenges."[ii] A second grant of $6.4

million in 2017 brought the total contribution of BMGF to CAS to $12 million. BMGF remains the primary funder of CAS to date, while fifteen additional institutional and individual contributors of $1000 or more are listed on the CAS website. CAS describes its main strategies as:

a. Establishing a global network
b. "Training with a purpose"
c. Developing multimedia communications on agricultural biotechnology

These strategies come together through its Global Leadership Fellows Program, a 12-week intensive training course held each year at Cornell bringing together 20–30 young professionals, mainly from the Global South, and particularly Africa. While the geographical reach of the program has been broadening, the majority of fellows (60.6% in 2019) were of African origin, in keeping with prior years (See Figure 1). Upon examination of the fellows' affiliations, multiple linkages with BMGF become apparent. Cross checking the fellows' affiliations with grant disbursement data provided on the BMGF website, we can see that 34% of all the African fellows from 2015–2019 were associated with organizations that received funding from BMGF. Together, organizations connected to the fellows received over $712 million from BMGF from 2003 through 2019.

The strong overlap between the groups funded by BMGF for agricultural development and the CAS fellows gives additional meaning to the CAS strategy of building a global network, begging the question, "Who does this network serve and toward what ends?"

Given these linkages, it comes as little surprise that there are strong parallels between the types of technologies promoted by BMGF through its agricultural investments and the messages coming from CAS and its fellows. In analyzing the work put out by CAS and its fellows, a striking pattern emerges of there being a singular focus and message running throughout almost all of it—an uncritical promotion of biotechnology. Furthermore, in a distortion of scientific methodology, this position is not vetted against any diverging ones. What adds power to the narratives of CAS it is that its messages are not coming from BMGF or from its agribusiness partners directly, but from mostly young, African voices that make up its

Fellowship Program, ostensibly informed by their lived experiences and claimed scientific rigor.

Through its funding for the Cornell Alliance for Science, the Bill and Melinda Gates Foundation is seeking to shape public opinion in favor of adopting GMOs and corporate agriculture. CAS is building a new generation of leaders to carry out BMGF's mission of spreading corporate biotechnology across the Global South, particularly Africa. A key communications strategy of coming at the same time as a mounting global scientific consensus around the CAS is to promote narratives in which biotechnology is equated with "science" and any critique of biotechnology is equated with being "anti-science." It is no coincidence that the attacks on agroecology by CAS are coming at the same time as a mounting global scientific consensus around the merits of agroecology. Studies have demonstrated that perceived scientific consensus is a key factor in influencing public support on a given issue and that this tends to encourage counter-efforts around "the 'manufacture of doubt' by political and vested interests."[iii] As momentum continues to build around agroecology, its advocates can be certain that attempts to manufacture doubt will continue. Ultimately, analyzing the Gates Foundation's networks of influence points to the need for the food sovereignty movement to develop robust communication strategies of our own.

APPENDIX I
AFFILIATIONS OF 2019 AFRICAN CAS FELLOWS

Universities
Ahmedu Bello University (Nigeria)
Purdue University
Cairo University
Jimma University (Ethiopia)
Wageningen University (Netherlands)
University of California, Davis
University of Callabar (Nigeria)
University of Dar es Salaam (Tanzania)
University of Ghana
University of Ibadan (Nigeria)
University of Rwanda
Chalimbana University (Zambia)
Makarere University (Uganda)

Michigan State University
Mississippi State University
Sokoine University of Agriculture (SUA) (Tanzania)

Research & Policy

Institute of Research in Applied Sciences and Technologies (IRSAT) Environmental Institute for Agricultural Research – Burkina Faso (INERA)
Ethiopian Biotechnology Institute
French Agricultural Research Center for International Development (CIRAD) Leibniz Institute of Plant Genetics and Crop Plant Research International Food Policy Research Institute (IFPRI)
Kenya Agricultural and Livestock Research Organization (KALRO)
Food and Agriculture Organization (FAO) of the UN
National Agricultural Research Organization (NARO)
National Crops Resource Research Institute (NaCRRI)
National Resource and Land Management – Lake Zone Agricultural Research Development Institute (LZARDI)
Uganda's National Agricultural Research Laboratories Institute (NARL)
Virus Resistant Cassava (VIRCA), part of the Donald Danforth Plant Science Center

Media Organizations

Ghana Agricultural and Rural Development Journalists Association (GARDJA)
Radio Maisha (Kenya)
Science and Development Network via Centre for Agriculture and Biosciences International (CAB)
TV7 (Rwanda)

Start-ups & Private Organizations

Real Green Gold Ltd – social enterprise specializing in organic farming of tropical fruits
Rwanda Youth in Agribusiness Forum – a platform established to bring together different youth organizations, individual youth farmers and entrepreneurs in the agriculture sector
Mnandi Africa – helps rural women combat poverty and malnutrition through skills development, market access and agro-technologies
AGCO Corporation – supports high-tech solutions for farmers

Government-Related

Open Forum on Agricultural Biotechnology (OFAB via AATF) Chamber of Agribusiness Ghana (CAG) National Science and Technology Council

Bt Brinjal:
Alliance for Crooked Science
& Corporate Lies

❦

FARIDA AKHTER

B RINJALS, LOCALLY CALLED Begun (in Bangla) by the people of
Bangladesh, are the most common and favorite vegetable. On
May 17, 2020, *New Age*, a national daily newspaper of Bangladesh
published an article of mine titled "Aubergine Story: Local varieties exist, not GMOs."[i] In the article, I argued that in the month of
Ramadan (month-long fasting of the Muslim communities) the
demand for brinjal (eggplant/aubergine) is the highest because it
is the main component of the most popular Iftar item, the Beguni.
From the rich to the poor, Iftar is incomplete without chola-peyaju-
beguni on the plate. In the market, local varieties of brinjals were
amply seen but not Bt brinjal. Promoters claimed that smallholder
farmers have rapidly adopted the crop, from just 20 in 2014 to more
than 27,000 in 2019 across all districts of Bangladesh.[ii]

The article referred to a UBINIG quick survey over telephone in
April and May 2020 with farmers in eight districts and consumers in
Dhaka to investigate how farmers were faring during the COVID-19
lockdown period with the marketing of brinjals. These were sold for
prices ranging from Tk 35 to Tk 80[1] a kilogram on the market. In
early May, at least 26 different local varieties with beautiful names,

---

1 At the time of publication, 1 Bangladeshi Taka = 0.012 United States Dollar.

specific to their agroecological locations, were found on the market. The prices of high yield variety (HYV) brinjals were between Tk 25 and 50, and that of hybrid was Tk 45 to 55 per kilogram. Commercial farmers grow the HYV varieties on a large scale, while the small farming households grow local varieties on a smaller scale on their small pieces of land. Interestingly, they are readily available on the market and have good demand. Local varieties fared much better than the HYVs and hybrid varieties.

Bt brinjal seeds (Bt brinjal 1, 2, 3, and 4) for the winter season were given to farmers in different areas during the period of December 2019 to January 2020. If the claim of the International Food Policy Research Institute (IFPRI) and the ministry of agriculture that 27,000 smallholding farmers were cultivating Bt brinjal across all districts of the country is true, then it is reasonable to expect that the new genetically modified crop would have grown enough in quantity to be visible in the market. The markets in eight districts and in Dhaka showed no presence of any Bt brinjal in late April–early May 2020. None of the sellers in the market could identify any Bt brinjal in their stock. None of the buyers interviewed in the Dhaka market could identify any aubergine which would be a GMO.

Could it be that they were in the market without any label? In that case, it is a clear case of violation of approval conditions of Bt brinjal in the country. We know that in October 2013, the National Committee on Biosafety (NCB) imposed seven conditions to be followed in the field cultivation of the four Bt brinjals. One of these conditions was labeling—if Bt brinjal is brought to the market, it must be labeled, i.e., it should be clearly stated that it is GMO. But the Director General of BARI, Dr. Rafiqul Islam Mondol, only agreed to label the sacks as "poison-free GM brinjal,"[2] which was also not followed.

Culturally, farmers have the tradition of naming the brinjals they grow with beautiful local names such as Hingla begun, Batka begun, Tal- begun, Kalo-khato begun, Laoitta begun, Sailla begun,

---

2 Akhter, 2016. Akhter, Farida "Put a label on it: Consumers have the right to know what they are buying" Dhaka Tribune, 4 March 2016 http://ubinig.org/index.php/home/showAerticle/86/english/Farida-Akhter/Bt- Brinjal:-Put-a-label-on-it

Ghritakanchan begun, Nayantara, and many others. Brinjal (*Solanum melongena*), also known as aubergine or eggplant) is one of the most common and important vegetables. It is an important solanaceous crop of the subtropics and tropics. In this rich diversity of brinjals, Bt brinjal is now a "bejat" name in the list of hundreds of diverse varieties of aubergine in the country because these are numbered like prisoners and are called Bt brinjal 1, 2, 3, and 4. The word bejat expresses the displacement in the order of crop varieties, implicating potential harm to agriculture, food system, and culture. In bejat, the original names of source materials have disappeared.

Local names of brinjals are always related to specific agroecological conditions where a variety could express their natural genetic traits. But Bt brinjal seeds are given to different geographical locations assuming a homogeneous agroecological environment where they do not belong. Now it is harder to decide where they belong, except in the gene-manipulating laboratories. Farmers cannot feel or determine any agroecological, culinary, or cultural connections to laboratory varieties. Therefore, farmers who received the seeds, having not being told the real name of the introduced Bt brinjal, called genetically engineered varieties as "Sarkrari Begun" or the "government brinjal."

The genetically modified Bt brinjal has been developed by inserting a gene cry1Ac from a soil bacterium called Bacillus thuringiensis through an Agrobacterium-mediated gene transfer. Four Bt brinjals are distributed to farmers for field cultivation. The original names of the varieties that had been selected for transgenic manipulation are Uttara (Bt brinjal 1), Kajla (Bt brinjal 2), Nayantara (Bt brinjal 3), and ISD-006 (Bt brinjal 4). These are some of the most popular commercial varieties, and they are grown as non-Bt varieties. There are elements of deception in the Bt brinjal field trial in selecting the most popular varieties; if farmers accept any transgenic variety, it could be claimed that genetic manipulation is a commercial success. But farmers' varieties, selected over hundreds of years, are already successful and proof of the brilliance of the farmers' knowledge.

Genetic manipulation is merely a trick for appropriation of farmers' knowledge.

Bangladesh has been a target country for Bt brinjal under the Agricultural Biotechnology Support Project II (ABSP II). The introgressions of Bt gene into nine Bangladeshi local variety brinjals were done at Maharashtra Hybrid Seed Company (MAHYCO), an Indian company, using their lab facility. MAHYCO has received the application rights of the Bt cry1Ac gene technology from the US company Monsanto which has a 26% stake in Mahyco-Monsanto Biotech (MMB). The Bangladeshi varieties were backcrossed at MAHYCO with transgenic brinjal containing cry1Ac. There was hardly any scope for knowledge and technology transfer from MAHYCO's proprietary technology to the scientists working in public research institutions of Bangladesh. The Bt brinjal is actually piracy of the local variety brinjals to be genetically modified for patenting by the Monsanto-Mahyco partnership. Under ABSPII, the three-country partnership arrangement was extended to the Indian Institute of Vegetable Research, Varanasi, University of Philippines in Los Banos, the Bangladesh Agricultural Research Institute (BARI), and a private seed company, East West Seeds. The ABSP II is funded by USAID and led by Cornell University.

On May 25, 2020, *Frontiers in Bioengineering and Biotechnology* published an article based on a 2019 study on Bt brinjal claiming that 83.1% of Bt brinjal growers were satisfied with the yields obtained, and 80.6% were satisfied with the quality of fruit, while 58.7% non-Bt brinjal growers were satisfied with their yields and 28% indicated that a large portion of their fruit was infested. Among the non-Bt brinjal growers, 39.6% had not heard of Bt brinjal.[iii]

Another article was published on May 28, 2020, in the *Cornell-CALS* by Joan Conrow, which referred to the same article, making a conclusive statement that "farmers in Bangladesh achieved significantly higher yields and revenues by growing insect-resistant, genetically engineered eggplant." The article also quotes Maricelis Acevedo, Director for the Feed the Future South Asia Eggplant Improvement Partnership: "This study provides more evidence that

Bt brinjal is being accepted in the market, but more work is needed to develop new varieties better adapted to local conditions and market preferences."[iv] It looks like they do not have updated information on the Bt brinjal farmers' performances this year; it was simply a deceptive tactic using previous studies with newer headlines. The question remains, why are they not visible in the market?

CORNELL UNIVERSITY & BT BRINJAL "SUCCESS" LIES

The Cornell Alliance for Science was launched in 2014 with a $5.6 million grant from the Bill and Melinda Gates Foundation to "add a stronger voice for science and depolarize the charged debate around agricultural biotechnology and genetically modified organisms (GMOs)."[v] Cornell University is home to the controversial Cornell Alliance for Science, which is publicizing the Bangladesh Bt brinjal project. Its partners include the GMO industry group ISAAA, which is funded by Monsanto, CropLife, and Bayer. Cornell gave Mark Lynas a visiting fellowship and a platform to voice his pro-GMO views. Lynas now promotes GMOs "to the exclusion of almost everything else." Cornell paid his travel expenses to the Philippines to write a pro-GMO article.[vi]

From the beginning, the role of the Bangladesh Agricultural Research Institute (BARI) was guided by the ABSPII project guidelines, and it had to provide its regional research stations for field testing and later on to get formal government approval for commercial cultivation in the farmers' fields. Started back in 2005, it took seven years to complete greenhouse trials. The national biosafety committee approved the contained field trial of Bt brinjal in 2007–2008.[vii]

However, the results of the contained field trial were not shared with relevant stakeholders before it was allowed for an open field trial. Later, open-field trials of Bt brinjal were conducted in various agroecological zones in the country for local adaptability of the crop. From the beginning, the field research was conducted by BARI/USAID/ABSPII and Cornell University. Monsanto hardly appeared on those signboards, as all the signboards were in English. As the implementing agency, it said: "Biotechnology Division, BARI, Gazipur ARS, USAID, ABSP-II & Cornell University." [viii]

The role of the government was limited to getting approval from the National Committee on Biosafety (NCB) under the Ministry of Environment & Forest (MOEF) as recommended by the National Technical Committee on Crop Biotechnology (NTCCB) under the Ministry of Agriculture. The report of the performance of the field trials in the BARI research stations was never published, nor is there any reference to it. UBINIG's investigation in the six regional stations of BARI showed that the trials were not very satisfactory. [ix]

A notification (in Bangla) on October 30, 2013, bearing a reference No.22.00.0000.073.05.003.2012-271 the Environment Section-2 of the Ministry of Environment and Forestry provisionally approved the petition of BARI to cultivate Bt begun varieties 1,2,3 and 4 in a limited scale at the field level with seven conditions. One of the conditions was for the applicant organization to take effective measures by labeling so that Bt brinjal can be marketed as per biosafety rules. The Ministry of Agriculture, until now, has not taken any such measure.

CORNELL UNIVERSITY'S STRATEGIES TO PROMOTE BT BRINJAL: ATTRACTING THE PRIME MINISTER

In May 2015, Cornell University Visiting Director, Ronnie Coffman, honored Prime Minister Sheikh Hasina with a citation at her office on behalf of the university's president, David J Skorton. The citation signed by the president of the university read: "Prime Minister Sheikh Hasina's continuous support for the improvement of agriculture sector in Bangladesh and attain self-sufficiency in food production as well as her keen interest in promoting science and technology."

Ronnie Coffman of Cornell University informed the Prime Minister that the new variety of the brinjal could withstand pest attacks and hence can be free from pesticides. Sheikh Hasina thanked Cornell University for the innovation of Bt brinjal. [x]

Although Bangladesh Agricultural Research Institute (BARI) is the responsible government institution in conducting the research and monitoring field cultivation. Unfortunately, it hardly provides information on the success or failure of Bt brinjal. For example, there is no information on BARI's website. The Department of Agricultural Extension (DAE), which is responsible for distributing the Bt brinjal seeds to farmers, also has no information on their website. They did not have to do any promotion of Bt brinjal, nor come up with any performance reports. No report has been published as research findings of the first two rounds of field cultivation except some propaganda campaigns. Even the International Service for the Acquisition for Agri-Biotech Applications (ISAAA) did not publish any report after its Brief 47: "The Status of Commercialized Bt Brinjal in Bangladesh in 2014. There is nothing reported in 2015 about the so-called success of the second round of field cultivation. In the second round, Bt brinjal seedlings were given to 108 farmers, of which 79 farmers were interviewed and were found to have had massive failures."[xi]

For Cornell University, despite having big named scientists and propaganda journalists like Mark Lynas, it was not very easy to establish the claims of the "success" of Bt brinjal cultivation in Bangladesh. Farmers' organizations like Nayakrishi Andolon, research organizations like UBINIG, environmental activist groups, and individual activist journalists always had different reports published before and after the approval of Bt brinjal. Areas including farmer's fields were followed up, and farmer's experiences of failures were documented. Repeatedly UBINIG and Nayakrishi proved that the false claim of success has no scientific and empirical basis. Today, the promoters of GMOs have failed to produce any scientific evidence that Bt brinjal field trials were successful, nor can they show that farmers have adopted their transgenic varieties. The false claims of success were, therefore, challenged.

The International Food Policy Research Institute (IFPRI) also undertook a study under the behest of the Ministry of Agriculture with 1,200 farmers in 2018. The report was released in 2019.[xii] The IFPRI study findings claimed, "farmers, who cultivated the GM versions gained by 55% higher income compared to their peers growing the non-Bt brinjal," over Tk 30,000 per hectare.[xiii]

In Bangladesh, 84% of farmers belong to small households, owning less than a hectare of land, and only 14% of households have between one and three hectares.[xiv] Brinjal farmers are mostly small-scale farmers and allocate less than a hectare of land to brinjal farming. Bt Brinjal farmers also fall into this category. In a 2019 UBINIG study, 71% of farmers receiving Bt brinjal seeds were small-scale farmers and only 25% of farmers were middle-scale farmers. However, they do not allocate all the land they own for brinjal farming and also not to Bt brinjal farming.

From 2015–2015, in the initial round of Bt brinjal farming, 89% of farmers allocated 33 decimals of land (less than one-third) of an acre for Bt brinjal. The land allocated by the farmer for Bt brinjal cultivation varied by a number of seedlings given. It was found that the allocated land was between 4 to 38 decimals. The land was selected, and the amount was determined by the DAE official himself.[xv] UBINIG field investigation showed a farmer cultivating Bt brinjal on land of 33 decimals incurred a loss of Tk 30,000, and another farmer had a loss of Tk 25,000, showing there is hardly any basis for IFPRI's claim.[xvi]

FALSE CLAIM: BT BRINJAL IS PESTICIDE-FREE

Bangladesh is a country that has a wide range of brinjal cultivars. Bangladesh has at least 248 Indigenous varieties of brinjals. Most of the varieties are resistant to major diseases and pests. The major pests of brinjal include insects, mites, fungi, nematodes, and bacteria. The fruit and shoot borer (*Leucinodes orbonalis*), for example, is one of the insect pests of brinjal. Some of the local varieties, including Jhumka 1 and 2, are highly resistant to fruit and shoot borer while Islampuri 3, BL 34, and Muktakeshi are fairly resistant. Singnath long and Singnath 4 are tolerant to brinjal shoot and fruit borer.[xvii]

Promoters claim that Bt brinjal is pesticide-free. It is called "*Poka bihin began*" (no-pest brinjal), meaning that it does not require use of pesticides for the most common pest, the fruit and shoot borer (FSB). Therefore, GM crops are claimed to be safe because they do not need applications of a huge amount of pesticides. Interestingly, the IFPRI study did not claim no use of pesticides but claimed there was 39% reduction in the quantity of pesticides applied and 51% reduction in the number of pesticide applications.[xviii] The major promotional message to the farmers was that Bt brinjal does not require any application of pesticides and not merely a reduction in the use of pesticides.

But the UBINIG field study found a different reality. The farmers had to use huge amounts of pesticides recommended by the supervising authorities of BARI and DAE. These included Comfidor, Ektara, Admasar, Dithane M-45, Bavistin, Thiovit, Basudin, Furadan, Borax, Demsa granular, Vim powder, Admire, 200sl (Bayer crop science), bleaching powder, Heckel, Salclox, Diazinon etc., among many other insecticides and fungicides sprayed, as provided by DAE. In the booklet distributed to some of the farmers, they recommended organic pesticides such as Neem seeds, Neem oil, powder soap, and Trix. Among the chemical pesticides, Malathion, Omite, and Bavistin were suggested for different pest/disease attacks. It seems that in real situations, the supervising authorities were giving more pesticides than those recommended because of the different kinds of pest attacks.

In the field investigation of Bt brinjal's second round of field cultivation, pesticide use was more prominent than in the first round. Different pesticides were used several times, beginning from transplanting to growth, development to bearing, and harvesting of fruits. The major pests observed in the Bt brinjal field included viruses, fungi, insects, and mites. The virus infection included tulshi virus and mosaic virus. The fungi appeared as root rot, stem rot, wilting, leaf spot, and fruit rot. The insects included aphids, leaf curlings, whiteflies, sucking insects, fruit and shoot borer, red mites, and many others. Thirty-five types of pesticides, including acaricide, insecticide, and fungicide, were sprayed several times in the Bt brinjal fields, as per the directions of the supervising officials.

Five banned insecticides, including Basudin, Bidrin, Darsbun, Diazinon and Furadan, were used in different Bt brinjal fields. Thirty other pesticides used were not from the list of 76 pesticides recommended for brinjal crop production in Bangladesh.[xix]

LIES AND PROPAGANDA INSTEAD OF EVIDENCE-BASED RESEARCH

Mark Lynas, a frequent contributor, and researcher at the Cornell Alliance for Science, visited Bangladeshi Bt brinjal farmers along with various scientists and others from Cornell University and the Bangladesh Agricultural Research Institute. His organized visit was aimed to make everything successful. He tried to counter the reports written by the Bangladeshi journalists as false![xx] He visited the same Bt brinjal farmer and found the crop in good health and the farmer happy.[xxi]

Media attention to Mark Lynas is generated by mostly the drama he draws from his own life. He claims his life begins as "the first anti-GMO activist in the world" but ends as an avid GMO supporter, desperate to make amends for the movement he started. The Bill Gates Foundation has set up a position for Mark Lynas at Cornell as part of the controversial Cornell Alliance for Science. This allows Lynas to do paid promotion for GMOs "to the exclusion of almost everything else."[xxii]

In response, Anne Lappe of Small Planet Institute published a letter to the Editor on May 4, 2015, saying, "Mark Lynas' profile of one farmer in Bangladesh does not represent the facts on the ground about the genetically engineered eggplant there. The trials of the new variety of eggplant have actually had very poor results: genetic engineering did not protect plants from most pests and have led to crop loss and debt for farmers". She revealed that "Mr. Lynas' Bangladesh visit was organized by the new Cornell Alliance for Science, funded by a $5.6 million grant from the Gates Foundation, that is promoting biotechnology, not dispassionately reviewing the science."

BBC PANORAMA: A SCANDALOUS PROMOTION
OF BT BRINJAL

BBC Panorama's program, *GM Food: Cultivating Fear,* aired on June 8, 2015, featured the pro-GMO campaigner Mark Lynas visiting an insecticidal Bt brinjal field in Bangladesh and enthusing about the performance of the crop, claiming 90% success for this controversial GMO. The presenter, Tom Heap, and his friend, Mark Lynas, grossly misrepresented the so-called success of the brinjal crop.

Faisal Rahman, staff correspondent for the United News of Bangladesh (UNB) and the author of the report titled "Bt brinjal turns out to be 'upset case' for farmers" based on field visits and telephone interviews with farmers growing Bt brinjal in the second year Bt brinjal cultivation, challenged that there is no evidence to support the claim.

Faisal Rahman's report concluded that "The cultivation of genetically engineered Bt brinjal in the country's several districts has cost the farmers their fortunes again this year as the plants have either died out prematurely or fruited very insignificantly compared to the locally available varieties." His evidence, together with subsequent investigations by GMWatch, casts serious doubt on the credibility of the BBC Panorama program.[xxiii]

The documentary featured the "success" story of a farmer Hafizur Rahman, who was visited by Mark Lynas before. Lynas claimed that the Bt brinjal had "nearly doubled" productivity and that Hafizur Rahman had been able to sell the crop labeled "insecticide-free." Lynas concluded, "Now, with increased profits, he looked forward to being able to lift his family further out of poverty." But after tracking down farmer Hafizur Rahman, UBINIG found almost every element of the Lynas narrative was misleading or false. Visiting Hafizur Rahman, UBINIG found that far from being a poor farmer that the GM crop is helping to lift out of poverty. As Lynas claimed, Hafizur Rahman is actually a "Polytechnic Graduate" and a "well off commercial vegetable farmer." The story about the GM crop enabling him to dispense with agrochemicals was far from the truth—multiple chemicals, including pesticides, were used on the crop. The farmer also complained that the Bt brinjal had a "rough surface and gets soft very quickly," unlike the traditional variety, which is "shiny and remains fresh for a longer time."[xxiv]

Two complaints were lodged to the Editorial Standard Committee (ESC) of the BBC Trust that its Panorama film *GM Food: Cultivating Fear*, broadcasted in June 2015, was biased and inaccurate and that it "misled the audience by making a claim of success for a GM aubergine crop which is not supported by the evidence." BBC failed to provide sources for the 90% success rate and only referred to Dr. Frank Shotkoski, director of the Agricultural Biotechnology Support Project II (ABSPII) program at Cornell University.[xxv]

CONCLUSION

Bt brinjal started with Monsanto as a proprietary owner of the technology, but the real game was played by ABSPII of USAID and Cornell University, backed by the Gates Foundation. Fortunately, Bangladeshi land and environment have rejected the seed. It simply does not grow or give fruits. That's why they need propagandists like Mark Lynas and so-called scientists to prove the 27,000 farmers of Bangladesh are happily cultivating Bt brinjal. Of course, you need Bill Gates to fund blatant lies, crooked science, commercial propaganda, and the destruction of agriculture and biodiversity in countries like Bangladesh.

AN EARTH-BASED
PHILOSOPHY

A Message From Gaia

I am Gaia. I am Bhoomi. I am Pachamama—the Living Earth.

For over four billion years, I have generated trillions of species, microbes, plants, and animals that mutually support each other, working through my patterns of interrelatedness and peace to foster life on Earth. When climate systems and temperatures gave rise to the evolution of humans on Earth some 200,000 years ago, human species began to evolve and thrive, co-creating in diversity, freedom, and reciprocity. My being is interconnectedness and harmony by which all life on Earth has evolved.

My expression is diversity.

Humanity has survived and sustained herself down the ages by caring for the Earth, maintaining her cycles of food and water, life, and energy while providing for people's needs. Living within planetary and ecological laws and boundaries is a precondition for humans to survive the unprecedented crises they face today for the future of humanity.

For millennia, Indigenous cultures and Earth citizens have known me as Mother Earth, *Terra Madre*, connected in body and spirit. They know themselves as my custodians and live according to established laws as an Earth Community—an Earth Family—not as masters, controllers, or owners.

Around 500 years ago, the notion of my inseparability and interconnectedness with humans began to fade in people's minds and the illusion of being separate and disconnected from the Earth took hold. With colonization and "civilizing missions," those who saw themselves as superior and masters of the Earth—blind to the vital, self-organizing life on Earth and to the people who have lived on and cared for the Earth for generations—declared lands to be empty, devoid of life, and dead. *Terra Madre* became seen as *Terra Nullius*, with insignificant people living on barren land.

Humans soon began violating Earth's planetary and ecological boundaries by burning, extracting, and plundering Earth's living resources, polluting the soils, land, water, and air, unaware that it was the path of self-destruction. Stubborn illusions of superiority, mastery, and being separate from Earth and intelligent, self-organizing living systems are at the root of the degradation and desertification of both the Earth and the human spirit. Violence and injustice are their consequences, which lead to war.

Forests are burning, chronic diseases are spreading, and long-gone pandemics have returned as an industrial poison-based agricultural system invades into forests and across vast agricultural lands, poisoning all life from the smallest microbes to plants, animals, and people. Indigenous peoples and concerned Earth citizens are today fighting for their survival as never before as my habitats and biodiversity are being ravaged in the relentless pursuit of profits, control, and power led by corporations and billionaires.

Rapacious systems of profit and power-hungry billionaires are anathema to my self-organizing, regenerative, and life-sustaining systems. Gates and those in his foundation falsely portray themselves as caring philanthropists of the poor, sick, and hungry while worsening extractive and destructive systems.

I grow diversity, and you impose monocultures and uniformity. I self-organize, self-create, maintain, and renew in interconnectedness. Their mechanized competitive mind imposes high-tech brutal controls. I promote harmony and freedom; they spawn violence and impose monopolies. I create cycles of renewal through living organisms; they impose inert genetically modified commodities and produce genetically modified seeds to be patented, sold, and traded for profit. I generate biodiversity that supports all life on Earth; they destroy biodiversity through poisons and create vast swathes of toxic monocultures. My ecological agriculture provides health and nutrition; their industrial agriculture creates disease, hunger, and malnutrition with so-called "humanitarian" projects that gain control over humanity's life-sustaining systems: seeds, agriculture, food, health, and knowledge. Whether they know it or not, the philanthrocapitalists of the world are creating an empire of disease.

Digital genomic patenting thwarts the regulations which have evolved to protect my biodiversity and the rights of those who sustain me. As a major backer of geoengineering, together with massive investments in the coal and oil industry's mining and extraction for fossil fuel energy, they poison Earth's atmosphere, disrupt Earth's ecosystems, violate my boundaries, and dangerously destabilize the climate. Channeling these vast sums, instead, to reduce carbon emissions to zero would be far more cost-effective to stop the warming of the planet.

They also assume the right to mutate life through gene drive technology and CRISPR, a high-risk and unpredictable new genetic extinction technology, which can lead to the deliberate modification of humans and living species. Life is not a Microsoft machine and cannot be cut and pasted. Nature's intelligence continues to evolve and fights back in unpredictable and unexpected ways as the world is witnessing today with the COVID-19 virus pandemic. Ethical and long-term implications for the future of humanity find no space in narrow self-absorbed, power-hungry minds that disrupt my life-sustaining systems and threaten the biodiversity I have evolved over billions of years.

They are not just rupturing the fabric I have woven, with colossal wealth and mechanistic minds, but they are blindly setting the course of humanity faster on the destructive path of ecological, social, and economic breakdown in this crucial and epoch changing time for the future of humanity. They are tearing apart the fabric of community and society that makes life livable—bringing human society itself to the brink of annihilation by destroying the conditions that guarantee life and freedom to all citizens. To them, I give the reminder that empires have come and gone.

I call on all citizens to take energy and creativity from me and rise to protect their communities, societies, their humanity, and future from you and your cohorts mechanical, robotic, thoughtless, toxic urge to control everything that is living and free. My laws are higher than the laws made by powerful men for their limitless greed and hubris. By following my laws and respecting my ecological boundaries, humanity can find its way toward the regeneration of hope, freedom, and life in abundance.

Reclaim the seeds I have given you. Reclaim the living food that nourishes us. Reclaim your life and freedom, in unity and solidarity, in community and interconnectedness, through diversity and self-organization. Draw from me the power to speak, act, and live the truth of life in freedom, compassion, love, and oneness. Co-create with me an age beyond empires, an age of generosity and well-being—an age of Gaia.

Contributors

Additional Research and Editing:

Carla Ramos Cortés, Elisa Catalini, Ruchi Shroff

Translations:

Elisa Catalini, Carla Ramos Cortés

Authors:

Adelita San Vicente, Doctor in Agroecology, Director General of the Primary Sector and Natural Resources, SEMARNAT, Mexico.

Aidé Jiménez-Martínez, MA in Sciences, Director of Regulations of Biosafety, Biodiversity and Genetic Resources, SEMARNAT, Mexico.

Chito Medina, founding member of MASIPAG (Farmers-Scientists Partnership For Development), and former National Coordinator of the network. Associate Professor of environmental science in a leading university in the Philippines.

Community Alliance for Global Justice/AGRA Watch. GM Watch.

Dru Jay, Coordinator of GeoengineeringMonitor.org, writer and activist in climate justice and Indigenous solidarity movements, based in Montreal, Canada.

Farida Akhter, founding Executive Director of UBINIG, Bangladesh.

Fernando Cabaleiro, Attorney at law (University of Buenos Aires), Naturaleza de Derechos, Argentina.

Jim Thomas, Co-Executive Director and Researcher, focusing on emerging technologies on human rights, biodiversity, equity, and food systems, ETC Group, currently based in Canada.

Jonathan Latham, molecular biologist and former genetic engineer. He now edits the website Independent Science News.

José Esquinas-Alcazar, former Secretary of the FAO Intergovernmental Commission on Genetic Resources for Food and Agriculture and Chairman of the FAO Ethics Committee for Food and Agriculture.

Mantasa, Indonesia.

Navdanya Team

Nicoletta Dentico, journalist, and director of the global health program of Society for International Development (SID).

Satish Kumar, Founder of Schumacher College, England, UK.

Seth Itzkan, Co-founder and Co-Director of Soil4Climate Inc.

Silvia Ribeiro, Uruguay, Journalist, lecturer, writer, and educator on emerging technologies, Latin American Director, ETC Group, based in Mexico City.

Tapsoba Ali de Goamma; Human rights activist; Ecologist; President of the Terre A Vie association; Spokesperson for the Collectif Citoyen pour l'Agroécologie (Citizen's Collective for Agroecology), Burkina Faso.

Timothy Wise, Senior Advisor at the Institute for Agriculture and Trade Policy (IATP).

Vandana Shiva, founder of Navdanya Research Foundation for Science, Technology and Ecology (India) and President of Navdanya International.

Zahra Moloo, Kenya, Investigative journalist, documentary filmmaker and researcher on extractive industries, land rights, conservation and security. ETC Group, based in Montreal, Canada.

Endnotes

❦

Disrupting a World of Traditional Knowledge, Sovereignty, and Biodiversity

i Gammage, Bill. *The Biggest Estate on Earth: How Aborigines Made Australia*. Main edition. Allen & Unwin, 2011. Bruce Pascow, Dark Emu: *Aboriginal Australia and the birth of agriculture*, Magabala Books, 2014.

ii University of Exeter. "Ancient Farmers Transformed Amazon and Left an Enduring Legacy on the Rainforest." *Phys.Org*, July 23, 2018. https://phys.org/news/2018-07-ancient-farmers-amazon-left-legacy.html

iii Steenhuysen, Julie. "Evidence of Ancient Farming Found in Andes." *Reuters*, June 28, 2007. https://www.reuters.com/article/us-farming-idUSN2842559620070628

iv "Native Potato Varieties." *International Potato Center*. https://cipotato.org/potato/native-potato-varieties/

v Onofre S.A. 2005, The floating gardens in México Xochimilco, world heritage risk site. City & Time 1 (3): 5. http://www.ceci-br.org/novo/revista/docs2005/CT-2005-34.pdf

vi O'Leary, Matthew. "Maize: From Mexico to the World." *CIMMYT*, May 20, 2016. https://www.cimmyt.org/blogs/maize-from-mexico-to-the-world/

vii Fischer, Nan. "Ancient Companion Planting: The Three Sisters." *Medium*, March 29, 2019. https://medium.com/nannie-appleseed/ancient-companion-planting-the-three-sisters-e1d3b5f34285

viii "First Evidence of Farming in Mideast 23,000 Years Ago: Evidence of Earliest Small-Scale Agricultural Cultivation." ScienceDaily, July 22, 2015. https://www.sciencedaily.com/releases/2015/07/150722144709.htm

ix Society, National Geographic. "The Development of Agriculture." National Geographic Society, August 19, 2019. http://www.nationalgeographic.org/article/development-agriculture/

x King, F. H. Farmers of Forty Centuries: Organic Farming in China, Korea, and Japan. Dover Ed edition. Mineola, N.Y: Dover Publications, 2004.

xi Dr.R.H. Richaria and S. Govindaswami, Rices of India, Academy of Development Science, Kashele, Maharashtra. 1990. https://www.pnas.org/content/103/25/9578

xii Navdanya International, The Law of the Seed (2013), https://navdanyainternational .org/publications/the-law-of-the-seed/

xiii "I.G. Farben." IG Farben German Industry and the Holocaust -www.Holocaust ResearchProject.org, n.d. http://www.holocaustresearchproject.org/economics/ igfarben.html.

xiv Shiva, V. (1991). The Violence of the Green Revolution: Third World Agriculture, Ecology, and Politics. Other India Press. https://books.google.it/books?id= jPNRPgAACAAJ

xv Dogra, B., & Richharia, R. H. (1991). The life and work of Dr. R.H. Richharia: The eminent rice scientist who struggled all his life for small farmers to protect them from big business and to preserve their heritage: Including the text of an action plan on rice prepared by Dr. Richharia. B. Dogra. http://books.google.com/ books?id=KUMFAQAAIAAJ

xvi Vandana Shiva et al. Reclaiming the Commons, Synergetic Press. New Mexico, 2020. Updated version of "Recovery and Enclosures of the Commons", Research Foundation for Science Technology and Ecology, 1997.

xvii Navdanya, Global Citizens reports on Seed Freedom https://navdanyainternational .org/publications/seed-freedom-global-report-2012/ - https://navdanyainternational .org/publications/seed-freedom-global-report-2014/

xviii "Navdanya International Report on Monsanto Tribunal and People's Assembly in The Hague." People's Assembly, December 13, 2016. https://peoplesassembly.net/ navdanya-international-report-on-the-monsanto-tribunal-and-peoples-assembly-in-the-hague/

xix "Monsanto and Bayer's Chemical Romance: Heroin, Nerve Gas and Agent Orange." Alternet.Org, February 17, 2017. https://www.alternet.org/2017/02/ monsanto-and-bayers-chemical-romance-heroin-nerve-gas-and-agent-orange/

xx "Navdanya." https://www.navdanya.org/site/

xxi Mcintyre, Beverly & Herren, Hans & Wakhungu, Judi & Watson, Robert. (2009). Agriculture at a Crossroads: The Global Report. https://www.researchgate.net/ publication/258099731_Agriculture_at_a_Crossroads_The_Global_Report

xxii Shiva, V. (1991). The Violence of the Green Revolution: Third World Agriculture, Ecology, and Politics. Other India Press. https://books.google.it/ books?id=jPNRPgAACAAJ

xxiii Alvares, Claude. "The Great Gene Robbery." Vijayvaani.Com, January 13, 2012. https://www.vijayvaani.com/ArticleDisplay.aspx?aid=2137

xxiv Shiva, V., Anilkumar, P., & Ahluwalia, U. (2020). Ag one: Recolonisation of agriculture. Navdanya/ RFSTE. https://navdanyainternational.org/publications/ ag-one-recolonisation-of-agriculture/

xxv "Investment into Research Must Double to Halt Climate and Food Crises by 2030." CGIAR, January 25, 2021. https://www.cgiar.org/news-events/news/ investment-into-research-must-double-to-halt-climate-and-food-crises-by-2030/.

xxvi FAO Commission on Genetic Resources for Food and Agriculture. "The State of the World's Biodiversity for Food and Agriculture 2019," 2019. http://www.fao.org/state-of-biodiversity-for-food-agriculture/en

xxvii IPBES. "UN Report: Nature's Dangerous Decline 'Unprecedented'; Species Extinction Rates 'Accelerating.'" UN | Sustainable Development, May 6, 2019. https://www.un.org/sustainabledevelopment/blog/2019/05/nature-decline-unprecedented-report

xxviii "Land Is a Critical Resource, IPCC Report Says". IPCC, August 8, 2019. https://www.ipcc.ch/2019/08/08/land-is-a-critical-resource_srccl/

xxix El Hage Scialabba, Nadia. "Feeding the Word: Delusion, False Promises and Attacks of Industrial Agriculture." Navdanya International, December 7, 2019. https://navdanyainternational.org/publications/feeding-the-word-delusion-false-promises-and-attacks-of-industrial-agriculture/

xxx "India Deposit to the Svalbard Global Seed Vault." Crop Trust, May 15, 2014. https://www.croptrust.org/blog/india-deposit-svalbard-global-seed-vault/

xxxi "Two contributions to an integrated, global, accession-level information system for ex situ conservation" | Input Paper to the ITPGRFA Consultation on the Global Information System on Plant Genetic Resources for Food and Agriculture (COGIS-PGRFA) Provided by: The Global Crop Diversity Trust. January 2015. IT/COGIS-1/15/Inf.4.a5. http://www.fao.org/3/a-be678e.pdf

xxxii "'DivSeek Initiative' Loses Support of the International Treaty on Plant Genetic Resources for Food and Agriculture." International Planning Committee for Food Sovereignty (IPC), February 28, 2017. https://www.foodsovereignty.org/divseek-initiative-loses-support-international-treaty-plant-genetic-resources-food-agriculture/

xxxiii Shiva, V., & Shiva, K. (2020). Oneness Vs. The 1 Percent: Shattering Illusions, Seeding Freedom. CHELSEA GREEN PUB. https://books.google.it/books?id=4TmTzQEACAAJ

xxxiv Herper, Matthew. "Bill Gates And 13 Other Investors Pour $120 Million Into Revolutionary Gene-Editing Startup." Forbes, August 10, 2015. Accessed September 8, 2020. https://www.forbes.com/sites/matthewherper/2015/08/10/bill-gates-and-13-other-investors-pour-120-million-into-revolutionary-gene-editing-startup/

An Overview of Bill & Melinda Gates Agricultural Innovations

i See also: Shiva, V., Anilkumar, P., Ahluwalia, U., "Ag One: Recolonisation of Agriculture", Navdanya/RFSTE, 2020, http://navdanya.org/site/latest-news-at-navdanya/703-ag-one-recolonoisation-of-agriculture

ii Gray, Bryce. "Gates Foundation Plans Crop Research Center in St. Louis." *Online Research Library: Questia | St Louis Post-Dispatch (MO)*, January 30, 2020. https://www.questia.com/newspaper/1P4-2348219385/gates-foundation-plans-crop-research-center-in-st iii"Overview: Bill & Melinda Gates Agricultural Innovations." Bill & Melinda Gates Foundation, January 2020. https://docs.gatesfoundation.org/Documents/GatesAg One_OverviewandFAQ.pdf

ivIbid.

v"Gates Foundation on Intention to Create Nonprofit Agricultural Research Institute." Bill & Melinda Gates Foundation | Press Releases, January 21, 2020. https://www. gatesfoundation.org/Media-Center/Press-Releases/2020/01/Gates-Foundation-Statement-on-Creation-of-Nonprofit-Agricultural-Research-Institute

viCheney, Catherine. "Exclusive: Gates Foundation Launches New Agriculture-Focused Nonprofit." Devex. Last modified January 21, 2020. https://www.devex. com/news/sponsored/exclusive-gates-foundation-launches-new-agriculture -focused-nonprofit-96384

viiIbid.

viiiIbid.

ix "Microsoft y El IICA Definieron Hoja de Ruta Para La Transformación Digital Del Agro de Las Américas." Instituto Interamericano de Cooperación Para La Agricultura (IICA). https://www.iica.int/en/node/16190

x "About." Global Center on Adaptation. https://gca.org/about

xi "Global Coalition Promises More than $650 Million to Accelerate CGIAR Efforts to Help 300 Million Smallholder Farmers Adapt to Climate Change." CGIAR, September 23, 2019. https://www.cgiar.org/news-events/news/uncas-global-coalition-funds-cgiar/

xii Ibid.

xiii Ibid.

xiv"The Next Agribusiness Takeover: Multilateral Food Agencies." ETC Group. Last modified February 12, 2020. https://www.etcgroup.org/content/next-agribusiness -takeover-multilateral-food-agencies

xv"Agricultural Development." Bill & Melinda Gates Foundation. https://www. gatesfoundation.org/What-We-Do/Global-Growth-and-Opportunity/Agricultural -Development

xvi"About Us." Digital Green. https://www.digitalgreen.org/about-us/

xvii Lucchi, N. (2013). Understanding genetic information as a commons: From bio-prospecting to personalized medicine. International Journal of the Commons, 7(2), 313–338. DOI: http://doi.org/10.18352/ijc.399

xviii Masucci M., Un accordo per tutelare la biodiversità agricola, Terra Nuova, 16 February 2020, https://www.terranuova.it/Il-Mensile/Un-accordo-per-tutelare-la-biodiversita-agricola/

The Bill & Melinda Gates Foundation and the International Rice Research Institute Alliance

xixCheney, Catherine. "Exclusive: Gates Foundation Launches New Agriculture-Focused Nonprofit." Devex, January 21, 2020. https://www.devex.com/news/sponsored/exclusive-gates-foundation-launches-new-agriculture-focused-nonprofit-96384

i McFarlan, Franklin Warren. "Planned Giving and Foundations." Essay. In *Effective Fundraising the Trustees Role and Beyond*, 176. Hoboken, NJ: Wiley, 2021.

ii 2014 CGIAR Annual Report.

iii IRRI 2016 Audited Financial Report.

iv Awarded Grants / Agricultural Development. P. 4" Bill & Melinda Gates Foundation. https://www.gatesfoundation.org/How-We-Work/Quick-Links/Grants-Database (accessed June 15, 2020)

v IRRI 2016 Audited Financial Report.

vi Essay. In *Sowing the Seeds of Change: an Environmental Teaching Pack for the Hospitality Industry*, 021. Paris: UNEP, 2001.

vii IRRI World Rice Statistics, 2004

viii WRI, UNEP and IUCN, 2002

Seed Ownership Through New Gene Editing Technologies

i Shiva, V., & Shiva, K. (2020). Oneness Vs. The 1 Percent: Shattering Illusions, Seeding Freedom. CHELSEA GREEN PUB.

ii Stoye, Emma. "Crispr-Edited Mushroom Dodges Regulation." *Chemistry WorApril* 26l 26, 2016. https://www.chemistryworld.com/news/crispr-edited-mushroom-dodges-regulation/1010298.article

iii Pollack, Andrew. "Jennifer Doudna, a Pioneer Who Helped Simplify Genome Editing." The New York Times, May 11, 2015, sec. Science. https://www.nytimes.com/2015/05/12/science/jennifer- doudna-crispr-cas9-genetic-engineering.html

iv Sanders, Robert. "Gates Foundation Awards $100,000 Grants for Novel Global Health Research." Berkeley News, May 10, 2010. https://news.berkeley.edu/2010/05/10/gates-foundation/

v "What Is CRISPR-Cas9?" Yourgenome, n.d. https://www.yourgenome.org/facts/what-is-crispr-cas9

vi Otieno MO (2015) CRISPR-Cas9 Human Genome Editing: Challenges, Ethical Concerns and Implications. J Clin Res Bioeth 6: 253.doi: 10.4172/2155-9627.10002. https://www.longdom.org/open-   access/crisprcas9-human-genome-editing-challenges-ethical-concerns-and-implications-2155- 9627-1000253.pdf

vii Latham, Jonathan. "God's Red Pencil? CRISPR and Myths of Precise Genome Editing." Independent Science News | Food, Health and Agriculture Bioscience News, April 25, 2016. https://www.independentsciencenews.org/science-media/gods-red-pencil-crispr-and-the-three- myths-of-precise-genome-editing/

viii Herper, Matthew. "Bill Gates And 13 Other Investors Pour $120 Million Into Revolutionary Gene-Editing Startup." Forbes, August 10, 2016. https://www.forbes.com/sites/

matthewherper/2015/08/10/bill-gates-and-13-other-investors-pour-120-million-into-revolutionary-gene-editing-startup/

ix Begley, Sharon. "CRISPR Patent Fight: The Legal Bills Are Soaring." STAugust 16t 16, 2016. https://www.statnews.com/2016/08/16/crispr-patent-fight-legal-bills-soaring/

x "Bngo -Company Profile." BCIQ. https://bciq.biocentury.com/companies/bngo

Gene Editing: Unexpected Outcomes and Risks

xi Sanders, Robert. "Twelfth CRISPR Patent Awarded to UC Team." Berkeley NeSeptember 3er 3, 2019. https://news.berkeley.edu/2019/09/03/twelfth-crispr-patent-awarded-to-uc-team/ "Crispr-Cas Component Systems, Methods and Compositions for Sequence Manipulation," n.d. https://patents.google.com/patent/EP2840140A1/en.

xii Shiva, Vandana. "Gene Edited Foods Are GMOs: New Research." *Seed Freed-September* 7er 7, 2020. https://seedfreedom.info/gene-edited-foods-are-gmos-new-research-establishes-that-gene-editing-is-not-natural-that-it-can-be-tested-and-should-be-regulated-for-biosafety-as-a-gmo/

xiii Court of Justice of the European Union, PRESS RELEASE No 111/18, Luxembourg, 25 July 2018, Judgment in Case C-528/16, Confédération paysanne and Others v Premier ministre and Ministre de l'Agriculture, de l'Agroalimentaire et de la Forêt, *Organisms obtained by mutagenesis are GMOs and are, in principle, subject to the obligations laid down by the GMO Directive.* https://curia.europa.eu/jcms/upload/docs/application/pdf/2018-07/cp180111en.pdf

xiv Citizen Action: https://www.gmfreeze.org/current-actions/ask-ministers-to-reject-plans-toderegulate-genome-editing/ Action briefing: https://www.gmfreeze.org/publications/action-briefing-on-agriculture-billamendment-to-deregulate-genome-editing/ Political briefing: https://beyond-gm.org/wp-content/uploads/2020/07/Genome-Editing-_Ag-Bill_Political-Briefing_030720-FINAL_updated.pdf

xv Hruska , Joel . "CRISPR Gene Editing May Have Unanticipated Side Effects." ExtremeTeJuly 24y 24, 2018. https://www.extremetech.com/extreme/274110-study-suggests-crispr-gene-editing-could-have-unanticipated-side-effects

xvi Licholai, Greg "Is CRISPR Worth the Risk?" *Yale InsighAugust* 21t 21, 2018. https://insights.som.yale.edu/insights/is-crispr-worth-the-risk

xvii Creighton, Jolene "Gene Drives: Assessing the Benefits & Risks." *Future of Life Institute*, n.d. https://futureoflife.org/gene-drives-assessing-the-benefits-risks/

i Eckerstorfer, Michael F., Marion Dolezel, Andreas Heissenberger, Marianne Miklau, Wolfram Reichenbecher, Ricarda A. Steinbrecher, and Friedrich Waßmann. "An EU Perspective on Biosafety Considerations for Plants Developed by Genome Editing and Other New Genetic Modification Techniques (NGMs)." Frontiers in Bioengineering and Biotechnology 7 (2019). https://www.frontiersin.org/articles/10.3389/fbioe.2019.00031/full; Gelinsky, Eva, and Angelika Hilbeck. "European Court of Justice Ruling Regarding New Genetic Engineering Methods Scientifically Justified:

A Commentary on the Biased Reporting about theRecent Ruling." Environmental Sciences Europe 30, no. 1 (December 20, 2018): 52. https://enveurope.springeropen. com/articles/10.1186/s12302-018-0182-9

ii Kawall, Katharina. "New Possibilities on the Horizon: Genome Editing Makes the Whole Genome Accessible for Changes." Frontiers in Plant Science 10 (2019). https:// www.frontiersin.org/articles/10.3389/fpls.2019.00525/full3

iii Wolt, Jeffrey D., Kan Wang, Dipali Sashital, and Carolyn J. Lawrence-Dill. "Achieving Plant CRISPR Targeting That Limits Off-Target Effects." The Plant Genome 9, no. 3 (2016): plantgenome2016.05.0047. https://acsess.onlinelibrary.wiley.com/doi/ full/10.3835/plantgenome2016.05.0047; Zhu, Changfu, Luisa Bortesi, Can Baysal, Richard M. Twyman, Rainer Fischer, Teresa Capell, Stefan Schillberg, and Paul Christou. "Characteristics of Genome Editing Mutations in Cereal Crops." Trends in Plant Science 22, no. 1 (2017): 38–52. https://www.ncbi.nlm.nih.gov/pubmed/27645899

iv Tuladhar, Rubina, Yunku Yeu, John Tyler Piazza, Zhen Tan, Jean Rene Clemenceau, Xiaofeng Wu, Quinn Barrett, et al. "CRISPR-Cas9-Based Mutagenesis Frequently Provokes on-Target MRNA Misregulation." Nature Communications 10, no. 1 (September 6, 2019): 1–10. https://www.nature.com/articles/s41467-019-12028-5; Smits, Arne H., Frederik Ziebell, Gerard Joberty, Nico Zinn, William F. Mueller, Sandra Clauder-Münster, Dirk Eberhard, et al. "Biological Plasticity Rescues Target Activity in CRISPR Knock Outs." Nature Methods 16, no. 11 (November 2019): 1087–1093. https://www.nature.com/articles/s41592-019-0614-5

v Tang, Xu, Guanqing Liu, Jianping Zhou, Qiurong Ren, Qi You, Li Tian, Xuhui Xin, et al. "A Large-Scale Whole-Genome Sequencing Analysis Reveals Highly Specific Genome Editing by Both Cas9 and Cpf1 (Cas12a) Nucleases in Rice." Genome Biology 19, no. 1 (July 4, 2018): 84. https://genomebiology.biomedcentral.com/ articles/10.1186/s13059-018-1458-5

vi Norris, Alexis L., Stella S. Lee, Kevin J. Greenlees, Daniel A. Tadesse, Mayumi F. Miller, and Heather A. Lombardi. "Template Plasmid Integration in Germline Genome-Edited Cattle." Nature Biotechnology 38, no. 2 (February 2020): 163–164. https://www.nature.com/articles/s41587-019-0394-6

i"Convention on Biodiversity." United Nations. United Nations, n.d. https://www. un.org/en/observances/biological-diversity-day/convention.

iiUnit, Biosafety. "Article 1. Objectives." Convention on Biological Diversity. Secretariat of the Convention on Biological Diversity, November 2, 2006. https://www.cbd. int/convention/articles/?a=cbd-01.

iiiUnit, Biosafety. "Article 2. Convention Text." Convention on Biological Diversity. Secretariat of the Convention on Biological Diversity, November 2, 2006. https:// www.cbd.int/convention/articles/?a=cbd-02.

ivA Betancourt., (2016). The Cancun Summits: The Conservation of Biodiversity, Clashing Paradigms and Debate Between the Commercialization and Safeguarding of Nature [online]. Heinrich Böll Stiftung. [Viewed 4 July 2020]. Available from: https://mx.boell.org/es/2016/06/16/

las-cumbres-de-cancun-conservacion-de-la-biodiversidad- choque-de-paradigmas-y-debate

vThe Secretariat of Environment and Natural Resources (SEMARNAT), (2018). Varieties of Native Mexican Maize/Corn Capture Nitrogen thereby Leading to a Departure from Chemical Fertilizers [online]. Mexico: SEMARNAT. [Viewed 4 July 2020]. Available from: https://www.gob.mx/semarnat/prensa/variedad-de-maiz-nativo-mexicano-captura-nitrogeno- con-lo-que-se-evitarian-fertilizantes-quimicos

viBöll Heinrich Fundación, (2016). Four Steps Forward and one Step Back in the Global Regulation of Synthetic Biology [online]. Heinrich Böll Stiftung. [Viewed 4 July 2020]. Available from: https://mx.boell.org/es/2016/12/21/cuatro-pasos-adelante-y-uno-hacia-atras-en-la-regulacion- global-de-la-biologia-sintetica

viiUnit, Biosafety. "Article 1. Objectives." Convention on Biological Diversity. Secretariat of the Convention on Biological Diversity, November 2, 2006. https://www.cbd.int/convention/articles/?a=cbd-01.

Megadiverse Countries as Providers of Genetic Resources &
Digital Sequence Information

viii The Convention of Biological Diversity., (2016). Decision Adopted by the Conference of the Parties to the Convention on Biological Diversity. Xiii/16 Digital sequence information on genetic resources [online]. The Convention of Biological Diversity. [Viewed 22 June 2020]. Available from: https://www.cbd.int/doc/decisions/cop-13/cop-13-dec-16-en.pdf

ixBöll Heinrich Fundación, (2016). Four Steps Forward and one Step Back in the Global Regulation of Synthetic Biology [online]. Heinrich Böll Stiftung. [Viewed 4 July 2020]. Available from: https://mx.boell.org/es/2016/12/21/cuatro-pasos-adelante-y-uno-hacia-atras-en-la-regulacion- global-de-la-biologia-sintetica
x Toledo M., Manuel V., y Barrera B, N., (2008). La Memoria Biocultural: la importancia ecológica de los saberes tradicionales. Icaria Editorial. Barcelona.

xiA Betancourt., (2016). The Cancun Summits: The Conservation of Biodiversity, Clashing Paradigms and Debate Between the Commercialization and Safeguarding of Nature [online]. Heinrich Böll Stiftung. [Viewed 4 July 2020]. Available from: https://mx.boell.org/es/2016/06/16/las-cumbres-de-cancun-conservacion-de-la-biodiversidad- choque-de-paradigmas-y-debate xii Nuel, C., (2013). Carlos Slim and Bill Gate inaugurate the Centre for the Improvement of Maize and Wheat in Texcoco [online]. Xataka Mexico. [Viewed 4 July 2020]. Available from: https://www.xataka.com.mx/eventos/carlos-slim-y-bill-gates-inauguran-el-centro-de-mejoramiento-del-maiz-y-trigo-en-texcoco xiiiNuel, C., (2013). Carlos Slim and Bill Gate inaugurate the Centre for the Improvement of Maize and Wheat in Texcoco [online]. Xataka Mexico. [Viewed 4 July 2020]. Available from: https://www.xataka.com.mx/eventos/carlos-slim-y-bill-gates-inauguran-el-centro-de- mejoramiento-del-maiz-y-trigo-en-texcoco

iCapturing 'Climate Genes.'" ETC Group, October 21, 2010. https://www.etcgroup. org/content/gene-giants-stockpile-patents-%E2%80%9Cclimate-ready%E2% 80%9D-crops-bid-become-biomassters-0

ii"Food and Climate Change: The Forgotten Link." Grain, September 28, 2011. https://www.grain.org/e/4357Biopiracy of Climate Resilient Seeds

iii Vogel, E., Donat, M. G., Alexander, L. V., Meinshausen, M., Ray, D. K., Karoly, D., Meinshausen, N., & Frieler, K. (2019). The effects of climate extremes on global agricultural yields. Environmental Research Letters, 14(5), 054010. https://doi.org/ 10.1088/1748-9326/ab154b

iv "2017 South Asian Floods." Wikipedia. https://en.wikipedia.org/wiki/2017_South_ Asian_floods

v Van Oort, P. A. J., & Zwart, S. J. (2018). Impacts of climate change on rice production in Africa and causes of simulated yield changes. Global Change Biology, 24(3), 1029–1045. https://doi.org/10.1111/gcb.13967

vi "STRASA Legacy Site - Flood-Tolerant." IRRI STRASA Legacy Site. https://sites. google.com/irri.org/strasalegacy/varietal-releases/submergence

vii Saikat Kumar Basu (2011) Earth grab: geopiracy, the new biomassters and capturing climate genes, by Diana Bronson, Hope Shand, Jim Thomas and Kathy Jo Wetter, Biodiversity, 12:4, 274-275, DOI: 10.1080/14888386.2011.643575viii "Smart Breeding." Greenpeace International, October 28, 2014. https://www. greenpeace.org/international/publication/7075/smart-breeding

ix Le, Vincent. "New Flood-Tolerant Rice Offers Relief for World's Poorest Farmers." The Ronald Laboratory, May 8, 2015. https://cropgeneticsinnovation.ucdavis.edu/ new-flood-tolerant-rice-offers-relief-worlds-poorest-farmers

Biopiracy Case Studies

i Queensland University of Technology. "Golden bananas high in pro-vitamin A developed: Research has produced a golden-orange fleshed banana, rich in pro-vitamin A." ScienceDaily. ScienceDaily, 7 July 2017. https://www.sciencedaily.com/ releases/2017/07/170707095806.htm

ii Quoted in Food Biofortification: no answer to ill-health, starvation or m alnutrition By Bob Phelps http://www.freshfruitportal.com/opinion-biofortification-is-an-obstacle-to-food-justice

iii Navdanya. "GMO Banana Petition – Letter to Prime Minister of India." Seed Freedom, October 5, 2014. https://seedfreedom.info/gmo-banana-petition-letter-to-prime-minister-of-india/iv Mantasa."OUR SEEDS, OUR FUTURE: Strengthening

Indonesia's Food Sovereignty." Seed Freedom, August 14, 2014. https://seedfreedom.info/events/our-seeds-our-future-strengthening-indonesias-food-sovereignty/

v Ibid.

vi"Fraley Lecture Opposition – Iowa, USA." Seed Freedom, November 11, 2014. https://seedfreedom.info/fraley-lecture-opposition-iowa-usa/

viiGalvis, Ana. "Over 57,000 Express Concern with Human Feeding Trials of GMO Bananas." Food First. Last modified November 2, 2016. https://foodfirst.org/over-57000-express-concern-with-human- feeding-trials-of-gmo-bananas/

viii Gmobanana, Seed Freedom, https://seedfreedom.info/tag/gmobanana/

ix Englberger, L., Darnton-Hill, I., Coyne, T., Fitzgerald, M.H. and Marks, G.C. 2003. Carotenoid-rich bananas: A potential food source for alleviating vitamin A deficiency. Food and Nutrition Bulletin 24(4):303-318. http://www.musalit.org/seeMore.php?id=8855

x Coghlan, Andy. "Orange Banana to Boost Kids' Eyes." New Scientist, July 10, 2014. https://www.newscientist.com/article/dn6120-orange-banana-to-boost-kids-eyes/

xi Radford, Tim. "Carrot-like Banana Could Save Lives in the Tropics." The Guardian, July 8, 2004. http://www.theguardian.com/uk/2004/jul/08/research.health

xii "Asupina." The Banana Knowledge Platform of the ProMusa Network. http://www.promusa.org/Asupina

xiii Mlalazi, Bulukani, Welsch, Ralf, Namanya, Priver, Khanna, Harjeet, Gei-jskes, Jason, Harrison, Mark, Harding, Rob, Dale, James, & Bateson, Marion (2012). Isolation and functional characterisation of banana phytoene synthasegenes as potential cisgenes. Planta, 236(5), pp. 1585-1598. https://eprints.qut.edu.au/52937/ & http://eprints.qut.edu.au/52937/1/Mlalazi_2012_-_Accepted_PSY_draft_manuscript_-_ePrints_version.pdf

The Recolonization of Agriculture

i Vidal, John. "Why Is the Gates Foundation Investing in GM Giant Monsanto?". The Guardian, September 29, 2010. http://www.theguardian.com/global-development/poverty-matters/2010/sep/29/gates-foundation-gm-monsanto

ii Schwab, Tim. "Bill Gates's Charity Paradox." The Nation, March 17, 2020. https://www.thenation.com/article/society/bill-gates-foundation-philanthropy/

iii Burwood-Taylor, Louisa. "Bill & Melinda Gates Foundation Makes First Agtech Investment in AgBiome's $34.5m Series B." AgFunderNews, August 20, 2015. https://agfundernews.com/bill-melinda-gates-foundation-first-agtech-investment-agbiome-011.html

iv Vinluan, Frank. "Pivot Bio Gets $70M, Led by Bill Gates's Fund, to Replace Fertilizer - Page 2 of 2." Xconomy. Last modified October 2, 2018. https://xconomy.com/san-francisco/2018/10/02/pivot-bio-gets-70m-led-by-bill-gatess-fund-to-replace-fertilizer/

v "Microsoft e IICA Firmaron Un Acuerdo Para Potenciar El Uso de Tecnología En El Agro | Solo Campo." Last modified December 24, 2018. http://solocampo.com.ar/

index/microsoft-e-iica-firmaron-un-acuerdo-para-potenciar-el-uso-de-tecnologia-en-el-agro/

vi "El IICA y Bayer firman acuerdo para promover seguridad alimentaria en América." Nuevos Papeles, February 7, 2019. https://www.nuevospapeles.com/nota/17625-el-iica-y-bayer-firman-acuerdo-para-promover-seguridad-alimentaria-en-america

vii "Acuerdo entre Corteva Agriscience y el IICA fortalecerá producción de alimentos de calidad en las Américas." Instituto Interamericano de Cooperación Para La Agricultura (IICA), October 31, 2019. https://iica.int/es/prensa/noticias/acuerdo-entre-corteva-agriscience-y-el-iica-fortalecera-produccion-de-alimentos-de

viii "Syngenta y el IICA se unen para impulsar la innovación en la agricultura de las Américas." Instituto Interamericano de Cooperación Para La Agricultura (IICA), July 7, 2020. https://iica.int/es/prensa/noticias/syngenta-y-el-iica-se-unen-para-impulsar-la-innovacion-en-la-agricultura-de-las

ix Curtis, M. 2016. Gated Development: Is the Gates Foundation Always a Force for Good? Second Ed., Global Justice Now. June 2016. Pg. 31. https://www.globaljustice.org.uk/sites/default/files/files/resources/gjn_gates_report_june_2016_web_final_version_2.pdf

x Wise, Timothy A. "AGRA at Ten Years: Searching for Evidence of a Green Revolution in Africa," November 2017. https://afsafrica.org/wp-content/uploads/2019/10/agrawiseprelimfindings2017.pdf

xiSlideshow: Bill Gates on Agricultural Innovations - YouTube, 2009. https://www.youtube.com/watch?v=xXcB8k7Ysk4

xii"Hungry for Land: Small Farmers Feed the World with Less than a Quarter of All Farmland." Grain, May 28, 2014. https://www.grain.org/article/entries/4929-hungry-for-land-small-farmers-feed-the- world-with-less-than-a-quarter-of-all-farmlandxiii HLPE. 2019. Agroecological and other innovative approaches for sustainable agriculture and food systems that enhance food security and nutrition. A report by the High Level Panel of Experts on Food Security and Nutrition of the Committee on World Food Security, Rome. http://www.fao.org/3/ca5602en/ca5602en.pdf

xivAltieri M.A., Nicholls C., Henao A., Lana M., Agroecology and the design of climate change- resilient farming systems, 869 – 890, 35 (3), SN 1773-0155, Springer, Agronomy for Sustainable Development, 2015, https://link.springer.com/article/10.1007/s13593-015-0285-2xv D'Annolfo, Raffaele & Gemmill-Herren, Barbara & Graeub, Benjamin & Garibaldi, Lucas. (2015). Social and economic performance of Agroecology. https://www.researchgate.net/publication/283721240_Social_and_economic_performance_of_Agroecology

xviFAO 2010. The Second Report on the State of the World's Plant Genetic Resources for Food and Agriculture. Rome. http://www.fao.org/3/i1500e/i1500e.pdfxvii How Data-Driven Farming Could Transform Agriculture | Ranveer Chandra | TEDxUniversityof Rochester - YouTube. TEDx TALKS, 2018. https://youtu.be/dpVylFjT-Cw

xviii IPBES (2019): Global assessment report on biodiversity and ecosystem services of the Intergovernmental Science-Policy Platform on Biodiversity and Ecosystem Services. E. S. Brondizio, J. Settele, S. Díaz, and H. T. Ngo (editors). IPBES secretariat, Bonn, Germany. https://ipbes.net/global-assessment

xix Sánchez-Bayo, F., & Wyckhuys, K. A. G. (2019). Worldwide decline of the entomofauna: A review of its drivers. Biological Conservation, 232, 8–27. https://doi.org/10.1016/j.biocon.2019.01.020 Goulson, D., Insect decline and why they matter, Wildlife Trusts, 2019, https://www.somersetwildlife.org/sites/default/files/2019-11/FULL%20AFI%20REPORT%20WEB1_1.pdf; Brain RA, Anderson JC. The agro-enabled urban revolution, pesticides, politics, and popular culture: a case study of land use, birds, and insecticides in the USA. Environ Sci Pollut Res Int. 2019;26(21):21717-21735. doi:10.1007/s11356-019-05305-9, https://pubmed.ncbi.nlm.nih.gov/31129901/; Gabbatiss, J., 'Shocking' decline in birds across Europe due to pesticide use, say scientists, The Independent, 21 march 2018, https://www.independent.co.uk/environment/europe-bird-population-countryside-reduced-pesticides-france-wildlife-cnrs-a8267246.html

xx La Vía Campesina and GRAIN. "Food Sovereignty: Five Steps to Cool the Planet and Feed Its People." Grain, December 15, 2014. https://www.grain.org/article/entries/5102-food-sovereignty-five-steps-to-cool-the-planet-and-feed-its-people

xxi Mateo-Sagasta, J., Marjani Zadeh, S., & Turral, H. (2018). More people, more food... worse water? - Water Pollution from Agriculture: a global review. FAO. http://www.fao.org/documents/card/en/c/CA0146EN ; Rodríguez-Eugenio, N., McLaughlin, M. and Pennock, D. 2018. Soil Pollution: a hidden reality. Rome, FAO. 142 pp. http://www.fao.org/3/I9183EN/i9183en.pdf

xxii "Organic vs Conventional." Rodale Institute. https://rodaleinstitute.org/why-organic/organic- basics/organic-vs-conventional/

xxiii   "Food and Climate Change: The Forgotten Link." Grain, September 28, 2011. https://www.grain.org/e/4357

xxivIbid.xxv Renmatix. "Renmatix Secures $14M Investment from Bill Gates and Total, the Global Energy Major, In Concert with Signing of 1 Million Ton Cellulosic Sugar License," September 15, 2016. https://renmatix.com/uploads/renmatix-bulletin-gates-press-release.pdf

xxvi "Sugar Cane, Palm Oil, and Biofuels in the Amazon." Yale School of the Environment | Global Forest Atlas, n.d. https://globalforestatlas.yale.edu/amazon/land-use-and-agriculture/biofuels

xxvii Ibid.

xxviii Ibid.

xxix Ibid.

xxx Shiva, V. (1991). The Violence of the Green Revolution: Third World Agriculture, Ecology, and Politics. Other India Press. https://books.google.it/books?id=jPNRPgAACAAJ.

xxxi ICTworks. "Digital Technologies Are Part of the Climate Change Problem." *ICTworks*, February 20, 2020. https://www.ictworks.org/digital-technologies-climate-change-problem/

xxxii   Akbar, Syed. "One Agriculture-One Science: Partnership to Revitalize Global Farm Education | India News - Times of India." The Times of India, July 22, 2014. https://timesofindia.indiatimes.com/india/One-agriculture-one-science-Partnership-to-revitalize- global-farm-education/articleshow/38867896.cms

xxxiii "$120 Million-Investment for CRISPR Technology From Bill Gates and Other 13 Investors." CD Genomics, October 16, 2018. https://www.cd-genomics.com/blog/120-million-investment-for-crispr-technology-from-bill-gates-and-other-13-investors/

A Treaty to Protect Our Agricultural Biodiversity

i FAO Newsroom, Treaty on biodiversity to become law, 31 March 2004 - Rome, http://www.fao.org/newsroom/en/news/2004/39887/index.html

Ag Tech: Bill & Melinda Gates Agricultural Innovations in Argentina

i "Microsoft e IICA Firmaron Un Acuerdo Para Potenciar El Uso de Tecnología En El Agro | Solo Campo." Last modified December 24, 2018. http://solocampo.com.ar/index/microsoft-e-iica-firmaron-un-acuerdo-para-potenciar-el-uso-de-tecnologia-en-el-agro/; "El IICA y Bayer firman acuerdo para promover seguridad alimentaria en América." Nuevos Papeles, February 7, 2019. https://www.nuevospapeles.com/nota/17625-el-iica-y-bayer-firman-acuerdo-para-promover-seguridad-alimentaria-en-america; "Acuerdo entre Corteva Agriscience y el IICA fortalecerá producción de alimentos de calidad en las Américas." Instituto Interamericano de Cooperación Para La Agricultura (IICA), October 31, 2019. https://iica.int/es/prensa/noticias/acuerdo-entre-corteva-agriscience-y-el-iica-fortalecera-produccion-de-alimentos-de; "Syngenta y el IICA se unen para impulsar la innovación en la agricultura de las Américas." Instituto Interamericano de Cooperación Para La Agricultura (IICA), July 7, 2020. https://iica.int/es/prensa/noticias/syngenta-y-el-iica-se-unen-para-impulsar-la-innovacion-en-la-agricultura-de-las

ii "Alianzas Estratégicas ." Instituto Interamericano de Cooperación Para La Agricultura (IICA). https://www.iica.int/es/strategic-alliances; "Microsoft y el IICA definieron hoja de ruta para la transformación digital del agro de las Américas." Instituto Interamericano de Cooperación Para La Agricultura (IICA). https://www.iica.int/es/prensa/noticias/microsoft-y-el-iica-definieron-hoja-de-ruta-para-la-transformacion-digital-del-agro; Instituto Interamericano de Cooperación Para La Agricultura (IICA). "Acuerdo Microsoft-IICA Potenciará La Innovación y El Uso de Tecnología En El Sector Del Agro de Las Américas." Laboratorio Nacional de GeoInteligencia (GeoINT), n.d. http://mid.geoint.mx/site/publicacion/id/55.html

iii"Microsoft y el IICA definieron hoja de ruta para la transformación digital del agro de las Américas." Instituto Interamericano de Cooperación Para La Agricultura (IICA).

https://www.iica.int/es/prensa/noticias/microsoft-y-el-iica-definieron-hoja-de-ruta-para-la- transformacion-digital-del-agro ; Instituto Interamericano de Cooperación Para La Agricultura (IICA). "Acuerdo Microsoft-IICA Potenciará La Innovación y El Uso de Tecnología En El Sector Del Agro de Las Américas." Laboratorio Nacional de GeoInteligencia (GeoINT), n.d. http://mid.geoint.mx/site/publicacion/id/55. html iv "El ministro Basterra abrió el ciclo virtual 'El Impacto Científico Tecnológico en el desarrollo del Sector Agropecuario.'" Argentina.gob.ar. Last modified July 1, 2020. https://www.argentina.gob.ar/noticias/el-ministro-basterra-abrio-el-ciclo-virtual-el-impacto-cientifico-tecnologico-en-el

v Loboguerrero, A. M., Birch, J., Thornton, P., Meza, L., Sunga, I., Bong, B. B., Rabbinge, R., Reddy, M., Dinesh, D., Korner, J., Martinez-Baron, D., Millan, A., Hansen, J., Huyer, S., & Campbell, B. (2018). Feeding the world in a changing climate: An adaptation roadmap for agriculture (October 2018). Global Commission on Adaptation. https://cdn.gca.org/assets/2018- 10/18_WP_GCA_Agriculture_1001_Oct5.pdf

vi"La agricultura mundial dispone de un nuevo instrumento para la adaptación efectiva al cambio climático." Instituto Interamericano de Cooperación Para La Agricultura (IICA), October 25, 2018. https://www.iica.int/es/prensa/noticias/la-agricultura-mundial-dispone-de-un-nuevo-instrumento- para-la-adaptaci%25C3%25B3n-efectiva The Golden Rice Hoax

i Everding, Gerry. "Genetically Modified Golden Rice Falls Short on Lifesaving Promises | ." The Source | Washington University in St. Louis, June 2, 2016. https://source.wustl.edu/2016/06/genetically-modified-golden-rice-falls-short-lifesaving-promises/

ii Hilbeck, Angelika, and Hans Herren. "Millions Spent and No Vitamin A Deficiency Relieved." Independent Science News | Food, Health and Agriculture Bioscience News, August 10, 2016. https://www.independentsciencenews.org/health/millions-spent-who-is-to-blame-failure-gmo-golden-rice/

iii U.S. Food & Drug Administration. Biotechnology Notification File No. 000158 | Note to the File. May 8, 2018. https://www.fda.gov/downloads/Food/Ingredients PackagingLabeling/GEPlants/Submissions/ucm6 07450.pdf

iv *0.50-2.35ug/g (FDA 2018a). That is, beta-carotene levels in Golden Rice are both low and variable. This compares to beta-carotene levels measured in non-GMO foods such as fresh carrot (13.8-49.3ug/g6); Asian greens (19.74-66.04 ug/g7); and spinach (111ug/g). FDA notes the mean value of beta-carotene for GR2E is 1.26ug/g. This is, paradoxically, less beta-carotene than the 1.6ug/ g measured for the original iteration of Golden Rice (Ye et al. 2000)."*

v Chandra-Hioe MV, Rahman HH, Arcot J. 2017. Lutein and β-Carotene in Selected Asian Leafy Vegetables. J Food Chem Nanotechol3(3): 93-97.

vi GRAIN, MASIPAG and Stop Golden Rice! Network. "Don't Get Fooled Again! Unmasking Two Decades of Lies about Golden Rice." Grain, November 21, 2018. https://www.grain.org/en/article/6067-don-t-get-fooled-again-unmasking-two-decades-of-lies-about-golden-rice vii Masipag National Office. "Farmer-Scientist Group Deplore Secretive Visit of Bill Gates to IRRI, Golden Rice Commercialization Possible Agenda." Masipag.Org, April 14, 2015. https://masipag.org/2015/04/farmer-scientist-group-deplore-secretive-visit-of-bill-gates-to-irri-golden-rice-commercialization-possible-agenda/

viii Masipag. "Philippines: Corporate science subdues the poor." Grain, July 8, 2016. https://www.grain.org/fr/article/entries/5509-philippines-corporate-science-subdues-the-poor

ix Robinson, Claire. "Pro-GMO Campaign Exploits Nobel Laureates in 'Golden Rice' Greenpeace Attack," July 4, 2016. https://theecologist.org/2016/jul/04/pro-gmo-campaign-exploits-nobel-laureates-golden-rice-greenpeace-attack

x Chow, Lorraine. "Greenpeace to Nobel Laureates: It's Not Our Fault Golden Rice Has 'Failed as a Solution.'" EcoWatch, June 30, 2016. https://www.ecowatch.com/greenpeace-to-nobel-laureates-its-not-our-fault-golden-rice-has-failed-1896697050.html

xi Masipag National Office. "Farmer-Scientist Group Condemns Golden Rice Approval." Masipag.Org, December 19, 2019. https://masipag.org/2019/12/farmer-scientist-group-condemns-golden-rice-approval/

xii Stop Golden Rice Network (SGRN). "Why We Oppose Golden Rice." Independent Science News | Food, Health and Agriculture Bioscience News, August 7, 2020. https://www.independentsciencenews.org/health/why-we-oppose-golden-rice/

xiii Arellano, Elnard. "'Business as Usual' For Agrochemical Industry Damaging To Biodiversity, Farmers." Pesticide Action Network Asia Pacific, May 22, 2020. https://panap.net/2020/05/business-as-usual-for-agrochemical-industry-damaging-to-biodiversity-farmers/xiv Masipag National Office. "Farmers and Consumers Urge Regulatory Body to Halt Golden Rice Release." Masipag.Org, October 16, 2019. http://masipag.org/2019/10/farmers-and-consumers-urge-regulatory-body-to-halt-golden-rice-release/

xv Medina, Charito P. "Comments Regarding Consolidated Report of PHILRICE and IRRI's GR2E Rice Application for Direct Use as Food and Feed, or for Processing," October 16, 2019. https://bioscienceresource.org/wp-content/uploads/2020/03/Golden-Rice_DFFP_Medina-comments.pdf

The Dystopia of the Green Revolution in Africa

i "AGRA." https://agra.org/

ii "GlobalAlliance forImproved Nutrition (GAIN)." https://www.gainhealth.org/homepage

iii Moench-Pfanner R. e Van Ameringen M., "The Global Alliance for Improved Nutrition (GAIN): A decade of partnerships to increase access to and affordability of nutritious foods for the poor", in Food & Nutrition Bulletin, Vol. 33, supplement 3, pp. 373-380.

iv Martens J., and Saetz K., Philanthropic Power and Development: who shapes the agenda?, p. 42.

v Ibid.em, pp. 5-6.

vi AGRA, Planting the Seeds of a Green Revolution in Africa, 2014, https://reliefweb. int/sites/reliefweb.int/files/resources/agrapassreporthires.pdf

vii Rockefeller Foundation, "Africa Turn: the Green Revolution for the 21st Century", White Paper, Rockefeller Foundation, 2006.

viii Ibid. em

ix "Malawi Agrodealer Strengthening Program." CNFA. https://www.cnfa.org/ program/malawi-agrodealer-strengthening-program/

x "About Us." Cultivating New Frontiers in Agriculture (CNFA). https://www.cnfa. org/about-us/

xi Bennet N., "Government ministers should ban Roundup – not sing its praises", in The Guardian, 14 August 2018, https://www.theguardian.com/commentisfree/2018/ aug/14/roundup-government-uk-minister-ban-glyphosate. On the same subject, see also: Gillam C., "Formulations of glyphosate-based weed killers are toxic, tests show", in The Guardian, 23 gennaio 2020, https://www.theguardian.com/business/2020/jan/23/ formulations-glyphosate-based-weedkillers-toxic-tests.

xii Action Aid, Assessing the Alliance for the Green Revolution in Africa, Action Aid International Report, 2009, p. 14.

xiii "Agricultural Development." Bill & Melinda Gates Foundation. https:// www.gatesfoundation.org/What-We-Do/Global-Growth-and-Opportunity/ Agricultural-Development

xiv Daño E., Unmasking the New Green Revolution in Africa: Motives, Players and Dynamics, paper by Church Development Services (EED), Third World Network and African Centre for Biosafety, published by Third World Network, 2007, https://www. twn.my/title2/books/green.revolution.in.africa.htm

xv Voices from Africa: African Farmers & Environmentalists Speak Out Against a New Green Revolution in Africa. Oakland Institute, 2009. https://www.oaklandin- stitute.org/voices-africa-african-farmers-environmentalists-speak-out-against-new- green-revolution-africa

xvi As the Action Aid International report explains, Cfr. Action Aid, Assessing the Alliance for the Green Revolution in Africa, p. 15-16.

xvii "African Agricultural Technology Foundation (AATF)." https://www.aatf-africa. org/

xviii "One Agriculture-One Science': A New Partnership to Revitalize Global Agri- cultural Education." || ICRISAT ||Press Releases 2014. Last modified July 21, 2014. http://www.icrisat.org/newsroom/news-releases/icrisat-pr-2014-media22.htm

xix Martens J. e Seitz K., Philanthropic Power and Development, op. cit. pp. 50-52.

xx Rock J., "We are not starving". Challenging Genetically Modified Seeds and Devel- opment in Ghana", in Culture, Agriculture, Food and Environment. The Journal of Culture and Agriculture, Vol. 41, Issue 1, June 2019, pp. 15-33, https://anthrosource. onlinelibrary.wiley.com/doi/full/10.1111/cuag.12147 .

xxi McKeon N., Food Security Governance: Empowering Communities, Regulating Corporations, Routledge, London and New York, 2015, pp. 13-30.

xxii "Ghana Has New Biosafety Law." Afri-Law, May 31, 2015. https://www.afri-law.com/ghana-has-new-biosafety-law/

xxiii Bill & Melinda Gates Foundation, Agricultural Development Grant Overview, 2011, https://docs.gatesfoundation.org/documents/agricultural-development-grant-overview.pdf Curtis M., Gated Development, op. cit, p. 36.

xxiv Mcintyre, Beverly & Herren, Hans & Wakhungu, Judi & Watson, Robert. (2009). Agriculture at a Crossroads: The Global Report. https://www.researchgate.net/publication/258099731_Agriculture_at_a_Crossroads_The_Global_Report

i Wise, Timothy A.. "Failing Africa's Farmers: New Report Shows Africa's Green Revolution Is Failing on Its Own Terms."" Global Development and Environment Institute - TuftsUniversity, July 2020. Working PaperNo.20-01.https://sites.tufts.edu/gdae/files/2020/07/20-01_Wise_FailureToYield.pdf

ii Mkindi, A. R., Maina, A., Urhahn, J., Koch, J., Bassermann, L., Goïta, M., Nketani, M., Herre, R., Tanzmann, S., Wise, T. A., Gordon, M., & Gilbert, R. (2020). False promises: The alliance for a green revolution in africa (Agra). Biodiversity and Biosafety Association of Kenya(BIBA), Brot für die Welt, FIAN Germany, German NGO Forum on Environment and Development, INKOTA-netzwerk e.V., Institut de Recherche et de Promotion des Alternatives en Développement (IRPAD), PELUM Zambia, Rosa Luxemburg Stiftung Southern Africa, Tanzania Alliance for Biodiversity (TABIO), Organic Agriculture Movement (TOAM). https://www.rosalux.de/en/publication/id/42635 The Gates Foundation's Green Revolution Fails Africa's Farmers

iii Pretty, J. N., Noble, A. D., Bossio, D., Dixon, J., Hine, R. E., Penning de Vries, F. W. T., & Morison, J. I. L. (2006). Resource-conserving agriculture increases yields in developing countries. Environmental Science & Technology, 40(4), 1114–1119. https://doi.org/10.1021/es051670d

Seeds of Surveillance Capitalism

i Trotter, Greg. (2016). Monsanto venture capital group brings tech-world approach to agribusiness. Chicago Tribune. Available at: http://www.startribune.com/monsanto-venture-capital-group-brings-tech-world-approach-to-agribusiness/407653476/

ii Zuboff, S. (2019). The age of surveillance capitalism: The fight for a human future at the new frontier of power. Profile Books. Pg. 15

iii Ahuja, A. 2018. CropIn Technology raises $8 million from Chiratae Ventures, Gates Foundation. Livemint. Available at: www.livemint.com/Companies/X5TRE10YbgUlqgvhN2IDBL/CropIn-Technology-raises-8-million-from-Chiratae-Ventures.html. Accessed on 20 August 2019.

iv Economic Times. 2019. SaaS-based agri-tech company CropIn registers 300% growth. Available at: https://economictimes.indiatimes.com/small-biz/startups/newsbuzz/saas-based-agri-tech-company-cropin-registers-300-growth/articleshow/68147881.cms?from=mdr. Accessed on 23 August, 2019. v How CropIn is helping the farmer ecosystem. 2018. Available at: http://smartceo.co/cropin-helping-farmer-ecosystem/. Accessed on 28th August 2019.

The Problems with Lab Made Food

i "Food for Health Manifesto." Navdanya International, May 1, 2019. https://navdanyainternational.org/publications/manifesto-food-for-health/

ii CDC. "CDC and Breastfeeding." Centers for Disease Control and Prevention. Last modified August 14, 2020. https://www.cdc.gov/breastfeeding/index.htm

iii "Improving Breastfeeding, Complementary Foods and Feeding Practices." UNICEF. https://www.unicef.org/nutrition/index_breastfeeding.html

iv "IBFAN – International Baby Foods Action Network," n.d. https://www.ibfan.org/

v Brady, June Pauline. "Marketing Breast Milk Substitutes: Problems and Perils throughout the World." Archives of Disease in Childhood 97, no. 6 (March 14, 2012): 529–532, https://www.ncbi.nlm.nih.gov/pmc/articles/PMC3371222/;WHO. "Countries Failing to Stop Harmful Marketing of Breast-Milk Substitutes, Warn WHO and UNICEF." Last modified May 27, 2020. https://www.who.int/news-room/detail/27-05-2020-countries-failing-to-stop-harmful-marketing-of-breast-milk-substitutes-warn-who-and-unicef

vi Roy, Aditi. "Bill Gates' Climate-Change Investment Firm Bets on Lab-Produced Breast Milk." CNBC. Last modified June 16, 2020. https://www.cnbc.com/2020/06/16/biomilq-raises-3point5-million-from-bill-gates-investment-firm.html; "Mother Cultured Breastmilk | BIOMILQ | United States." BIOMILQ. https://www.biomilq.com

vii Watson, Elaine,. "BIOMILQ Raises $3.5m to Fund Mammary Cell-Cultured Human Breastmilk Platform, Disrupt Infant Nutrition Market." Foodnavigator-Usa.Com. Last modified June 16, 2020. https://www.foodnavigator-usa.com/Article/2020/06/16/BIOMILQ-raises-3.5m-to-fund-mammary-cell-cultured-human-breastmilk-platform-disrupt-infant-nutrition-market

viii Shiva, Vandana. "Fake Food, Fake Meat: Big Food's Desperate Attempt to Further the Industrialisation of Food." Navdanya International, June 18, 2019. https://navdanyainternational.org/fake-food-fake-meat-big-foods-desperate-attempt-to-further-the-industrialisation-of-food/

ix "Engineering an Environmental Disaster." Earthjustice. Last modified March 27, 2015. https://earthjustice.org/features/engineering-an-environmental-disaster-2

x Ellis, Glenn. "Argentina's Bad Seeds." Al Jazeera. Last modified March 14, 2013. https://www.aljazeera.com/programmes/peopleandpower/2013/03/201331313434142322.html; Shiva, Vandana. "The Pulse of Life." The Asian Age. Last modified January 27, 2016. http://www.asianage.com/columnists/pulse-life-681

xi Honeycutt, Zen. "GMO Impossible Burger Positive for Carcinogenic Glyphosate." Moms Across America. Last modified May 16, 2019. https://www.momsacrossamerica.com/gmo_impossible_burger_positive_for_carcinogenic_glyphos ate

xii Benbrook, Charles M. "Trends in Glyphosate Herbicide Use in the United States and Globally." Environmental Sciences Europe 28, no. 1 (February 2, 2016): 3. https://enveurope.springeropen.com/articles/10.1186/s12302-016-0070-0

xiii Shiva, Vandana. "Biodiversity , GMOs, & Gene Drives of the Militarised Mind." Seed Freedom. Last modified July 7, 2016. https://seedfreedom.info/

biodiversity-gmos-gene-drives-of-the-militarised-mind/https://seedfreedom.info/
biodiversity-gmos-gene-drives-of-the-militarised-mind/

xiv Mitroff, Sarah. "Where to Get the Impossible Burger: Red Robin, Burger King,
White Castle, Little Caesars and More." CNET. https://www.cnet.com/health/
where-to-buy-the-impossible-burger-2-0-fast-food-and-chain-restaurants/

xv Shiva, Vandana. "Monsanto vs Indian Farmers." Seed Freedom. Last modified
March 27, 2016. https://seedfreedom.info/monsanto-vs-indian-farmers/; "Patents
Assigned to Monsanto Technology LLC -Justia Patents Search". https://patents.justia.
com/assignee/monsanto-technology-llc

xvi Itzkan, Seth. "Opinion: Software to Swallow — Impossible Foods Should Be
Called Impossible Patents." Medium. Last modified May 27, 2020. https://medium.
com/@sethitzkan/opinion-software-to-swallow-impossible-foods-should-be-called-
impossible-patents-71805ececode

xvii "Bayer Sees Potential Future Business in Plant-Based Meat Market."   Reuters,   August   1,   2019.   https://www.reuters.com/article/
us-bayer-agriculture-food-idUSKCN1UR5SF

xviii Pointing, Charlotte. "Vegan Meat Category Is a '$3 Trillion Opportunity.'" LIVE-
KINDLY, March 6, 2019. https://www.livekindly.co/vegan-meat-category-3-trillion-
opportunity/

xix "Poison-Free Food and Farming 2030." Navdanya International, January 30,
2019. https://navdanyainternational.org/cause/poison-free-food-and-farming-2030/;
Hedlund, Baum. "Roundup Cancer Study Summaries | Glyphosate Linked to Health
Issues." Baum Hedlund, n.d. https://www.baumhedlundlaw.com/toxic-tort-law/mon-
santo-roundup-lawsuit/roundup-cancer-study/ .

xx Shiva, Vandana. "Ecological Reflections on the Corona Virus." Jivad – The Vandana
Shiva Blog, March 18, 2020. https://www.navdanya.org/bija-refelections/2020/03/18/
ecological-reflections-on-the-corona-virus/

xxi "Organic Diet Intervention Significantly Reduces Urinary Glyphosate Levels in
U.S. Children and Adults." Environmental Research (August 11, 2020): 109898.

Bill Gates' Climate "Solutions": Funding for Geoengineering

i "Innovating to Zero! | Bill Gates - YouTube." https://www.youtube.com/watch?v=JaF-
fq2Zn7I

ii The Planet Remade: How Geoengineering Could Change the World, by Oliver
Morton (2015), page 102

iii "Crude-by-Rail Shipments Hit Record High over 400,000 Bpd in January."
630CHED.   https://globalnews.ca/news/6708937/crude-by-rail-shipments-hit-
record-high-over-400000-bpd-in-january/

v "Lac-Mégantic Rail Disaster." Wikipedia, July 25, 2020. https://en.wikipedia.org/w/
index.php?title=Lac-M%C3%A9gantic_rail_disaster&oldid=969494782

vi "Federal Govt. Should Respect Labour Rights in CN Strike | National Union of
Public and General Employees." https://nupge.ca/content/federal-govt-should-
respect-labour-rights-cn-strike

vii "Cascade Investment." Wikipedia, June 16, 2020. https://en.wikipedia.org/w/index.php?title=Cascade_Investment&oldid=962804357

viii "CNI - Canadian National Railway Co Shareholders - CNNMoney.Com." https://money.cnn.com/quote/shareholders/shareholders.html?symb=CNI&subView=institutional

ix "CNR Dividend Yield, History & Payout Ratio (Canadian National Railway)." https://www.marketbeat.com/stocks/TSE/CNR/dividend/; Cascadia holds 101,400,770 shares; Bill and Melinda Gates Foundation holds 17,126,874 shares, for a total of 118,527,644 shares. At an annual dividend of CAD$2.19 per share, that's around US$190 million (based on conversion rates of July 15, 2020).

x "Crude-by-Rail and Container Traffic Push CN Rail to Record Revenues of Nearly $4B." Global News. https://globalnews.ca/news/5675640/record-cn-revenues-crude-by-rail/

xi "Microsoft's Climate Bullshit | REDD-Monitor." https://redd-monitor.org/2020/03/29/microsofts-climate-bullshit/

xii "Azure for Energy | Microsoft Azure." https://azure.microsoft.com/en-ca/industries/energy/

xiii Wood, Charlie. "An Anonymous Microsoft Engineer Appears to Have Written a Chilling Account of How Big Oil Might Use Tech to Track Its Workers' Every Move." Business Insider. https://www.businessinsider.com/microsoft-engineer-says-big-oil-surveilling-oil-workers-using-tech-2019-11

xiv 118,527,644 shares at a value of CAD$125.06 is CAD$14.8 billion, or US$10.9 billion (based on share prices and conversion rates of July 15, 2020).

xv Fiona Harvey Environment correspondent, "What Is the Carbon Bubble and What Will Happen If It Bursts?" The Guardian, June 4, 2018, sec. Environment. https://www.theguardian.com/environment/2018/jun/04/what-is-the-carbon-bubble-and-what-will-happen-if-it-bursts

xvi "Fuel to the Fire: How Geoengineering Threatens to Entrench Fossil Fuels and Accelerate the Climate Crisis (Feb 2019)." Center for International Environmental Law, n.d. https://www.ciel.org/reports/fuel-to-the-fire-how-geoengineering-threatens-to-entrench-fossil-fuels-and-accelerate-the-climate-crisis-feb-2019/

xvii "Microsoft Will Be Carbon Negative by 2030." The Official Microsoft Blog. Last modified January 16, 2020. https://blogs.microsoft.com/blog/2020/01/16/microsoft-will-be-carbon-negative-by-2030/

xviii Hamilton, Clive. "The Clique That Is Trying to Frame the Global Geoengineering Debate | Clive Hamilton." The Guardian. Last modified December 5, 2011. http://www.theguardian.com/environment/2011/dec/05/clique-geoengineering-debate

xix "Fund for Innovative Climate and Energy Research." https://keith.seas.harvard.edu/FICER

xx Vidal, John, environment editor. "Bill Gates Backs Climate Scientists Lobbying for Large-Scale Geoengineering." The Guardian, February 6, 2012, sec. Environment. https://www.theguardian.com/environment/2012/feb/06/bill-gates-climate-scientists-geoengineering

xxi "SRMGI – Solar Radiation Management Governance Initiative Is an International, NGO-Driven Project That Seeks to Expand the Global Conversation around the Governance of SRM Geoengineering Research," n.d. https://www.srmgi.org/

xxii Blackstock, J. J., D. S. Battisti, K. Caldeira, D. M. Eardley, J. I. Katz, D. W. Keith, A. A. N. Patrinos, D. P. Schrag, R. H. Socolow, and S. E. Koonin. "Climate Engineering Responses to Climate Emergencies." arXiv:0907.5140 [physics] (July 31, 2009). http://arxiv.org/abs/0907.5140

xxiii The Planet Remade: How Geoengineering Could Change the World, by Oliver Morton (2015), page 102

xxiv "David Keith - The Colbert Report (Video Clip)." Comedy Central. http://www.cc.com/video-playlists/kw3fjo/the-opposition-with-jordan-klepper-welcome-to-the-opposition-w--jordan-klepper/lvohd2

xxv "Superfreakonomics: Everything You Know about Global Warming Is Wrong." Carolina Huddle. https://www.carolinahuddle.com/boards/topic/34241-superfreak-onomics-everything-you-know-about-global-warming-is-wrong/

xxvi "NotOnlyIstheWarmingHidingintheOcean,It'sHidingintheFutureToo."WattsUp With That? Last modified October 1, 2013. https://wattsupwiththat.com/2013/09/30/not-only-is-the-warming-hiding-in-the-ocean-its-hiding-in-the-future-too/

xxvii "What If the Most Vulnerable Nations Decided to Hack the Climate?" Undark Magazine. Last modified July 18, 2016. https://undark.org/2016/07/18/plan-b-for-bangladesh-geoengineering-climate-change/

xxviii "Climate Science » Intellectual Ventures Lab." Last modified March 11, 2013. https://web.archive.org/web/20130311145011/http:/intellectualventureslab.com/?page_id=258

xxix Ibid.em

xxx Gates, Bill. "Is There a Crisis in Capitalism?" Gatesnotes.Com. https://www.gatesnotes.com/Books/The-Future-of-Capitalism

Driven to Exterminate: How Bill Gates Brought Gene Drive Extinction Technology Into the World

i "Self-Sustaining." Target Malaria | Our Work. https://targetmalaria.org/our-work/self-sustaining/

ii Dunning, Hayley . "Malaria Mosquitoes Eliminated in Lab by Creating All-Male Populations." Imperial College London | News, May 11, 2020. https://www.imperial.ac.uk/news/197394/malaria-mosquitoes-eliminated-creating-all-male-populations/

iii Regalado, Antonio. "Bill Gates Is Betting Big on a Technology That Could Make MosquitoesExtinct." Business Insider | MIT Technology Review , September 7, 2016. https://www.businessinsider.com/bill-gates-foundation-gene-drive-kill-mosquitoes-2016-9; "Gene Drive Files Expose Leading Role of US Military in Gene Drive Development." Gene Drive Files | Synbiowatch. Ref. 3. http://genedrivefiles.synbiowatch.org/2017/12/01/us-military-gene-drive-development/#3

iv O'Mahony, Jennifer. "Science Moves Closer to Killing Malaria with Mutant Mosquitos." Wired UK, n.d. https://www.wired.co.uk/article/mosquito-gene-drive-malaria

v Esvelt KM, Smidler AL, Catteruccia F, Church GM. Concerning RNA-guided gene drives for the alteration of wild populations. Elife. 2014;3 pii:e03401 10.7554/eLife.0340. https://www.ncbi.nlm.nih.gov/pmc/articles/PMC4117217/

vi Perkes, Courtney . "UCI Mosquito Project Receives $2 Million from Gates Foundation to Fight Malaria." Orange County Register, May 10, 2017. https://www.

ocregister.com/2017/05/09/uci-mosquito-project-receives-2-million-from-gates-foundation-to-fight-malaria/

vii Kotecki, Peter. "Mosquito-Borne Diseases Kill Millions of People Each Year. A Team of Scientists Think Genetic Manipulation Could Wipe out the Worst of Them." Business Insider, January 16, 2019. https://www.businessinsider.com/target-malaria-wants-to-end-mosquito-borne-disease-using-gene-drives-2019-

viii "Search Results 'Gene Drive.'" Bill & Melinda Gates Foundation. https://www.gatesfoundation.org/search#q/k=%22gene%20drive%22

ix Thomas, Jim. "What Is Synthetic Biology?" ETC Group, n.d. https://www.etcgroup.org/sites/www.etcgroup.org/files/files/synbio_comics-complete_letter_size_rev.pdf

x "Synthetic Biology Explained." Biotechnology Innovation Organization. https://www.bio.org/articles/synthetic-biology-explained

xi Levy, Steven. "Geek Power: Steven Levy Revisits Tech Titans, Hackers, Idealists." Wired, April 19, 2010. https://www.wired.com/2010/04/ff_hackers/5/

xii Kanellos, Michael. "Gates Foundation to Promote Synthetic Biology." CNET. Last modified November 12, 2005. https://www.cnet.com/news/gates-foundation-to-promote-synthetic-biology/

xiii Kanellos, Michael. "Gates Foundation to Promote Synthetic Biology." ZDNet. Last modified November 18, 2005. https://www.zdnet.com/article/gates-foundation-to-promote-synthetic-biology/

xiv Sanders, Robert. "Launch of Antimalarial Drug a Triumph for UC Berkeley, Synthetic Biology." Berkeley News, April 11, 2013. https://news.berkeley.edu/2013/04/11/launch-of-antimalarial-drug-a-triumph-for-uc-berkeley-synthetic-biology/

xv Thomas, Jim. "Synthetic Anti-Malaria Compound Is Bad News for Artemisia Farmers | Jim Thomas." The Guardian, April 12, 2013. http://www.theguardian.com/global-development/poverty-matters/2013/apr/12/synthetic-malaria-compound-artemisia-farmers

xvi Peplow, Mark. "Synthetic Biology's First Malaria Drug Meets Market Resistance." Nature News 530, no. 7591 (February 23, 2016): 389. https://www.nature.com/news/synthetic-biology-s-first-malaria-drug-meets-market-resistance-1.19426

xvii Cumbers, John. "Meet Eight Tech Titans Investing In Synthetic Biology." Forbes. Last modified September 14, 2019. https://www.forbes.com/sites/johncumbers/2019/09/14/meet-the-8-tech-titans-investing-in-synthetic-biology/

xviii ETC Group. "Forcing the Farm," October 2018. https://www.etcgroup.org/sites/www.etcgroup.org/files/files/etc_hbf_forcing_the_farm_web.pdf

xix National Academies of Sciences, Engineering, and Medicine. (2016). Gene Drives on the Horizon: Advancing Science, Navigating Uncertainty, and Aligning Research with Public Values. The National Academies Press. https://doi.org/10.17226/23405

xx "Person Overview ‹ Kevin Esvelt." MIT Media Lab. https://www.media.mit.edu/people/esvelt/overview/

xxi Farrow, Ronan. "How an Élite University Research Center Concealed Its Relationship with Jeffrey Epstein." The New Yorker. Last modified September 7, 2019. https://www.newyorker.com/news/news-desk/how-an-elite-university-research-center-concealed-its-relationship-with-jeffrey-epstein xxii "Gates Foundation Paid PR Firm to Secretly Stack Expert Process on Controversial Extinction Technology." Gene Drive Files | Synbiowatch, December 1, 2017. http://genedrivefiles.synbiowatch.org/2017/12/01/gates_foundation_pr/

xxiii "160 Global Groups Call for Moratorium on New Genetic Extinction Technology at UN Convention." SynBioWatch. Last modified December 5, 2016. http://www.synbiowatch.org/2016/12/160-global-groups-call-for-moratorium-on-new-genetic-extinction-technology-at-un-convention/

xxiv "About." Outreach Network for Gene Drive Research. https://genedrivenetwork.org/#about

xxv "Do Not Betray Africa on SynBio and Gene Drives." ETC Group. Last modified November 19, 2018. https://www.etcgroup.org/content/do-not-betray-africa-synbio-and-gene-drives

xxvi Gakpo, Joseph Opoku . "Africa Kicks against Proposed Gene Drive Moratorium at UN Biodiversity Conference." Alliance for Science, November 20, 2018. https://allianceforscience.cornell.edu/blog/2018/11/africa-kicks-proposed-gene-drive-moratorium-un-biodiversity-conference/

xxvii Brown, Evan Nicole. "How Algeria and Argentina Became Officially Malaria-Free." Atlas Obscura. Last modified May 30, 2019. http://www.atlasobscura.com/articles/algeria-argentina-malaria-free

Gates Foundation Hired a Public Relations Firm to Manipulate the UN Over Gene Drives

i "Emerging Ag Inc." https://emergingag.com/

ii Thomas, Jim. "The National Academies' Gene Drive Study Has Ignored Important and Obvious Issues." *The Guardian*, June 9, 2016, sec. Science. https://www.theguardian.com/science/political-science/2016/jun/09/the-national-academies-gene-drive-study-has-ignored-important-and-obvious-issues

iii "Agricultural Retail and Technology News." CropLife. https://www.croplife.com/
5 "Index of /Webdump/Genedrivefiles." http://www.pricklyresearch.com/webdump/genedrivefiles/

iv "Synthetic Biology." *J. Craig Venter Institute*. https://www.jcvi.org/research/synthetic-biology#team

v 7 Ibid.

vi "Prickly Research." http://www.pricklyresearch.com/

vii Callaway, Ewen. "Gene Drive Moratorium Shot Down at UN Meeting." *Scientific American*. Last modified December 22, 2016. https://www.scientificamerican.com/article/gene-drive-moratorium-shot-down-at-un-meeting/

viii "A Call for Conservation with a Conscience: No Place for Gene Drives in Conservation," September 2016. http://www.synbiowatch.org/wp-content/uploads/2016/09/letter_vs_genedrives.pdf

ix Latham, Jonathan. "Gene Drives: A Scientific Case for a Complete and Perpetual Ban." *Independent Science News | Food, Health and Agriculture Bioscience News*. Last modified February 13, 2017. https://www.independentsciencenews.org/environment/gene-drives-a-scientific-case-for-a-complete-and-perpetual-ban/

x "Agriculture and Food Systems Institute – Science to Enable Safe and Sustainable Agri-Food Systems." https://foodsystems.org/

xi Swetlitz, Ike, and STAT. "A Revolutionary Genetic Experiment Is Planned for a West African Village–If Residents Agree." *Scientific American*. Last modified March 14, 2017. https://www.scientificamerican.com/article/a-revolutionary-genetic-experiment-is-planned-for-a-west-african-village-if-residents-agree/

xii "20170601-Re_CBD Follow up -Reminder of Our Call Friday 2 June-240 (N0024131xC1D49)."PricklyResearch,GeneDriveFiles.http://www.pricklyresearch.com/webdump/genedrivefiles/20170601-Re_CBD%20follow%20up%20-%20reminder%20of%20our%20call%20Friday%202%20June-240%20%28N0024131xC1D49%29.PDF

xiii "20170530-Re_CBD Follow up -Reminder of Our Call Friday 2 June-136 (N0024130xC1D49)."PricklyResearch,GeneDriveFiles.http://www.pricklyresearch.com/webdump/genedrivefiles/20170530-Re_CBD%20follow%20up%20-%20reminder%20of%20our%20call%20Friday%202%20June-136%20%28N0024130xC1D49%29.PDF

xiv "Gates Foundation Grants Additional $6.4million to Cornell's Controversial Alliance for Science." *Independent Science News | Food, Health and Agriculture Bioscience News*. Last modified November 1, 2017. https://www.independentsciencenews.org/news/gates-foundation-grants-additional-6-4million-to-cornells-controversial-alliance-for-science/

xv HOW PUBLIC ARE THE PUBLIC RESEARCH LOBBYISTS OF PRRI? Corporate Europe Observatory, Briefing for COP/MOP, Bonn, 2008. https://corporateeurope.org/sites/default/files/sites/default/files/resource/prri.pdf

xvi "FOIA CFIA Syn Bio – PRRI Back up AHTEG." *Gene Drive Files -Synbiowatch*. http://genedrivefiles.synbiowatch.org/foia-cfia-syn-bio-prri-back-up-ahteg/

xvii "Piet van Der Meer." *IPBO VIB-UGent*, n.d. http://ipbo.

Targeting Palmer Amaranth: A Traditionally Nutritious and Culturally Significant Crop

i National Academies of Sciences, Engineering. *Gene Drives on the Horizon: Advancing Science, Navigating Uncertainty, and Aligning Research with Public Values*, 2016. https://www.nap.edu/catalog/23405/gene-drives-on-the-horizon-advancing-science-navigating-uncertainty-and

ii Thomas, Jim. "The National Academies' Gene Drive Study Has Ignored Important and Obvious Issues." *The Guardian*, June 9, 2016, sec. Science. https://www.theguardian.com/science/political-science/2016/jun/09/the-national-academies-gene-drive-study-has-ignored-important-and-obvious-issues

iii "Meet the Moralist Policing Gene Drives, a Technology That Messes with Evolution." *MIT Technology Review*. Last modified June 7, 2016. https://www.technologyreview.com/2016/06/07/8151/meet-the-moralist-policing-gene-drives-a-technology-that-messes-with-evolution/

iv Committee on Gene Drive Research in Non-Human Organisms: Recommendations for Responsible Conduct; Board on Life Sciences; Division on Earth and Life Studies; National Academies of Sciences, Engineering, and Medicine. Gene Drives on the Horizon: Advancing Science, Navigating Uncertainty, and Aligning Research with Public Values. Washington (DC): National Academies Press (US); 2016 Jul 28. 3, Case Studies to Examine Questions About Gene-Drive Modified Organisms. Available from: https://www.ncbi.nlm.nih.gov/books/NBK379273/

v Committee on Gene Drive Research in Non-Human Organisms: Recommendations for Responsible Conduct; Board on Life Sciences; Division on Earth and Life Studies; National Academies of Sciences, Engineering, and Medicine. Gene Drives on the Horizon: Advancing Science, Navigating Uncertainty, and Aligning Research with Public Values. Washington (DC): National Academies Press (US); 2016 Jul 28. 4, Charting Human Values. Available from: https://www.ncbi.nlm.nih.gov/books/NBK379278/

vi Ibid.

vii Ibid.

viii Janssen, Frederik, Anneleen Pauly, Ine Rombouts, Koen J. A. Jansens, Lomme J. Deleu, and Jan A.Delcour. "Proteins of Amaranth (Amaranthus Spp.), Buckwheat (Fagopyrum Spp.), and Quinoa(Chenopodium Spp.): A Food Science and Technology Perspective." *Comprehensive Reviews inFood Science and Food Safety* 16, no. 1 (2017): 39–58. https://onlinelibrary.wiley.com/doi/full/10.1111/1541-4337.12240;

Muchuweti, M & Kasiamhuru, A & Benhura, Mudadi & Chipurura, Batsirai & Amuna, Paul & Zotor,Francis & Parawira, Wilson. (2009). Assessment of the Nutritional Value of Wild Leafy VegetablesConsumed in the Buhera District of Zimbabwe: a Preliminary Study. Acta horticulturae. 10.17660/ActaHortic.2009.806.40.

https://www.researchgate.net/publication/233741670_Assessment_of_the_Nutritional_Value_of_Wild_Leafy_Vegetables_Consumed_in_the_Buhera_District_of_Zimbabwe_a_Preliminary_Study;

Sarker, Umakanta, and Shinya Oba. "Nutrients, Minerals, Pigments, Phytochemicals, and RadicalScavenging Activity in Amaranthus Blitum Leafy Vegetables." *Scientific Reports* 10, no. 1 (March 2,2020): 1–9. https://www.nature.com/articles/s41598-020-59848-w'

"HORT 281 :: Lecture 31 :: ORIGIN, AREA, PRODUCTION, VARIETIES, PACKAGE OF PRACTICES FOR

AMARANTHUS, PALAK AND GOGU." *Development of E-Courses for B.Sc (Agriculture)*.http://eagri.org/eagri50/HORT281/lec31.html

ix Loria, Kevin. "Bill Gates and Others Just Invested $120 Million in a Revolutionary Medical Startup." *Business Insider*. Last modified August 10, 2015. https://www.businessinsider.com/bill-gates-and-others-invest-in-editas-for-crispr-gene-editing-2015-8

x "Bayer Forms Gene Editing Partnership with CRISPR Therapeutics." *Reuters*, December 21, 2015. https://www.reuters.com/article/us-bayer-genetics-crispr-idUSKBN0U41US20151221

Global Resistance to Genetic Extinction Technology

i "Gene Drive Extinction Technology Is a War against the Planet and Biodiversity." Navdanya International, December 7, 2017. https://navdanyainternational.org/gene-drive-extinction-technology/

ii "160 Global Groups Call for Moratorium on New Genetic Extinction Technology at UN Convention." SynBioWatch, December 5, 2016. http://www.synbiowatch. org/2016/12/160-global-groups-call-for-moratorium-on-new-genetic-extinction-technology-at-un-convention/

iii "Call for a Global Moratorium on Gene Drives." SynBioWatch. http://www.synbio-watch.org/gene-drives/gene-drives-moratorium/

iv "ENB Report | CBD COP 13 | 2-18 December 2016 | Cancún, MX | IISD Reporting Services." http://enb.iisd.org/vol09/enb09678e.html

v "Gene Drive Files Reveal Covert Lobbying Tactics to Influence UN Expert Group." Corporate Europe Observatory, December 3, 2017. https://corporateeurope.org/ en/food-and-agriculture/2017/12/gene-drive-files-reveal-covert-lobbying-tactics-influence-un-expert

vi Court of Justice of the European Union, PRESS RELEASE No111/18, Luxembourg, 25 July 2018, Judgment in Case C-528/16, https://curia.europa.eu/jcms/upload/docs/ application/pdf/2018-07/cp180111en.pdf

vii Antoniou, Michael. "The EU Must Not De-Regulate Gene-Edited Crops and Foods." Www.Euractiv.Com, July 9, 2019. https://www.euractiv.com/section/agriculture-food/ opinion/the-eu-must-not-de-regulate-gene-edited-crops-and-foods/

viii ENSSER Statement on New Genetic Modification Techniques: Products of new genetic modification techniques should be strictly regulated as GMOs, European Network of Scientists for Social and Environmental Responsibility, 27 September 2017, https://ensser.org/publications/ngmt-statement/

ix "Open Letter to EU Commission to Support International Moratorium on Gene Drives." Navdanya International, October 26, 2018. https://navdanyainternational. org/gene-drives-morat-eu/

x "A Human Rights Analysis of Gene Drives." FIAN International, November 14, 2018. http://fian.org/en/publication/article/a-human-rights-analysis-of-gene-drives-2327

xi "Open Letter: We Need a Global Moratorium on the Release of Gene Drive Organisms." Friends of the Earth Europe, June 30, 2020. http://www.foeeurope.org/ global-moratorium-release-gene-drive-organisms

xii Citizen Action: https://www.gmfreeze.org/current-actions/ask-ministers-to-reject-plans-toderegulate-genome-editing/ Action briefing: https://www.gmfreeze. org/publications/action-briefing-on-agriculture-billamendment-to-de-regulate-genome-editing/

Political briefing: https://beyond-gm.org/wp-content/uploads/2020/07/Genome-Editing-_Ag-Bill_Political-Briefing_030720-FINAL_updated.pdf

xiii Amendment number 275 to Agriculture HL Bill (2019-21) 112 (i). https:// publications.parliament.uk/pa/bills/lbill/58-01/112/5801112(i).pdf

xiv "GE Deregulation Amendment Is Withdrawn – but There Is More Work to Do." Beyond GM. Last modified July 29, 2020. https://beyond-gm.org/ ge-deregulation-amendment-is-withdrawn-but-there-is-more-work-to-do/

xv "Emerging Ag Inc." https://emergingag.com/

xvi Thomas, Jim. "The National Academies' Gene Drive Study Has Ignored Important and Obvious Issues." *The Guardian*, June 9, 2016, sec. Science. https://www. theguardian.com/science/political-science/2016/jun/09/the-national-academies-gene-drive-study-has-ignored-important-and-obvious-issues xvii "BT Cotton Failure Case Witnesses from India and Burkina Faso." *P_e_o_p_l_e_'s_ _A_s_s_e_m_b_l_y_*, November 2, 2016. https://peoplesassembly. net/bt-cotton-failure-case-witnesses-from-india-and-burkina-faso/

xviii "BT Cotton Failure Case Witnesses from India and Burkina Faso." People's Assembly, November 2, 2016. https://peoplesassembly.net/bt-cotton-failure-case-witnesses-from-india-and-burkina-faso/

xix "Target Malaria," https://targetmalaria.org/

xx McKemey, Andrew. "Virtual Tours of Target Malaria's Insectaries to Celebrate World Mosquito Day." Target Malaria, August 20, 2020. https://targetmalaria.org/virtual-tours-of-target-malarias-insectaries-to-celebrate-world-mosquito-day/

xxi Gakpo , Joseph Opoku. "African Scientists Confident GMO Mosquitoes Will Be Game Changer in Fight to Control Malaria." Alliance for Science. Last modified September 13, 2018. https://allianceforscience.cornell.edu/blog/2018/09/african-scientists-confident-gmo-mosquitoes-will-game-changer-fight-control-malaria/

xxii "Civil Society Denounces the Release of GM Mosquitoes in Burkina Faso." ETC Group, July 2, 2019. https://www.etcgroup.org/content/civil-society-denounces-release-gm-mosquitoes-burkina-faso

xxiii Afrane, Y. A., Bonizzoni, M., & Yan, G. (2016). Secondary malaria vectors of sub-saharan africa: Threat to malaria elimination on the continent? Current Topics in Malaria. https://doi.org/10.5772/65359

xxiv "The Retreat from Monsanto Bt Cotton in Burkina Faso." Environmental Justice Atlas. Last modified August 17, 2017. https://ejatlas.org/conflict/the-retreat-from-monsanto-bt-cotton-burkina-faso.

The Philanthropic Monopoly of Bill & Melinda Gates

i "How Bill and Melinda Gates Are Transforming Life for Billions in the 21st Century." Fortune. https://fortune.com/longform/bill-melinda-gates-worlds-greatest-leaders/

ii Curtis M., Gated Development, op.cit. p.25.

iii "Financials." Last modified January 1, 2001. https://www.gatesfoundation.org/Who-We-Are/General-Information/Financials

iv "Buffett Donates $37bn to Charity," June 26, 2006. http://news.bbc.co.uk/2/hi/business/5115920.stm

v Gates, Bill and Melinda. "Warren Buffett's Best Investment." Gatesnotes.Com. https://www.gatesnotes.com/2017-Annual-Letter

vi "History." Last modified January 1, 2001. https://www.gatesfoundation.org/Who-We-Are/General-Information/History"EDGARFilingDocumentsfor0001104659-17-002579." https://www.sec.gov/Archives/edgar/data/1166559/000110465917002579/0001104659-17-002579-index.htm m

vii

viii Bayliss K e Waeyenberge E., "Unpacking the Public Private Partnership Revival", in The Journal of Development Studies, 54(4), 2017, pp. 577-593, https://www.tandfonline.com/doi/full/10.1080/00220388.2017.1303671?src=recsys

ix "About IFFIm | Supporting Gavi, The Vaccine Alliance." https://iffim.org/about-iffim

x Ciavoni, Carlo. "Ebola, così gli investitori privati speculano sull'epidemia nella Repubblica Democratica del Congo e non solo." la Repubblica, March 2, 2020. https://www.repubblica.it/solidarieta/cooperazione/2020/03/02/news/ebola-250013502/

xi "Cameroon Cataract Bond." The Government Outcomes Lab. https://golab.bsg.ox.ac.uk/knowledge-bank/case-studies/cameroon-cataract-bond/.

xii Bayliss K. e Waeyenberge E., op. cit., p 6. The IFC reports entitled "Business of Health in Africa" (2008) and "Landscape of Inclusive Business Models of Healthcare in India" (2014), have been instrumental in promoting and expanding private health-care industry financing.

xiii Ibid.em, p. 6.

xiv McClelland, Colin . "Abraaj Seeks Shelter From Africa's Economic Woes in Health Care." Bloomberg -Economics, September 20, 2016. https://www.bloomberg.com/news/articles/2016-09-20/abraaj-seeks-shelter-from-africa-s-economic-woes-in-health-care

xv Bayliss K. e Waeyenberge E., op. cit., p. 7.

xvi Hunter B. and Murray S., "Deconstructing the Financialization of Healthcare," Development and Change o(o), 2019, pp. 1269.

xvii Hunter BM e Marriott A., "Development Finance Institutions and the (In)coherence of their Investments in Private Health Companies", in The Reality of Aid 2018, Quezon City, 2018, IBON International, pp. 33-44.

xviii Bank D., "Leveraging the Balance Sheet: A conversation with Julie Sanderland, founding director of Program Related Investments at the Bill & Melinda Gates Foundation", in Stanford Social Innovation Review, supplement funded by the Bill & Melinda Gates Foundation, summer 2016, https://ssir.org/articles/entry/leveraging_the_balance_sheet.

xix The first donation amounted to $100 million.

xx "Bill and Melinda Gates Announce a $100 Million Gift to Establish the Bill and Melinda Gates Children's Vaccine Program." Last modified January 1, 2001. https://www.gatesfoundation.org/Media-Center/Press-Releases/1998/12/Bill-and-Melinda-Gates-Childrens-Vaccine-Program

xxi "The Bill & Melinda Gates Foundation." https://www.gavi.org/investing-gavi/funding/donor-profiles/bill-melinda-gates-foundation

xxii "Strategy." https://www.gavi.org/our-alliance/strategy

xxiii "Vaccine Coalition Unveils Ambitious Plan to Immunize 300 Million Children." STAT, August 29, 2019. https://www.statnews.com/2019/08/29/gavi-vaccine-alliance-ambitious-plan/

xxiv WHO, "Access to COVID-19 Tools (ACT) Accelerator." https://www.who.int/publications/m/item/access-to-covid-19-tools-(act)-accelerator 30 Martens J. e Seitz K., Philantropic Power and Development, op. cit. , p. 29.

xxv Martens J. e Seitz K., *Philantropic Power and Development*, op. cit., p. 29.

xxvi Storeng TK, "The GAVI Alliance and the "Gates Approach" to Health System Strengthening", in Global Public Health: An International Journal for Research, Policy and Practice, 9(8):1-15, August 2014.

xxvii Dentico N., "Advanced Market Commitments: Un nuovo meccanismo di aiuto allo sviluppo? " in Salute Globale e Aiuti allo Sviluppo. Diritti, ideologie, inganni, 3°

Rapporto Osservatorio Italiano sulla Salute Globale, Edizioni ETS, Pisa, 2008, pp. 279-285. On this subject, see also the recent report by Doctors Without Borders, Analysis and Critique of the Advanced Market Commitment (AMC) for Pneumococcal Conjugate Vaccines (PCVs) and Impact on Access, June 2020, MSF Access Campaign, https://msfaccess.org/sites/default/files/2020-06/Executive-Summary_Gavi-AMC-PCV-critique_MSF-AC.pdf

xxviii In the 1990s, the WHO suffered the reduction of compulsory contributions from Western governments, which directed their funding towards voluntary approaches, and for programmes chosen by the governments themselves, so as to reduce the operating margin of the WHO. The downturn in funding is counterbalanced by an important shift in the political scenario. The World Bank takes the lead over the WHO as a multilateral actor entitled to set strategies and provide funding for health in low-and middle-income countries. The World Bank's framework for action is consistent with the structural adjustment plans imposed as a condition for new development loans, and the provision of guarantees to make debt payments sustainable. In those same years the WHO was subjected to an unprecedented invective by the British Medical Journal, which recognized the United Nations agency's limited scope of intervention to health security and the control of infectious diseases on a scale. See in this regard: Godlee F., "WHO in retreat: is it losing its influence", in BMJ, December 1994, 309, pp. 1491-1495, https://www.bmj.com/content/309/6967/1491.full;Godlee F., "The World Health Organization: WHO at country level: a little impact, no strategy", in BMJ, December 1994, 309, pp. 1636-1639, https://www.ncbi.nlm.nih.gov/pmc/articles/PMC2542000/; Godlee F., "The World Health Organization: WHO in crisis", in BMJ, November 1994, 309, pp. 1424-1428, https://www.bmj.com/content/309/6966/1424

xxix Dentico N., "L'incerto futuro dell'Oms" in Salute Internazionale, 1 March 2017, https://www.saluteinternazionale.info/2017/03/lincerto-futuro-delloms/. In 2002, the annual budget of the WHO was lower than what Coca Cola and Pepsi Cola combined had spent on their marketing. Cfr. Lang, T., Rayner G. e Kaelin E., The food industry, diet, physical activity and health: A review of reported commitments and practice of 25 of the world's largest food companies. Report to the World Health Organization. City University Centre for Food Policy, 2006.; Clift C., "What's the World Health Organization For?", Final Report from the Centre on Global Health Security, Working Group on Health Governance, Chatham House Report, May 2014, https://www.chathamhouse.org/sites/default/files/field/field_document/20140521WHO HealthGove rnanceClift.pdf.

xxx World Bank, World Development Report 1993 : Investing in Health, 1993, New York, Oxford University Press, World Bank. https://openknowledge.worldbank.org/handle/10986/5976.

xxxi Birn AE, "Philanthrocapitalism Past and Present: The Rockefeller Foundation, the Gates Foundation, and the setting(s) of the international/global health agenda", in Hypothesis Journal, Vol. 12, No 1, November 2014, p. 10, https://www.hypothesisjournal.com/wp-content/uploads/2014/11/HJ229—FIN_Nov1_2014.pdf.

xxxii McCoy D., Kembhavi G., e altri, "The Bill and Melinda Gates Foundation's grant-making programme for global health", in The Lancet, Vol 373, 9 May 2009, https://www.thelancet.com/journals/lancet/article/PIIS0140-6736(09)60571-7/fulltext.

xxxiii https://www.politico.eu/article/bill-gates-who-most-powerful-doctor/.

xxxiv As of December 2019, the Bill & Melinda Gates Foundation is reported to support more than 30 public-private initiatives in the field of global health. From the foundation's website: https://www.gatesfoundation.org/how-we-work/quick-links/grants-database#q/k=Public-%20private%20partnerships%20in%20global%20health&page=2.

xxxv www.gatesfoundation.org/what-we-do.

xxxvi Ibid.em

xxxvii Birn AE, "Philanthrocapitalism Past and Present; op. cit. , p. 27.

xxxviii According to authoritative WHO representatives interviewed during the years of my work with Doctors Without Borders in Geneva, the creation of the Global Fund was a very hard and debilitating blow for the UN health agency. The attention of governments and funders was diverted to this new reality, often in competition with the WHO, albeit illegitimately, given that the Global Fund has a much more limited and agile governance structure and a much narrower operational mandate, limited to funding the fight against 3 diseases. Incredibly, UNAIDS and the WHO sit on the board of the Global Fund, but without voting rights. Private sector investors, including pharmaceutical companies and philanthropic foundations, instead have the right to vote.

xxxix Yamey G., "WHO's management struggling to transform a "fossilised bureaucracy"", in British Medical Journal, BMJ, 2002, 325:1170, https://www.bmj.com/content/325/7373/1170

xl "20 Years After the Battle of Seattle: Vandana Shiva & Lori Wallach on Historic 1999 WTO Protests." Democracy Now! Last modified November 27, 2019. https://www.democracynow.org/2019/11/27/1999_wto_protests_20_years_later

xli "Vandana Shiva Speaking at the Seattle IFG Teach-In, 11/26/99." © 1999 International Forum on Globalization, n.d. https://ratical.org/co-globalize/ifg112699VS.html

xlii Towards the end of his term of office, Nelson Mandela had pushed the South African government to adopt a new law on pharmaceuticals that would introduce all the safeguards of the WTO Agreement on Intellectual Property and pave the way for greater access to essential therapies (Medicines Act, 1997), especially in the areas of HIV and tuberculosis. At that time, South Africa was the country with the highest prevalence of HIV-positive people in the world, and the highest level of multi-resistant tuberculosis to treatments available. The launch of the Medicines Act in 1997 led to the immediate opposition of 39 pharmaceutical companies, which filed a controversial lawsuit against the South African government that lasted until 2001. When the Chief Justice of the South African Supreme Court asked the pharmaceutical companies to show their budgets to demonstrate the damage the law would do to them, the companies unanimously decided to withdraw from the case in 2001. It was estimated that if the Medicines Act had not been challenged in 1997, it would have saved the lives of 700,000 people in the four years of the trial. See in regard: Dentico N., "Globalizzazione e accesso alle cure: un'insolente storia di apartheid sanitario: Il ruolo delle industrie farmaceutiche, le responsabilità dei governi", in Salute e Globalizzazione: primo rapporto dell'Osservatorio Italiano sulla Salute Globale, La Feltrinelli, Milano, 2004, pp. 180-181.

xliii Legge D., "Protecting the right to health through action on the social determinants of health", presentation at an event on the eve of the World Conference on Social Determinants of Health, 18 October 2011, Rio de Janeiro, Brazil.

xliv Doctors Without Borders has carefully monitored and taken a position several times on specific features of the public-private partnerships created by the Gates Foundation. In particular, it focused its attention on GAVI, highlighting the need for transparency in the negotiations between GAVI and the pharmaceutical companies in relation to the price of vaccines. It stressed the oddity of the presence on the Boards of Directors of health initiatives such as the Global Fund and GAVI of representatives of multinationals that derive industrial benefits from the operational choices of these entities, which they are able to influence directly. The GAVI Board of Directors, for example, provides for the presence of 9 independent representatives on the board, people "without professional connections to the work of GAVI", but the people chosen come exclusively from the financial sector, audit firms, banks. See Martens J. E Saetz K., op. cit. p. 30.

xlv People's Health Movement, Medact, Third World Network et al., "Money talks at the World Health Organization", in Global Health Watch 4: An Alternative World Health Report, Zed Books Ltd., London, 2017, pp. 245-262.

xlvi Dentico N., "La riforma dell'Oms: tutta una questione di soldi", in Oms e diritto alla salute: quale futuro, 5° Rapporto dell'Osservatorio Italiano sulla Salute Globale, by Adriano Cattaneo andNicoletta Dentico, May 2013, p. 189.

xlvii Dentico N., "Il Finanziamento all'Oms. La Sfida di Tedros", in Salute Internazionale, 12 September 2018, https://www.saluteinternazionale.info/2018/09/il-finanziamento-alloms-la-sfida-di-tedros/ . In the period 2015-2017, voluntary contributions to the WHO accounted for 80% of the agency's funds, with 13.5% of these contributions coming from the Gates Foundation, second only to the US contribution (18%).

xlviii WHO, Results Report Programme Budget 2016-2017, A71/28 SEVENTY-FIRST WORLD HEALTH ASSEMBLY, Provisional agenda item 15.1, https://www.who.int/about/finances-accountability/budget-portal/rr_2016-17.pdf .

xlix WHO, Financial Estimate for the 13th General Programme of Work (2019-2023), White Paper, 16 May 2018, https://www.who.int/docs/default-source/documents/gpw/white-paper-financial-estimate-gpw13-may2018-en.pdf

l Jay Wenger, director of the foundation's polio program, responds to widespread criticism from the public health community about the Gates' huge investment in polio eradication, including within the WHO, with some interesting arguments. See: Wenger, By Jay. "Too Expensive, Too Slow, Too Discriminatory, and Other Myths about the Polio Eradication Program." Last modified September 10, 2018. https://www.gates-foundation.org/TheOptimist/Articles/health-systems-why-eradicate-polio-vaccine

li Clift C. e Røttingen JA, "New approaches to WHO financing: the key to better health", in British Medical Journal, 2018, 361:k2218, doi:10.1136/bmj.k2218.

lii Storeng TK, "The GAVI Alliance and the "Gates Approach" to Health System Strengthening", op. cit. p

liii Roberts, Leslie, and Martin Enserink. "Did They Really Say ... Eradication?" Science 318, no. 5856 (December 7, 2007): 1544–1545, https://www.ghdonline.org/uploads/1544.full.pdf

liv McNeil D., "Gates Foundation's Influence Critized", in The New York Times, 16 February 2008, https://www.nytimes.com/2008/02/16/science/16malaria.html

lv Ibid.em

lvi Njanji, Tinashe. "Melinda Gates Addresses the World Health Assembly: Civil Society Registers Its Protest – Peoples' Health Movement South Africa," n.d. https://

www.phm-sa.org/melinda-gates-addresses-the-world-health-assembly-civil-society-registers-its-protest/

lvii The Gates Foundation has promoted the approach by also supporting evaluation studies on scientific research conducted through public-private partnerships. For example, it commissioned several surveys from McKinsey on the determinants of the effectiveness of partnerships with the private sector. In 2014, it awarded $7.5 million to Population Services International "to demonstrate the benefits of engaging the private sector to meet India's 2020 family planning goals, and to improve the knowledge of key Indian influencers and policy makers about the need for efficient public-private alliances in the field of family planning", in Marten J. e Saetz K., op cit., p. 37-38.

lviii Tucker TJ e Makgoba M., "Public Private Partnerships and Scientific Imperialism", in Science, 320(5879):1016-7 June 2008, DOI:10.1126/science.1156720.

lix Doughton S. and Heim K.: "Does Gates Funding of Media Taint Objectivity? ." The Seattle Times. Last modified February 23, 2011. https://www.seattletimes.com/seattle-news/does-gates-funding-of-media-taint-objectivity/

lx "What We Do." Last modified January 1, 2001. https://www.gatesfoundation.org/what-we-do

lxi Bunce M., (2016) 'Foundations, philanthropy and international journalism', in Townded J., Muller D., Lance Keeble R., (edt.), Beyond Clickbait and Commerce: The Ethics Possibilities and Challenges of Not-For-Profit Media, in The International Journal of Communication Ethics, Vol. 13, N.2/3 2016, pp. 6-15.

lxii "Solutions Journalism Network." Wikipedia, May 5, 2020. https://en.wikipedia.org/w/index.php?title=Solutions_Journalism_Network&oldid=955083732

lxiii "Showcase Projects." Innovation. https://innovation.journalismgrants.org/

lxiv "FAIR" FAIR. https://fair.org

i Cornell Alliance for Science. Our Mission. https://allianceforscience.cornell.edu/about/mission/

ii Shackford, S. 2014. New Cornell Alliance for Science gets $5.6 million grant. https://news.cornell.edu/stories/2014/08/new-cornell-alliance-science-gets-56-million-grant.

iii Lewandowsky, S., Gignac, G.E. and Vaughan, S., 2013. The pivotal role of perceived scientific consensus in acceptance of science. Nature Climate Change, 3(4), pp.399-404. https://www.nature.com/articles/nclimate1720 Bt Brinjal: Alliance for Crooked Science & Corporate Lies

i Akhter, 2020. Akhter, Farida Aubergine Story: Local Varieties exist, not GMOs The New Age, 17 May, 2020 https://www.newagebd.net/article/106595/local-varieties-exist-not-gmos

ii Conrow, 2019. Conrow, Joan, Study confirms that GMO eggplant cuts pesticide use in Bangladesh, Cornell Alliance for Science, 7 March, 2019 https://allianceforscience.cornell.edu/blog/2019/03/study-confirms-gmo-eggplant-cuts-pesticide-use-bangladesh/

iii Shelton, et al, 2020. Shelton AM, Sarwer SH, Hossain MJ, Brookes G and Paranjape V (2020) Impact of Bt Brinjal Cultivation in the Market Value Chain in Five Districts of Bangladesh. Front. Bioeng. Biotechnol. 8:498. doi: 10.3389/fbioe.2020.00498, 25 May, 2020

iv Conrow, 2020. Conrow, Joan "Bangladeshi farmers reap higher yields, profits from Bt eggplant" , CornellCALS, May 28, 2020 https://cals.cornell.edu/news/bangladeshi-farmers-reap-higher-yields-profits-bt-eggplant

v CCR, 2015. Corporate Crime Reporter; Gates Foundation Backed Pro-GMO Cornell Alliance for Science On the Attack, March 5, 2015 https://www.corporatecrimereporter.com/news/200/gates-foundation-backed-pro-gmo-cornell-alliance-science-attack/

vi GMW, 2015. GM Watch, "Propaganda over facts? BBC Panorama and Bt brinjal 28 July, 2015 https://gmwatch.org/en/news/latest-news/16320

vii Ahmed, 2013. Ahmed, Reaz Brinjal modified: Bangladesh set to join elusive club of 28 GM crop growing countries Daily Star July 11 2013. http://www.thedailystar.net/beta2/news/brinjal-modified/

viii UBINIG, 2013. UBINIG, "Bangladesh does not need Bt brinjal: The approval story" 20 November 2013 unpublished

ix UBINIG, 2013. UBINIG, "Bangladesh does not need Bt brinjal: The approval story" 20 November 2013 unpublished

x NTV, 2015. NTV online, "US University honors Sheikh Hasina" 20 May, 2015 https://en.ntvbd.com/bangladesh/4584/US-univ-honours-Sheikh-Hasina

xi UBINIG, 2015. UBINIG, "Bt brinjal under Life Support" Experiences of farmers in the second round field cultivation http://ubinig.org/index.php/home/showAerticle/134/english/UBINIG-/Bt-Brinjal-Is-Under-%E2%80%98LIFE-SUPPORT%E2%80%99

xii Ahmed, 2019. Ahmed, Reaz, "5-yr after releasing its first GM crop Bangladesh says farmers gain by adopting Bt brinjal" Dhaka Tribune, 7 March, 2019 https://www.dhakatribune.com/business/2019/03/07/5-yr-after-releasing-its-first-gm-crop-bangladesh-says-farmers-gain-by-adopting-bt-brinjal

xiii IFPRI, 2019. IFPRI, Bt Brinjal Study: Pesticide Use Falls, But Risk Remains March 7, 2019 http://bangladesh.ifpri.info/2019/03/07/bt-brinjal-study-pesticide-use-falls-but-risk-remains/

xiv BBS, 2014. Statistical Pocketbook, Bangladesh 2014, Bangladesh Bureau of Statistics, Ministry of Planning, GOB

xv UBINIG, 2019. UBINIG 'Adoption' & abandoning of Bt brinjal cultivation: Farmers' Experience Survey: On farm Trials on Bt brinjal Varieties during 2014-15; January, 2019, unpublished http://ubinig.org/index.php/home/showAerticle/207/english/UBINIG/%E2%80% 98Adoption%E2%80%99-&-abandoning-of-Bt-brinjal-cultivation:-Farmers%E2%80%99-Experience-Survey

xvi Jony & Sobhan, 2016. Jony, Jahangir Alam & M.A. Sobhan "Bt brinjal failed in farmers' field" August 2016 http://ubinig.org/index.php/home/showAerticle/87/english/Jahangir-Alam-Jony-and-M.-A.-Sobhan/Bt-brinjal-failed-in-farmers'-field

xvii Mannan et al, 2003. Mannan et al, "Screening of Local and Exotic Brinjal Varieties/Cultivars for Resistance to Brinjal Shoot and Fruit Borer, Leucinodes orbonalis Guen" Pakistan Journal of Biological Sciences 6(5): 488-492, 2003 Screening of Local and Exotic Brinjal Varieties/Cultivars for Resistance to Brinjal Shoot and Fruit Borer, Leucinodes orbonalis Guen.

xviii IFPRI, 2019. Akhter, U. Ahmed et al "Impacts of Bt brinjal (eggplant) technology in Bangladesh", IFPRI, Bangladesh and USAID, August 2019

xix UBINIG, 2015. UBINIG, "Bt brinjal under Life Support" Experiences of farmers in the second round field cultivation http://ubinig.org/index.php/home/showAerticle/134/english/UBINIG-/Bt-Brinjal-Is-Under-%E2%80%98LIFE-SUPPORT%E2%80%99

xx New Age, 2014. New Age, "Bt brinjal cultivation ruins Gazipur farmers" May 7, 2014 http://www.newagebd.net/9116/bt-brinjal-farming-ruins-gazipur-farmers/

xxi Lynas, 2014. Lynas, Mark; "Bt brinjal in Bangladesh: The true story" 8 May, 2014 https://www.marklynas.org/2014/05/bt-brinjal-in-bangladesh-the-true-story/

xxii GMW, 2015. GM Watch, "Propaganda over facts? BBC Panorama and Btbrinjal 28 July, 2015 https://gmwatch.org/en/news/latest-news/16320

xxiii Robinson, 2015. Robinson, Claire, and GM Watch "GMO propaganda over facts? BBC Panorama and Bt brinjal" Ecologist 30 July, 2015 https://theecologist.org/2015/jul/30/gmo-propaganda-over-facts-bbc-panorama-and-bt-brinjal

xxiv GMW, 2015. GM Watch; Mark Lynas accused of fabricating story in the New York Times , 17 May 2015 https://www.gmwatch.org/en/news/latest-news/87-news/archive/2015/16175-mark-lynas-accused-of-fabricating-story-in-the-new-york-times

xxv GMW, 2015. GM Watch "Bangladesh NGO report challenges BBC claim of 90% success for Bt brinjal" 18 November 2015 https://www.gmwatch.org/en/news/archive/2015/16537-bangladesh-ngo-report-challenges-bbc-claim-of-90-success-for-bt-brinjal

Index

✴